VLASOV AND THE RUSSIAN
LIBERATION MOVEMENT

SOVIET AND EAST EUROPEAN STUDIES

Editorial Board

The National Association for Soviet and East European Studies exists for the purpose of promoting study and research on the social sciences as they relate to the Soviet Union and the countries of Eastern Europe. The Monograph Series is intended to promote the publication of works presenting substantial and original research in the economics, politics, sociology and modern history of the USSR and Eastern Europe.

SOVIET AND EAST EUROPEAN STUDIES

Генерал-лейтенант
АНДРЕЙ АНДРЕЕВИЧ ВЛАСОВ

LIEUTENANT-GENERAL
ANDREY ANDREYEVICH VLASOV

VLASOV AND THE RUSSIAN LIBERATION MOVEMENT

Soviet reality and émigré theories

CATHERINE ANDREYEV

FELLOW OF BALLIOL COLLEGE, OXFORD

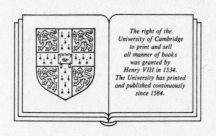

The right of the
University of Cambridge
to print and sell
all manner of books
was granted by
Henry VIII in 1534.
The University has printed
and published continuously
since 1584.

CAMBRIDGE UNIVERSITY PRESS

CAMBRIDGE

LONDON   NEW YORK   NEW ROCHELLE

MELBOURNE   SYDNEY

Published by the Press Syndicate of the University of Cambridge
The Pitt Building, Trumpington Street, Cambridge CB2 1RP
32 East 57th Street, New York, NY 10022, USA
10 Stamford Road, Oakleigh, Melbourne 3166, Australia

First published 1987

Printed in Great Britain at the University Press, Cambridge

British Library cataloguing in publication data
Andreyev, Catherine
Vlasov and the Russian Liberation Movement:
Soviet reality and émigré theories
(Soviet and East European Studies)
1. Russkoe osvoboditel'noe dvizhenie
I. Title   II. Series
940.53'47   R802.s65

Library of Congress cataloguing in publication data
Andreyev, Catherine, 1955–
Vlasov and the Russian Liberation Movement:
Soviet reality and émigré theories
(Soviet and East European Studies)
Based on the author's thesis (PhD) – University of Cambridge.
Bibliography
Includes index.
1. World War, 1939–1945 – Regimental histories – Soviet
Union. 2. Russkaĭa osvoboditel'naĭa armiĭa – History.
3. Komitet osvobozhdeniĭa narodov Rossii – History.
4. Vlasov, Andreĭ Andreevich, 1900–1946.
5. Anti-communist movement – Soviet Union.
I. Title.   II. Series.
D764.6.A664   1986   940.54'12'47   86–6823

ISBN 0 521 30545 4

To the memory of my father

Contents

Figures

Preface

I first became aware of the existence of the Russian Liberation Movement from the vivid recollections of Igor Novosiltsev. I am more than grateful to him for inspiring me to embark on further research on this subject.

The controversies and strongly held opinions surrounding this subject have continued to hold my attention and I hope that I have shown, at least, that even though forty years have elapsed since the end of the Second World War, many areas of the conflict, especially on the Eastern Front, not only provoke strong reactions but also raise questions which have not always been answered satisfactorily.

The question of the link between the ideology of the Russian Liberation Movement and political trends within the emigration allowed me to examine the hypothesis that the Russian émigrés after 1917 should not be regarded simply as an outmoded irrelevance but that sometimes they had valuable insights into developments within the USSR and must be treated as a part of the social history of their country.

This work would not have been possible without all those who agreed to be interviewed, who corresponded with me and who clarified many areas of the Russian Liberation Movement and who so generously gave me of their time and shared their knowledge with me. My heartfelt thanks are due to them. This book is a revised version of my doctoral thesis for Cambridge University and I would like once again to express my sense of great obligation to all who advised and helped me. In particular, I owe a deep debt of gratitude to the late Professor Leonard Schapiro for his encouragement, advice and that kindly and wise scholarship which so endeared him to his students. Dr Joachim Hoffmann's enthusiasm was infectious and I am most grateful for his assistance in dealing with archive collections in Germany.

To Professor John Erickson I am indebted for some most helpful advice. I would also like to thank all those at Harvard University, Darwin College, Cambridge and at the Russian Institute, Columbia University who enabled me to pursue my research. Needless to say, I alone am responsible for any errors of fact and judgement.

My family has been a constant support and I would also like to thank the Master and Fellows of Balliol College for providing a friendly and stimulating environment in which to complete this work.

Balliol College,
Oxford

CATHERINE ANDREYEV

Abbreviations

Organisations

KONR	*Komitet Osvobozhdeniya Narodov Rossii*: Committee for the Liberation of the Peoples of Russia
NTS	*Natsional'no-Trudovoy Soyuz*: The National Labour Alliance
OKH	*Oberkommando des Heeres*: High Command of the German Armed Forces
OKW	*Oberkommando der Wehrmacht*: High Command of the German Army
RNNA	*Russkaya Narodnaya Natsional'naya Armiya*: Russian People's National Army or Osintorf Brigade
ROA	*Russkaya Osvoboditel'naya Armiya*: The Russian Liberation Army
ROD	*Russkoe Osvoboditel'noe Dvizhenie*: The Russian Liberation Movement
RONA	*Russkaya Osvoboditel'naya Narodnaya Armiya*: The Russian People's Army of Liberation or Kaminsky Brigade
ROVS	*Russkiy Obshche-Voinskiy Soyuz*: The Russian Union of Veterans
SBONR	*Soyuz Bor'by Osvobozhdeniya Narodov Rossii*: The Union of the Struggle for the Liberation of the Peoples of Russia
VS KONR	*Vooruzhennye Sily Komiteta Osvobozhdeniya Narodov Rossii*: Armed Forces for the Liberation of the Peoples of Russia
WPr	Wehrmacht Propaganda: OKW Propaganda staff section

Bibliographical References

Certain archive collections and works of reference are cited as follows:

BA   Bundesarchiv Koblenz:
            RFSS Persönlicher Stab Files, Ostministerium
            Files

BA–MA   Bundesarchiv–Militärarchiv, Freiburg im
            Breisgau:
            Oberkommando des Heeres/Generalstab des
            Heeres Files,
            Pozdnyakov Collection, Steenberg Collection

BAR   Bakhmeteff Archive, Columbia University, New
            York

FCO   Foreign and Colonial Office Archives, London:
            Captured German records

IVMV   *Istoriya vtoroy mirovoy voiny*, 12 vols., Moscow,
            1973–82

IVOVSS   *Istoriya Velikoy Otechestvennoy voiny Sovetskogo
            Soyuza*, 5 vols., Moscow, 1961–5

IZ   Institut für Zeitgeschichte, Munich: Thorwald
            Collection

PRO   Public Record Office, Kew, London:
            F.O. 371/36958; 36959; 36960; 43303; 47955;
            48004; 56710.
            W.O. 11119

TMWC   *Trial of the Major War Criminals*, 42 vols., Nurem-
            berg: International Military Tribunal, 1947–9

YIVO   YIVO Institute for Jewish Research, New York.
            Material on the occupied territories

Introduction

Almost at once after the outbreak of war between the USSR and the Third Reich on 22 June 1941, Soviet citizens in German hands, particularly prisoners-of-war and those civilians employed as forced labour by the Nazis, made clear their active opposition to Stalin and his regime. The history of this opposition to Stalin in the period 1941–5 generated interest and controversy both at its inception and after the war, amongst scholars and publicists. The differing attitudes of the various German authorities to the Russian opposition movement and the impact of these divergent views was made evident throughout German policy towards the Soviet Union during the war. Owing to the closure of their independent presses in émigré centres such as Berlin, Paris and Prague by the Nazis, émigré Russians were unable to express their opinions during the war but they have indulged in bitter exchanges and polemics on this subject ever since the articles of B. I. Nikolaevsky, a Menshevik politician, historian and archivist, appeared in 1948.[1] Nikolaevksy went to Germany immediately after the war in order to collect material, in the form of official documents and personal testimonies, on the experience and activities of the Soviet citizens who found themselves in Germany during the Second World War, supporting the campaign against Stalin.

The presence of these Soviet citizens within the Third Reich has engendered a long-standing discussion as to the extent to which they were collaborators, quislings and traitors. For some, there is no valid argument, for there is nothing to discuss: since these people were fighting against the Soviet state on the side of her armed enemy, they were clearly traitors.[2] For others, the position is less clear-cut. They argue that those who joined the anti-Stalinist opposition, which came

1

to be called the Russian Liberation Movement, were motivated by patriotism and that the members of the Movement remained loyal to their country, if not to the government.[3] In her discussion of various treason trials, Rebecca West considers that the law's definition of treachery is quite clear:

If a state gives a citizen protection it has a claim to his allegiance, and if he gives it his allegiance it is bound to give him protection.[4]

It can be argued, however, that the refusal of the Soviet government to sign the Geneva Convention deprived its citizens of the protection to which they were entitled. Consequently, they did not owe the state their allegiance and, *ipso facto*, they were not traitors.[5]

These Soviet citizens were also referred to as Vlasovites, members of the Vlasov movement and as members of ROA (*Russkaya Osvoboditel'naya Armiya*), the Russian Army of Liberation. The terms are inaccurate, and these inaccuracies have been perpetuated to the present day not only by the uninformed but also by those to whom the position was clear. The most accurate term with which to describe the Soviet citizens who found themselves under the jurisdiction of the Third Reich and who endeavoured to create a viable opposition movement, based in the first instance on military formations, is to refer to them by the generic term of ROD (*Russkoe Osvoboditel'noe Dvizhenie*), the Russian Liberation Movement. ROD then covers a variety of phenomena: military and civil, groups and individuals, in German or Russian formations, but all opposed to the Stalinist regime. ROA never in fact existed, it was a term coined by those Germans agitating for a change in Nazi policy towards the Soviet Union, and they created a mythical army in order that those Soviet citizens fighting in the ranks of the Wehrmacht should feel some kind of unity and have some concrete aim for which to fight. Many of these soldiers, in German formations, commanded and officered by Germans, did consider themselves to be part of this phantom army, fighting to liberate Russia, and sewed insignia to this effect on to their uniforms. However, a unified military formation, such as this, remained a desire and not a reality, despite widespread use of the term ROA. This opposition movement has also been named after its nominal leader, Lieutenant-General Andrey Andreyevich Vlasov. However, the 'Vlasov movement' is also a misleading term. Vlasov was not captured by the Germans until July 1942, whereas various military formations had been formed earlier, and attempts at opposition to Stalin and the Soviet regime had been made from the beginning of hostilities. Despite all his hopes, and those of his advisers, Vlasov was retained merely as a propaganda weapon by the Nazis until January 1945 when he was finally allowed to form two divisions. These divisions were known as the Armed Forces of the Committee for the Liberation of the Peoples of Russia, VS KONR (*Vooruzhennye Sily Komiteta Osvobozhdeniya Narodov Rossii*), but are sometimes also referred to as ROA, since the ROA insignia was still worn on the uniforms. The troops were recruited for the most part directly from the prisoner-of-war camps and not from among those Russian troops which were already serving with the Wehrmacht and who considered themselves to be part of the Russian Liberation Army and under Vlasov's command, mythical though these entities were.

Both the supporters and detractors of the Russian Liberation Movement have confused the terms and the position of those involved. The supporters of the Liberation Movement, in the process of self-justification and polemic, have tended to gloss over its shortcomings and emphasise rather its scope and support, whereas its detractors have lumped together a variety of sins and individuals under the heading of 'Collaboration', and have not deemed it necessary to clarify points of potential ambiguity nor to examine possible mitigating circumstances. Nikolaevsky's two articles (which analysed the development of the Russian Liberation Movement up to 1943) gave rise to long-lasting and bitter exchanges on the nature of defeatism (*Porazhenchestvo*). Nikolaevsky attacked the Soviet claim of total unity and unanimous patriotism within the country during the war, by showing that defeatism did exist, a fact which the Soviet authorities had denied. Defeatism, the doctrine that urges soldiers to weaken their own side so that the regime might be more easily overthrown, was exhibited on a much larger scale in 1941 than could ever be considered normal. Before the beginning of the First World War, defeatism in Russia had been common only to small groups of ideologists, and Nikolaevsky asserted that during the First World War the effect of Bolshevik propaganda, in this respect, was in general not to make troops cross to the German side, but merely to lay down their arms and to go home. In the Second World War, on the contrary, defeatism took on the character of a mass movement as Soviet citizens prepared to join the enemy in order to ensure the collapse of the Soviet regime. Nikolaevsky's articles then proceeded to scrutinise the nature of the Movement with the aim of showing that defeatism was inspired by political antipathy to the Stalinist regime. These articles aroused such ire and controversy, that Nikolaevsky became embroiled in the mesh of émigré politics and passions, lost heart and did not complete the series.[6]

The exchanges of views between Nikolaevsky and his chief critics, Boris L. Dvinov and G. Ya. Aronson, two fellow Mensheviks, were published in the United States in the journal, *Novy zhurnal*, in the New York daily paper, *Novoe Russkoe Slovo*, and in *Sotsialisticheskiy vestnik*, the Menshevik journal. Dvinov, in articles in *Novoe Russkoe Slovo* and *Novy zhurnal*, and in his book,[7] attacked Nikolaevsky's contention that the defection of Soviet citizens to the Wehrmacht took place for political reasons and riposted that those who fought with the Germans did so only to save their own skins, while Vlasov himself was an opportunist ably exploited by the Nazis. Aronson[8] took a similar line, attacking the idea that those in the Vlasov movement could adhere in any way to democratic principles as they were obviously tools of the Germans. Aronson made much of anti-semitic remarks in newspapers, particularly those in *Parizhskiy vestnik*,[9] which had supported Vlasov; but Aronson failed to appreciate that this was not an official ROD publication and that the view of the editors did not necessarily reflect the views of the Movement's leaders. Dvinov and Aronson also failed to take into account the lack of homogeneity in the Third Reich. They viewed it as a monolithic block, whereas within the Nazi state a whole range of institutions carried out policy and frequently clashed over the priorities and the methods used to enact such policies. (This multiplicity of authority, indeed, was instrumental in the survival of the Russian Liberation Movement.) Aronson and Dvinov insisted that all Russians saw Hitler as the primary enemy. They argued that the fighting spirit exhibited by the Red Army in the later stages of the war proved this point. Aronson and Dvinov insisted that those who saw Stalin as the greater danger to democratic freedoms alleged this from motives of opportunism and treachery. Ekaterina D. Kuskova, another émigré (who had been attacked by Lenin for her 'Economist' ideas in the 1890s) entered into the debate as to who was the greatest enemy: Stalin or Hitler.[10] She considered that most émigrés erred on the optimistic side in their estimates of disaffection within the USSR. In a series of articles on the nature of the Russian Revolution and on ROD she emphasised that all societies develop loyalties and ties which counter tendencies to disaffection. This approach was followed by the work of George Fischer who argued that the initial Soviet defeats and defections of Red Army troops occurred, not because of their political views and expectations, but because they were apolitical in their aspirations and were reduced to a state which Fischer called 'inertness'. In his view,

Inertness, the exclusion of individual initiative in anything related to politics, had become the central feature of the political behaviour of the individual.[11]

Fischer considered that this passivity was an integral part of Soviet society and the mental make-up of the Soviet individual. It had arisen because of the totalitarian nature of the Soviet state, which supervised all actions in minute detail and explained, to his way of thinking, both the progress of the war in the USSR, and the behaviour and weaknesses of those who were members of the Russian Liberation Movement.

Fischer's approach seems somewhat condescending, and he underplays the problems faced by the Movement's supporters both in the Soviet Union and in the Third Reich. Available evidence suggests that those who became involved in the Russian Liberation Movement devoted much careful thought to the courses of action open to them. It is now clear that many of the weaknesses of the Russian Liberation Movement stemmed from a lack of information about the true nature of Nazism and that that this was further exacerbated by patterns of thought which had been inculcated as a result of living under the Stalinist system. That their actions might be circumscribed by certain preconceptions is not to say that the supporters of the Movement could not or were unwilling to take initiatives. Supporters made conscious decisions and were not merely passive adjuncts to political developments. It is, therefore, misleading to define their activity in terms of 'inertness'. Furthermore, the reaction of the Soviet authorities to the Russian Liberation Movement would suggest that they, at least, recognised the potential threat posed by the Movement and discerned no lack of decisiveness within it.

While the emigration argued as to whether or not democratic ideas in the opposition movement had existed, and scrutinised its connection with Nazism, the problem was also approached from another angle by a German journalist, Jurgen Thorwald. His book[12] was based on German sources and the testimony of Germans, particularly those connected with *Fremde Heere Ost* (the branch of the General Staff dealing with intelligence in the USSR). He provided a great deal of fresh material, but unfortunately it is not possible to disentangle fact from the fictionalised interludes in his book. Moreover, this volume was commissioned by the head of *Fremde Heere Ost*, Reinhard Gehlen, to exonerate himself and the organisation from charges of sympathising with Nazi aims. The whole question of Nazi policy in the East has been analysed in great detail by Alexander Dallin.[13] In his work he showed very clearly the contradictions and the pluralities of authority within the Nazi machine and the struggles for power by the various agencies: the Ostministerium, the SS, the Wehrmacht, the Foreign Office and the Nazi party, particularly when related to policy towards the Soviet Union and the Russian Liberation Movement. Dallin based his study on German documents and the scope and clarity of his work has enabled it to remain the best secondary source on this subject. Gerald Reitlinger[14] re-examined much of the material used by Dallin, but his tone is more didactic and partisan, and he added little of fundamental importance to the picture already provided. Lately much attention has been focused on various specific areas of *Ostpolitik* and the Eastern Front. Christian Streit,[15] for instance, has made a meticulous study of the basic living conditions of and policies enacted towards Soviet prisoners-of-war, but does not examine their utilisation in or aspirations for political propaganda. Joachim Hoffmann,[16] of the Institut für Militärgeschichtliches Forschungsamt, has provided an analysis of the Eastern Legions (*Ostlegionen*). His *Die Geschichte der Wlassow-Armee* (discussed below) is a major contribution to the military history of the Movement and also clarifies the issue of the political significance of this opposition.

The existence of the Russian Liberation Movement is an interesting by-product of the cross currents within the Third Reich and provides a most vivid picture of the conditions on the Eastern Front and of various attempts to alter policy there. German sources have enabled historians to conduct a fairly thorough investigation of the circumstances and difficulties surrounding and encountered by the creators of the Movement.

The significance of the Russian Liberation Movement, however, does not consist only in its ambiguous position *vis-à-vis* the Nazi authorities. The Movement was also important as a means of expressing views held by those Russians involved with it. For the first time since 1922, a mass movement had produced a political programme and had discussed various questions pertaining to Soviet society. This took place in circumstances which made the programme accessible to the Western scholar, yet unfortunately those aspects of the Movement which can be described as being a reflection of the concerns of the Soviet citizen – rather than those which deal with their relationship with the German authorities – have received relatively little attention. To a large extent this is because so few archives have survived.

While it is difficult to provide an exact figure for adherents to the Russian Liberation Movement – the Nazi authorities would only allow it to exist as a propaganda exercise until November 1944 – support for this venture was considerable. By 1944, approximately one million Soviet citizens were serving in the Wehrmacht and there were about three million forced labourers working in the Third Reich. Although most of these people were not allowed to join Vlasov, many of them considered themselves to be part of the Movement. They read the publications of Vlasov's propaganda unit at Dabendorf, *Zarya* and *Dobrovolets*, and wore, as of right, the insignia[17] of the non-existent Russian Army of Liberation on their German uniforms. In addition, at the point of furthest German advance into the USSR, territory with a population of some sixty million was occupied. Judging from the warm welcome accorded to Vlasov during trips to the occupied territories in the spring of 1943, given favourable circumstances, many of these people might well have supported him. It is, therefore, in terms of potential support from the beginning of hostilities, rather than from the numbers of those actually allowed to enrol in Vlasov's divisions in the winter of 1944, that the Russian Liberation Movement must be considered a mass movement.

Much documentation was destroyed, both by Allied bombing and by the participants themselves, since it was feared that important papers might fall into Soviet hands. In particular, minutes of KONR meetings and lists of names of members or those wishing to enrol in the KONR forces are known to have been destroyed for this reason. A member of Vlasov's secretariat, Lev Rahr, explained that he spent two days burning these documents, and then flushing the ashes away, before KONR personnel were evacuated from Berlin.[18] Records from Vlasov's personal secretariat seem to have suffered a similar fate.

Colonel Kromiadi, the head of Vlasov's secretariat, was sent on 9 April 1945[19] to Füssen in Bavaria to find accommodation for Vlasov and his entourage. Kromiadi took with him papers from Vlasov's secretariat. On the way south, the train was bombed at Pilsen. Kromiadi was badly wounded, and the carriage carrying the boxes of papers suffered a direct hit, with the consequent destruction of all these documents. N. A. Noreikis, who worked in the press department at Dabendorf, claimed that he rescued a suitcase of KONR documents, when he evacuated Berlin, but had to abandon this suitcase at a later stage.[20] This wholesale destruction of documents has made the historian's task more difficult.

However, in the wake of scholarly assessments came the memoirs of participants. Initially, survivors of the Russian Liberation Movement were reluctant to confess their involvement since the fear of repatriation to the Soviet Union, or of other retaliation, remained; but with time, events receded from public memory and from the forefront of the political arena and became part of history. In addition, retirement not only provided the opportunity for relating experiences, but sharpened the desire that facts should not be submerged and that events should be shown up in their true light before the eyewitnesses disappeared. Of these memoirs, which have appeared not only in book form but frequently as articles, of unique importance and interest were those of Captain Wilfried Strik-Strikfeldt,[21] the German officer who became Vlasov's friend and protector, who was involved in the Vlasov enterprise from the beginning, and who was privy to the many twists in its development. Michael Schatoff, at one time a member of Vlasov's bodyguard, edited a bibliography[22] of all known published material on the Russian Liberation Movement, and another volume of memoirs and documents.[23] The bibliography is haphazardly arranged and does not indicate the significance of its constituent parts. Schatoff felt it necessary to stress the positive aspects of the Liberation Movement and so his work is somewhat tendentious. Nevertheless, Schatoff actively encouraged the publication of other evidence relating to the Russian Liberation Movement, since he established an archive in New York dedicated to the Movement. Colonel V. Pozdnyakov, one of Vlasov's aides-de-camp, and in charge of KONR's security, has fulfilled a valuable service by publishing two volumes consisting of documents and memoirs. These volumes, *Rozhdenie ROA*[24] (*The Birth of ROA*) and *General Vlasov*,[25] are useful sources. They can be supplemented by the memoirs of the head of Vlasov's secretariat, Colonel K. G. Kromiadi[26] and those of Professor F. P. Bogatyr-chuk,[27] who became a member of KONR[28] and chairman of KONR's Ukrainian Committee. Father Alexander Kiselev[29] writes of Vlasov's spiritual development and Father Dimitri Konstanti-nov[30] addresses himself to problems of pastoral care encountered in his work among Soviet troops in the Wehrmacht. A. Kazantsev[31] expresses the views of an émigré as well as those of the NTS (National Labour Alliance – *Natsional'no-Trudovoy Soyuz*), an émigré political organisation of which he was a member. Kazantsev was closely involved with ROD from the time of Vlasov's capture by the Germans and became editor of the KONR newspaper *Volya naroda*. Colonel V. Artem'ev's *Pervaya Diviziya ROA*[32] (*The First Division of ROA*) describes the formation and military engagements of the 1st Division, while A. G. Aldan's[33] book deals mainly with the end of the whole enterprise, the surrender of VS KONR to the Americans, their experiences as prisoners and their subsequent repatriation to the Soviet Union. *Novy zhurnal*, one of the leading émigré journals, and the publications of the post-war ex-Vlasovite organisations have provided source material in the shape of documents and memoirs. In particular, the journals *Bor'ba* and *S narodom za narod*, produced by SBONR (Union of the Struggle for the Liberation of the Peoples of Russia – *Soyuz Bor'by Osvobozhdeniya Narodov Rossii*) – one of the post-war émigré organisations which bases its programme on the KONR Manifesto – are useful both for producing source material and for clarifying some of the attitudes of the participants.

The drawback of many of the memoirs of the participants is that they not only tend to exaggerate the role of the author, a common fault of this genre, but in the case of the Russian Liberation Movement in particular, the writers frequently – and not surprisingly – suffer from a feeling that they have been persecuted not merely by the Soviet authorities, but also by Western public opinion which, they claim, not only fails to appreciate their position, but condemns them without taking account of the circumstances. These writings accordingly suffer from the need or desire of the writer to exculpate himself and to justify his actions. Furthermore, in response both to émigré polemics, and to criticism and accusations made in Soviet publications, there is a marked tendency in some memoirs to present everything as whiter than white, with Vlasov painted in super-roseate colours as a martyr or godlike figure whose shortcomings and mistakes may not be mentioned. Similar faults can be laid at the door of oral reminiscences. The passage of time affects the memory and hindsight affects the judgements made. There is also a tendency toward self-justification on the part of the person being interviewed. But these weaknesses can be counteracted, not only by cross-reference with both printed and other oral evidence, but also by the intense desire of many of the participants to have facts accurately recorded by history. For all their shortcomings, apparent or unseen, without such memoirs and recollections it would be difficult to establish various details. Sven Steenberg's[34] biography of Vlasov is of particular interest in this respect because he consulted a large number of people, especially Germans involved in the Movement, whose testimonies are of importance, yet who died without recording their experiences.

Vlasov is regarded by the Soviet authorities as a dyed-in-the-wool traitor and opportunist. In mid 1943, when the Soviet propaganda campaign against Vlasov became more systematic, there were even accusations of his involvement and participation in the 'Trotskyite' conspiracy with Tukhachevsky. His name was not mentioned in Soviet post-war publications from the time of the appearance of the announcement in *Pravda* and *Izvestiya* in August 1946 of Vlasov's execution, until the late 1950s when the amnesty in 1955 liberated some of those who had been prisoners-of-war. When these former labour camp inmates returned to civilian life, the existence of the Russian Liberation Movement became more widely known, and the authorities found it necessary to denigrate the Movement.[35] The official history of the Second World War, published in 1961,[36] makes a one-line reference to Vlasov's treachery and cowardice which caused the loss of the 2nd Shock Army on the Volkhov Front, and this formula is repeated in other publications. However, various military memoirs by other army commanders, and especially those of Marshal K. A. Meretskov[37] who was the commander of the Volkhov Front, make it clear that it was not merely Vlasov's alleged moral turpitude which was to blame and that the reasons for defeat were not as clear as the authorities would wish to maintain for the purposes of propaganda. Soviet historiography, and this view is expounded in the four available reports[38] of Vlasov's trial, states that Vlasov sold himself to the fascist aggressors. It reiterates that the so-called Vlasov movement represented nothing except opportunism and the desire to betray fellow countrymen. Since fascism is described by Soviet

Marxism as the eventual logical outcome of capitalism, there is no detailed analysis of the Nazi regime, nor any indication of the contradictions within it. Because the Second World War is presented as the struggle between two opposing systems, and the logical conclusion to the development of capitalism, the clarity of the scheme collapses if it is admitted that the fascists did not always agree with each other and had different goals and methods. The framework of Soviet Marxism and some of the officially accepted concepts about the 'Great Patriotic War' necessitate this schematic method of approach by Soviet historians and preclude any very detailed analysis of the Nazi attitude to the Soviet Union or of their disagreements over actions and policies in the occupied territories.

Interest in the history of the Russian Liberation Movement does not lie solely in the denigration proffered by the adversaries of the enterprise during or after the war, nor in the military formations created and in the idealisation by the supporters of the venture. These facts relate to the conditions prevalent during hostilities and are of value as a case study into one of the less clear-cut areas of conflict during the Second World War. Rather it is more pertinent to ask whether a focal point for all the opponents of the Liberation Movement exists. A comparison of all the accusations shows that each one concludes with the statement that the Vlasovites produced no ideology of value and were dependent on the Nazis for their ideas as well as for all their material needs. Yet is this true and is it possible? From 1941 onwards a large number of Russians, or people of Russian culture, found themselves outside the confines of the Soviet Union and no longer constrained by the insistent demand – true of any totalitarian regime but particularly of Stalinist Russia in the 1930s – to acquiesce to the dogmata propounded by that regime. Once outside, albeit as prisoners-of-war, the Russians found unexpected freedom to discuss and question aspects of their regime. These discussions were, arguably, unsophisticated, and were not conducted at a particularly high intellectual level. But it has yet to be demonstrated that, because of their lack of experience in political discussion, the people who indulged in these arguments found no alternative but to latch on to the ideology of their captors, as their critics claim. Was this likely? The Nazi hierarchy maintained that the Russians were of less value than animals, and indeed, the lack of success met by Nazi policy in the East and subsequent German attempts to instigate modification in Nazi attitudes, arose because of the resistance of the population to being treated as subhumans (*Untermensch*). It is difficult to see what arguments could have encouraged captured Soviet soldiers to agree with their captors that they were only fit for exploitation and extermination.

Moreover, Soviet prisoners did not come into contact solely with a united front of convinced Nazis. They often encountered Germans critical of Nazi policies and occasionally even Russophile Germans actively hostile to the Nazis; perhaps most significantly for the development of the intellectual and political discussion, the Soviet prisoners met émigré Russians. Estimates of the size of the Russian emigration vary, but statistics in 1936 of the Russian Historical Archive Abroad,[39] the last contemporary Russian émigré statistics available on this question, state that outside the boundaries of the USSR, 108 Russian newspapers and 162 journals were being produced for a readership of more than two million. Owing to the circumstances in which the Bolsheviks had taken power and consolidated their authority, approximately one million Russian citizens had been made to leave their country. They resettled in a number of centres in Europe, most of them convinced that the Soviet regime would collapse in the near future and that they would be going home very soon. This attitude, nurtured in part by the difficulty of assimilating into the society of their host nations, meant that the Russian émigré community remained cut-off and separate from many developments in the host societies and consequently concentrated its thoughts on the political causes of departure from Russia and on those problems it would encounter on its return home. This activity manifested itself, on the one hand, in the formation of the Russian Union of War Veterans (*Russkiy Obshche-Voinskiy Soyuz – ROVS*) and, on the other, in intense intellectual activity. The Revolution had led to the expulsion of the pre-revolutionary intellectual, cultural and political elite. Once abroad, these individuals became involved in producing a tremendous variety of publications expressing a spectrum of views. Their convictions ranged from those which were more 'monarchistic' than the Imperial family (!) to those which supported Trotsky. As well as the continuance of the old political parties, new groups and movements appeared; all of which considered, discussed and produced solutions for various aspects of Russian society.

When by the mid 1930s the outbreak of war seemed inevitable, the emigration split into defeatists (*Porazhentsy*) and defencists (*Obo-*

rontsy). The *Porazhentsy*, which included most of the right-wing groupings in the emigration, considered that the first priority must be to overthrow Stalin, and if the Nazi regime was prepared to go to war with the Soviet Union, then the Nazi war effort must be supported. Their view was that they would be willing to seek an ally in the Devil himself if this would bring about the overthrow of Bolshevism. However, the support of the émigrés was not welcomed by the Nazi authorities. They refused, almost without exception, to accept Russian émigré volunteers into the Wehrmacht or to allow them to hold positions in the administration of the occupied territories. All Russians were subject to the theory of *Untermensch* and all Russians were consequently considered to be subhuman. The *Oborontsy* embraced a wide spectrum of individuals including: General Denikin, the commander-in-chief of the armed forces in South Russia during the Civil War; the Socialist Revolutionaries; the leader of Peasant Russia (*Krest'yanskaya Rossiya*), S. S. Maslov; and the leader of the right wing group of Eurasians, P. N. Savitsky. They believed that despite their antipathy to the Soviet regime, they must support their fellow countrymen when the latter were attacked by the Nazi aggressor. Some of them were also of the opinion that the reforms enacted by Stalin during the war showed that the regime was evolving to a more acceptable position. (At the end of the war, the Soviet authorities discounted patriotic expressions and pro-Soviet sympathies of those defencists who fell into their hands since they viewed these protestations as a sham and merely a cover for the reactionary views which all émigrés were supposed to hold.)

It would be natural to assume that the old emigration with its extensive and varied reservoir of political opinion and experience would meet and influence those Russians who now found themselves outside the Soviet Union, caught up in the flood-tide of the war. However, the onset of Nazism destroyed and dispersed the energies and opportunities of the older émigrés. Their independent press and publishing houses were closed by the Nazis. Furthermore, freedom of movement was greatly curtailed so that entry into the occupied territories of the Soviet Union was very difficult. No one could travel without permission between states which were part of the 'New Europe', under the control of the Third Reich, and permission was not easily granted, especially to non-Aryans. Therefore, it became increasingly difficult to sustain the life of the émigré community, to maintain links between the different centres of émigré activity or for the émigrés to find out what was happening within the confines of the USSR. This has resulted in a scarcity of evidence concerning this older generation during the war. Oral tradition claims that those who thought about ROD with any seriousness, believed that Vlasov would try and follow the example of Marshal Pilsudsky. During the First World War, Pilsudsky used the Austro-Hungarians to arm his Polish forces, but then turned against the Central Powers to achieve independence for Poland.

The only group which managed, to some extent, to get round these exceedingly restrictive regulations and continued to operate, albeit clandestinely, was the NTS. This organisation had originated in Belgrade in 1930, and consisted mostly of a younger generation of émigrés. Many of them had a scientific education or technical expertise, which enabled them during the war to get jobs, and therefore travel passes, to the occupied territories of the Soviet Union. Here they managed to get into contact with the local population, their Soviet compatriots. The NTS had already produced various preliminary political programmes but did not wish to finalise a platform until they had argued them through in dialogue with Russians from the Soviet Union, and, in fact, a programme was produced after just such dialogue. (See discussion, p. 189.) The NTS developed and changed their ideas after this illegal wartime contact with Soviet Russians, although some of these changes and their consequent influence were much criticised in the post-war period. Nevertheless, the NTS fulfilled a very important role as a focus for and purveyor of ideas amongst their Soviet compatriots, some of whom joined the organisation. It is, however, an exaggeration to state, as some members have done, that the NTS were the only ideological influence on the Russian Liberation Movement. Such an interpretation ignores the variety of ideas to be found within the Movement itself, and implies much greater unanimity of opinion than was the case. It also underplays the effect on the individual living within the Soviet Union, which was crucial to an understanding of the attitudes expressed in the programme of the Movement.

Writers on this history of the wartime opposition to Stalin have established the course of events, as far as the surviving documents will allow. Historians have examined Nazi policy, and demonstrated both its own rationale and its inherent contradictions. This has clarified the reasons for the creation of a Soviet opposition movement within the Third Reich and has provided an explanation for its erratic development there.[40] The survivors of the Vlasov enterprise have described their own state of mind. Initially, they expected great things from Germany, but disenchantment gradually set in and their hopes of the West were blighted too. For the West, contrary to their expectations, was not only uninformed but also uninterested in their position and plight.

The military aspects of the Vlasov enterprise, the extent and circumstances of its military formations, have been described in memoirs and by military historians. Two recent publications have made notable contributions in this area. Stanislav Ausky,[41] a Czech, served in the second regiment of the 1st Division of VS KONR. He has used Russian, Czech and German sources to make a detailed study of operations during those last months and, in particular, of the role of the 1st Division in Prague in May 1945. Ausky shows that the decision to intervene was made partly in response to requests for help from the Czech nationalists, and he considers that the participation of the division prevented the rising from being crushed on 6 May, i.e. on the second day. At the same time Ausky rejects claims made by those who wish to idealise the conduct of the 1st Division. He does not consider the division to have been militarily very successful, and says that morale was not very good. He argues that the intervention of the division in the Prague rising in fact made the German response more brutal and therefore caused greater suffering for the civilian population. At the same time he rebuts counter-claims made on behalf of the Red Army. Since both KONR forces and German troops had left Prague, it is misleading to state that the Red Army 'liberated' the city.

Joachim Hoffmann in his book, *Die Geschichte der Wlassow-Armee*, has also analysed the military aspects of the Movement, particularly as they developed in the closing stages. He argues that the Movement had a wider political significance than the military operations alone would indicate and that this must be understood within the context of the Soviet wartime and post-war response to the Russian Liberation Movement. Hoffmann considers that the official Soviet attitude, whereby the lives of soldiers, whether in the front line or in POW camp, were expendable, was crucial in persuading Soviet citizens to align themselves with Vlasov. In his opinion, the inability of Soviet historians to discuss the Liberation Movement provides further proof that the authorities find certain aspects of the wartime opposition still pertinent in contemporary politics.

Hoffmann's conclusions and his emphasis on the political aspects of the Russian Liberation Movement might appear unpalatable to those accustomed to viewing the forces involved in the war simply in terms of black and white, fascist and anti-fascist. Yet Hoffmann's approach is undeniably the right one since for the participants of the Russian Liberation Movement the focus of activities was directed towards the situation within the Soviet Union and these people did not see fascism as the only enemy facing them. The importance of the wider Soviet context and the seriousness with which the Soviet authorities view the subject has also been affirmed by Michael Geller and Alexander Nekrich. In their history of the Soviet Union,[42] they state that the problem of wartime opposition remains one of the most complex for Soviet historians of the war, not least because it is a forbidden subject for research.

This present study treats the human tragedy of those caught between Nazism and Stalinism in general outline. Such problems as the plight of refugees, forced labour, atrocities committed by either side and repatriation are dealt with in a summary manner since others have discussed these issues in detail elsewhere. This research addresses two important questions. First, the role of Vlasov[43] himself: was he a traitor and opportunist, or was he a man of great political wisdom and a martyr who died for his followers and his country? Second, what did the Russian Liberation Movement stand for? And since the members of the Russian Liberation Movement were products of Soviet history, how should the ideas which they expressed be understood within that society? Although the whole attempt to create a Russian Liberation Movement has been the target of constant criticism, with the motives and intentions of the participants the object of particular scorn, their aims and aspirations have not, hitherto, received a detailed analysis.

NOTES

1 Nikolaevsky, B. I. 'Porazhenchestvo 1941–5 godov i gen. A. A. Vlasov', *Novy zhurnal*, 18 (1948), pp. 209–34 and *Novy zhurnal* 19 (1948), pp. 211–47.
2 See, for example, Calvocoressi, P. and Wint, G., *Total War*, London (1979), p. 471.
3 Kiselev, A., *Oblik generala Vlasova*, New York (1977), pp. 12–15.
4 West, R., *The Meaning of Treason*, revised edn, London (1982), p. 413.
5 Solzhenitsyn, A. I., *Archipelag GULag 1918–56*, vols. 1–2, Paris (1973), p. 266.

6 Interview: A. M. Bourgina. She was B. I. Nikolaevsky's widow and archivist.

7 Dvinov, B. L., *Vlasovskoe dvizhenie v svete dokumentov*, New York (1950).

8 Aronson, G. Ya, *Pravda o vlasovtsakh, problemy novoy emigratsii*, New York (1950).

9 Aronson, G. Ya., 'Parizhskiy vestnik. Progitlerovskiy organ na russkom yazyke', *Novy zhurnal*, 18 (1948), pp. 331–41.

10 Kuskova, E. D., 'Emigratsiya i inostrantsy', *Novoe Russkoe Slovo* (28 October 1949). Kuskova, E. D., 'O russkikh pochemu', *Novoe Russkoe Slovo* (28 January 1950, 3 February 1950). Kuskova, E. D. 'Boleznennoe yavlenie', *Novoe Russkoe Slovo* (18 November 1950, 22 November 1950).

11 Fischer, G., *Soviet Opposition to Stalin*, Cambridge, Mass. (1952), p. 122.

12 Thorwald, J., *Wen sie verderben wollen . . .*, Stuttgart (1952).

13 Dallin, A., *German Rule in Russia 1941–5: A Study in Occupation Policies*, 1st edn, London (1957), 2nd edn, London (1981).

14 Reitlinger, G., *A House Built on Sand: Conflicts of German Policy in Russia 1939–1945*, London (1960).

15 Streit, C., *Keine Kamaraden*, Stuttgart (1978).

16 Hoffmann, J., *Die Ostlegionen 1941–1943*, Freiburg (1976).

17 The insignia consisted of a shield depicting the white diagonal cross of St Andrew on a blue background with a red edge. St Andrew was the patron saint of Russia, white, blue and red were the national colours of pre-revolutionary Russia. The letters ROA were above the shield.

18 Interview: L. A. Rahr.

19 Kromiadi, K. G., *Za zemlyu, za volyu . . .*, San Francisco (1980), pp. 208–13. Interview: K. G. Kromiadi.

20 Interview: N. A. Noreikis.

21 Strik-Strikfeldt, W., *Against Stalin and Hitler*, London (1970).

22 Schatoff, M., *Bibliografiya Osvoboditel'nogo Dvizheniya Narodov Rossii v gody vtoroy mirovoy voiny 1941–45*, New York (1961).

23 Schatoff, M., *Materialy i dokumenty ODNR v gody vtoroy mirovoy voiny 1941–45*, New York (1966).

24 Pozdnyakov, V. V., *Rozhdenie ROA*, Syracuse (1972).

25 Pozdnyakov, V. V., *Andrey Andreyevich Vlasov*, Syracuse (1973).

26 Kromiadi, K. G., *Za zemlyu, za volyu . . .*

27 Bogatyrchuk, F. P., *Moy zhiznennyi put' k Vlasovu i Prazhskomu Manifestu*, San Francisco (1978).

28 *Komitet Osvobozhdeniya Narodov Rossii* (Committee for the Liberation of the Peoples of Russia) see pp. 60–3.

29 Kiselev, A., *Oblik generala Vlasova*.

30 Konstantinov, D., *Zapiski voennogo svyashchennika*, Canada (1980).

31 Kazantsev, A. S., *Tret'ya sila*, 2nd edn, Frankfurt am Main (1974).

32 Artem'ev, V. P., *Pervaya Diviziya ROA*, London (Ontario) (1974).

33 Aldan, A. G., *Armiya obrechennykh*, New York (1969).

34 Steenberg, S., *Wlassow, Verräter oder Patriot?* Cologne (1968), translated by Farbstein, A., *Vlasov*, New York (1970).

35 For a comprehensive discussion of this question see Hoffmann, J., *Die Geschichte der Wlassow-Armee*, Freiburg (1984), pp. 362–86.

36 *IVOVSS*, 2, p. 470.

37 Meretskov, K. A., *Na sluzhbe narodu*, Moscow (1968).

38 Samoylov, E. M., 'Sud nad predatelyami', *Verkhovny Sud SSSR*, ed. Smirnov, L. N., Kulikov, V. V., Nikiforov, B. S., Moscow (1974), pp. 371–80. Tishkov, A. V., '"Predatel" pered sovetskim sudom', *Sovetskoe gosudarstvo i pravo*, 2 Moscow (1973), pp. 89–98. Titov, F., 'Klyatvoprestupniki', *Neotvratimoe vozmezdie*, ed. Chistyakov, N. F., Karyshev, M. E., Moscow (1973), pp. 214–34. Titov, F., 'Delo Vlasova i drugikh', *Na strazhe sotsialisticheskoy zakonnosti*, ed. Chistyakov, N. F., Moscow (1968), pp. 372–90.

39 Okuntsev, I. K., *Russkaya emigratsiya v Severnoy i Yuzhnoy Amerike*, Buenos Aires (1967), p. 311.

40 For a concise exposition of the problems raised in the study of the Russian Liberation Movement, see Volkmann, H-E., 'Das Vlasov-Unternehmen zwischen Ideologie und Pragmatismus', *Militärgeschichtliche Mitteilungen*, 2 (1972), pp. 117–55.

41 Ausky, S. A., *Vojska Generala Vlasova v Cechach 1944–45*, Russian translation as *Predatel' stvo i izmena. Voyska generala Vlasova v Chekhii*, San Francisco (1982).

42 Geller, M., and Nekrich, A., *Utopiya u vlasti*, vol. 2, London (1982), p. 149.

43 Buchbender, O., *Das tönende Erz*, Stuttgart (1978), p. 365, fn. 296.

I

Foundations

Until the regime in the USSR changes its policy on access to archives, the biographer of Andrey Andreyevich Vlasov must operate with the barest minimum of material. Vlasov left no personal documents[1] and almost everything that is known about his early life stems from his own accounts to his friends and followers during the Second World War after he had become the so-called leader of the Russian Liberation Movement. Most of the reports and anecdotes originate from individuals who met Vlasov for the first time during the war, since few knew him before that period of common adversity which began with their capture by the Germans.

Surviving photographs of Vlasov show a very tall, dark and rather gaunt individual with horn-rimmed spectacles, holding himself very erect. Early in his captivity he had a crew cut, but from later photographs it appears that he allowed his hair to grow and brushed it back.

Unlike his subordinates, Vlasov never wore a German uniform. A plain jacket of military cut and deep cuffs made out of brown cloth had been obtained for him by his German sponsors – who had great difficulty in finding clothes which were large enough – and a pair of uniform trousers with general's stripes down the side. His buttons were plain and he wore neither badges of rank nor medals, nor do any photographs show him wearing the ROA sleeve badge. His greatcoat was, unlike those of German officers, waisted, beltless and with wide lapels. On the front of his general's uniform cap he wore the white, blue and red cockade of the Russian Liberation Army.

Andrey Vlasov was born in 1900,[2] the thirteenth and youngest son of a peasant, the grandson of a serf. His father wanted to provide all his children with an education and worked to supplement his income by taking in tailoring. Despite these efforts Vlasov's father still remained badly off and his youngest son's education had to be paid for by Andrey's eldest brother, Ivan. Ivan sent Andrey to a church school and later to a seminary in Nizhni Novgorod. Here, the education offered did not differ from that provided by a classical 'gymnasium' except for additional courses in psychology and an introduction to philosophy.[3] This course of study was cut short by the Revolution. With its onset, the church could no longer offer Andrey real career possibilities, at which, no doubt, his brother had aimed. In 1918 Vlasov entered an agricultural college but agriculture, too, was in a state of disarray and uncertainty. However, in the spring of 1919 Vlasov was called up, and conscripted into the 27th (*Privolzhsky*) Rifle Regiment. He served throughout the Civil War in the Red Army to which, as far as can be ascertained, he devoted all his energies. He seems to have been a good soldier and to have got on well with his comrades. He rapidly gained promotion and made steady upward progress through the ranks. After a few weeks of service he was sent on an officer training course. Four months of training later, he became a platoon commander and was sent to the Southern Front. Vlasov served with a regiment of the 2nd Don Division which was fighting against General Denikin on the Don and Manych. Early in 1920, when the White Armies had been driven out of the Ukraine and the Caucasus, the 2nd Don Division was transferred to the Crimea to fight General Wrangel's forces. Here Vlasov commanded a company and after a few months he was transferred to the divisional staff as assistant to the chief of operations. His next appointment was in command of a mounted infantry reconnaissance section in one of the regiments of the division. By November 1920 the Red Army was in control of the Crimea. At that point Vlasov was given command of a detachment in the Ukraine which fought against Makhno and other anti-Bolshevik groups, or armed bandit gangs, still in existence there. From 1921 to 1923 the Red Army was reduced considerably in strength, but Vlasov had decided to remain a professional soldier and became a company commander in the forces, now reorganised by Trotsky. He was congratulated by the Soviet chief of staff, P. P. Lebedev, when the latter inspected the North Caucasus military district, on his excellent work in training his men. On the fifth anniversary of the formation of the Red Army, Vlasov was presented with an inscribed silver watch. In 1924 he was appointed commander of the regimental training depot of the 26th Infantry Regiment. In 1928 he was sent to Moscow to attend an infantry tactics course after which he returned as a battalion commander. In 1930, in the same year as he entered the Communist party, he became a tactics instructor at the Leningrad Officers' School for further professional training. Shortly afterwards he was sent to Moscow on an instructors' course. He then returned to Leningrad as assistant to the chief instructor. Very shortly afterwards he was transferred to the mobilisation department of the Leningrad military region. In 1935, an inspection of the region with the deputy commander, General Primakov, found the 11th Infantry Regiment of the 4th Turkestan Division in poor condition. Vlasov was given command of this regiment which, shortly afterwards, was officially recognised as the best in the Kiev military region. Vlasov was promoted deputy commander of the 72nd Division. In 1938 Timoshenko, then commanding the Kiev military district, appointed Vlasov to his staff. In the autumn of 1938 Vlasov was sent to China.

The Soviet Union was pursuing a dual policy in China.[4] On the one hand it supported Chiang Kai-shek against the Japanese, and on the other the Comintern supported the Chinese communists. Vlasov, who used the pseudonym Volkov[5] while serving in China, was appointed chief of staff to the Soviet military adviser, General Cherepanov. His duties included lecturing on tactics to the Chinese military commanders. From February to May 1939 Vlasov served as adviser to General Yen Hsi-shan, Governor of Shansi. Vlasov's job was to persuade him of the necessity of joining Chiang Kai-shek's operations against the Japanese. After the recall of General Cherepanov to Moscow, Vlasov performed the duties of chief military adviser to Chiang Kai-shek. In November 1939, after the arrival of the new military adviser in China, General Kachanov, Vlasov was recalled to Moscow. Chiang Kai-shek decorated Vlasov with the Golden Order of the Dragon. Apparently Madame Chiang Kai-shek also gave Vlasov a watch, but both watch and decoration were taken from him by Soviet officials when he crossed the border on his way home. On his return from China in 1939, he was reappointed to the Kiev military district, once again under Timoshenko's command. This suggests that his superiors found him a useful subordinate. He was made commander of the 99th Infantry Division which was notorious for its disarray, due in part to its being composed of a motley assortment of various nationalities. In 1940 Vlasov was given a gold watch[6] and the Order of Lenin[7] for his work in retraining and reforming the division. The division, too, received an award, the Red Banner, and was officially acclaimed the best in the Kiev military district;[8] Marshal Timoshenko called it the best in the army. In 1940, following official recognition of his work with and successful leadership of the 99th Division, Vlasov published an article[9] in which his practical attitude to military matters can be clearly seen. He quotes Suvorov[10] and emphasises the importance of constant training and practice. Another article[11] eulogises Vlasov and strongly commends his military capabilities, his understanding and care of the men under his command, and his vigilance and accuracy in carrying out his military tasks. No mention whatsoever is made of Vlasov's involvement with or interest in the Communist party or in politics of any kind.

Vlasov's war service was of an exemplary nature. When war broke out Vlasov was on the Ukrainian Front in command of the 4th Mechanised Corps, where Soviet troops came under heavy pressure from Field Marshal von Runstedt's Army Group South. The defence of Lvov was entrusted to Vlasov, and after its fall, he had to fight his way out of repeated encirclement.[12]

In August and September 1941 Vlasov was in command of the 37th Army defending Kiev. The official Soviet history of the war mentions the 37th Army but does not name its commander. On 17 September, Lieutenant-General M. P. Kirponos, the commander of the Kiev military district, ordered all armies to break out of the encirclement. These orders were transmitted to all armies except the 37th with whom contact had been lost: 'Not having any links with the front, the troops of the 37th Army continued the stubborn fight for Kiev. Outflanked by the enemy the 37th Army only left the capital of the Ukraine on 19 September and started to fight its way out [successfully] of the encirclement.'[13]

In November 1941 Vlasov was summoned to Moscow to help with the defence of the capital. His orders were to report to Stalin at midnight on 10 November. It was his first meeting with Stalin. When Vlasov was asked what he thought of the situation, he said that the mobilisation of untrained workers without the support of the trained military reserves, i.e. the crack troops stationed in Siberia, was useless. Stalin is supposed to have replied that 'anyone can defend Moscow with reserves'[14] but gave Vlasov fifteen tanks, the full sum of what was available.

In describing the defence of Moscow, Professor Erickson writes of Vlasov as 'one of Stalin's favourite commanders', and it would appear that Vlasov was indeed a most able leader doing his utmost in an impossible situation and being given commands of increasing importance. During the defence of Moscow, Vlasov commanded the 20th Army, which is mentioned in *IVOVSS* but again without a reference to its chief. The 20th Army was part of the Northern Group defending Moscow. In the Soviet counter-attack at the beginning of December, Vlasov's troops and Rokossovsky's 16th Army fought their way to the Istra River and then to Solnechnogorsk and Volokolamsk.

Vlasov was interviewed by an American journalist, Larry Lesueur,[15] on 16 December 1941, after he had captured Solnechnogorsk and before the attack on Volokolamsk. Lesueur mentions Vlasov's popularity with his men and his optimistic frame of mind. He was going to capture Volokolamsk that night and he was going to drive the Germans back as far as possible. The French journalist, Eve Curie, working for the American press, saw Vlasov after his capture of Volokolamsk. She writes of him as: 'One of the young army commanders whose fame was rapidly growing among the people of the USSR'.[16] She mentions that Vlasov was a military man who, after twenty-three years' service, judged everything from a purely strategic point of view. When speaking of strategy he instanced Napoleon and Peter the Great as examples of outstanding military commanders. He showed a keen interest in Charles de Gaulle and Guderian as contemporary strategists. Eve Curie (somewhat naively) adds that Vlasov viewed Stalin as his direct superior, both militarily and politically, and was emphatic that the fascists must be annihilated. By January 1942, Vlasov's Army spearheaded the main attack in the Soviet counter-offensive whose final objective was to surround the German forces in the Mozhaisk-Gzhatsk-Vyazma area.

On 13 December 1941 the Soviet Informburo published a communiqué describing the German repulse from the gates of Moscow together with the photographs of those commanders who had made an outstanding contribution to the defence of the city. One of these was of Vlasov.[17] On 24 January 1942 he was awarded the Order of the Red Banner and promoted to the rank of lieutenant-general.[18]

A picture of Vlasov as a talented military commander emerges. The fact that foreign correspondents were allowed to meet him denotes that he was seen as a success by the authorities and must also indicate the high degree of trust they had in him. Once again, however, the emphasis is laid on the military side of Vlasov's achievements; there is no mention of any kind of political activity on his part.

In March 1942, Vlasov was made deputy commander of the Volkhov Front. General Meretskov, the front commander, mentions Vlasov in his memoirs as a difficult, unwilling and ambitious subordinate, lacking in initiative.[19] This statement can be assessed as one prescribed at a later date, by the Soviet authorities, who by that time were demanding that all mention of Vlasov be critical. But this statement may also be based on truth and could indicate that some personal animosity or professional rivalry existed between Meretskov and Vlasov.[20] Nevertheless, the fact that Vlasov arrived from General Headquarters (*Stavka*) in an aeroplane with Voroshilov, Malenkov and the deputy commander of the air force, A. A. Novikov, must indicate that Vlasov's appointment was seen as one of considerable importance. It must be stressed that the claims of Soviet historiography, which lay blame for the defeat of the 2nd Shock Army solely on Vlasov's cowardice and treachery, cannot be sustained. All available evidence shows that the situation on the Volkhov Front had been exceptionally difficult from the very beginning.

On 12 December 1941, Meretskov was called to GHQ and told of the creation of the Volkhov Front. The 4th and 52nd Armies had been assigned to it as well as the 2nd Shock (*udarnaya*) Army and the 59th Army which were in the process of being formed. Meretskov had asked that the 54th Army, which was part of the Leningrad defences, should be transferred to his command. The 54th Army's area of operations was adjacent to the Volkhov front, and the 54th Army was separated from the main Leningrad command by the besieging German forces. The military commander of the Leningrad Front, Lieutenant-General M. S. Khozin, and the city's political controller, A. A. Zhdanov, argued that this was not an obstacle; in any case the 54th Army could attack the German rear and relieve some of the pressure on Leningrad. On the other hand, Meretskov argued that the overall objective of the Volkhov command was to give aid to Leningrad, and that co-ordination of attacks would be hindered considerably by the lack of a unified command in the German rear. GHQ supported Khozin and Zhdanov. The 54th Army remained assigned to the Leningrad Front. Six months later, however, the position was reversed and the 54th Army, as well as the newly formed

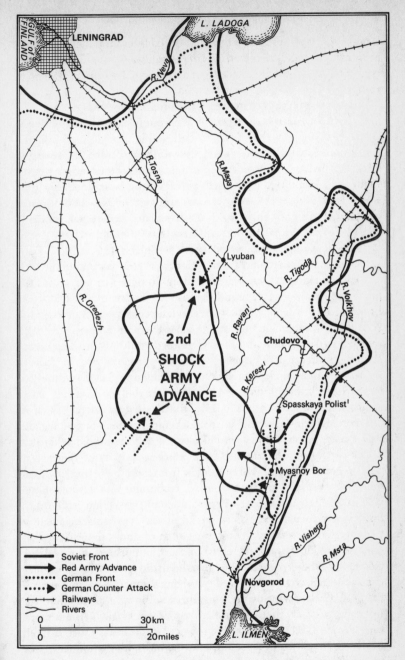

Figure 1 Sketch map of 2nd Shock Army operations, spring 1942

8th Army, was transferred to the Volkhov command. It would appear from this exchange that, from the beginning, friction existed between GHQ and Meretskov over the question of deployment of troops on the Volkhov Front. It is possible that this friction was an added element in later developments on the front, when GHQ did not respond to Meretskov's urgent demands for aid to the 2nd Shock Army.[21]

GHQ wished the troops of the Volkhov Front to continue advancing without any let-up, in order to ease the situation around Leningrad. On 13 January 1942 the armies of the Volkhov Front were thrown into the attack. German intelligence had advance warning of this and the defence was strong and the fire power heavy. The 2nd Shock Army and the 59th Army had been fully committed to the attack. Neither officers nor men were adequately trained. They lacked heavy artillery and ammunition, and were unused to the type of terrain – many of them were recruited from the steppes. It was the first time that they had found themselves in forests and they were frightened by this. In addition, there were constant complaints of the lack of air cover. The advance was slow. The 2nd Shock Army reached Myasnoy Bor and then GHQ ordered that the main attack should be directed on Lyuban and Spasskaya Polist'. Meretskov says of this campaign: 'The Staff at the front and I had overestimated the capacity of our troops.'[22] Meretskov decided that the 2nd Shock Army must be reinforced. GHQ complained about the lack of progress. Klykov, who had been commander of the 52nd Army and had replaced Lieutenant-General Sokolov as commander of the 2nd Shock Army on 10 January 1942, complained about the lack of reinforcements and air cover. Finally Meretskov went to the headquarters of the 2nd Shock Army and then to the operational headquarters with Klykov. Here he found that the problem of providing adequate reinforcements had not been solved, and that there were inadequacies in the supply of arms and rations to the front line troops. The casualty returns supplied by the chief of operations, Colonel Pakhomov, were in chaos. Furthermore, his inaccurate communiqués were confusing both the staff and the commander in the field. Orders were being transmitted so slowly that the front line troops were receiving them only after a 24-hour delay. As a result of this chaos, GHQ ordered the replacement of the chief of staff, Major-General V. A. Vizzhilin, and the chief of operations. Major-General Alfer'ev was appointed deputy commander of the 2nd Shock

Army. When Klykov became seriously ill, Vlasov was appointed commander of the 2nd Shock Army.

The advance was continued but with little success. With the spring thaw the position of the army became ever more difficult as communications and supplies were affected. Meretskov suggested three solutions for improving the position of the 2nd Shock Army. First, in order to take its objectives, the army must be heavily reinforced, and this before there was a complete thaw. Second, the army could be withdrawn and another method of achieving its objectives found. Third, the army could dig itself in until after the thaw, when the surface would become passable again, and having been reinforced, it could then renew its attack. Meretskov himself favoured the first course of action, which would allow the 2nd Shock Army to consolidate the gains of the winter campaign and would also relieve the pressure on Leningrad to some extent. The third course of action seemed completely unacceptable, as leaving the army in the swamps would endanger both its communication and supply routes and could result in its being surrounded by the Germans.

The Germans pressed home their attack and on 19 March cut the 2nd Shock Army's lines of communication. After a couple of days Meretskov obtained the necessary reinforcements, successfully counter-attacked and reopened the lines of communication. The Soviet attack was now concentrating on the Lyuban. Meretskov intended to reinforce the 2nd Shock Army with the 6th Guards Corps, which was in the process of being formed and was intended to be stronger than the 2nd Shock Army had been at its original formation. This, however, was not to be. On 23 April Meretskov heard, to his horror and astonishment, that the Volkhov Front had been disbanded. It was now to be known as the Volkhov Operational Group and had been subordinated to the Leningrad Front. Meretskov writes: 'I just could not understand why this unification had taken place. In my view there was no operational, political or any other kind of necessity for this action.'[23]

It then became apparent that General Khozin had persuaded Stalin that with this manoeuvre and these additional troops, he could lift the blockade of Leningrad.[24] Meretskov was ordered to join Zhukov on the Western Front. Before he left he telephoned GHQ to remind them of the necessity of sending the 6th Guards Corps to reinforce the beleaguered 2nd Shock Army. He was told not to worry. On 24 April he visited GHQ where, in the presence of Stalin and

Malenkov, Meretskov delivered a very blunt warning: 'The 2nd Shock Army is entirely played out. In its present state it can neither attack nor defend itself. Its communications are threatened by German attack. If nothing is done, then a catastrophe is inevitable.'[25] He suggested that if it was not possible to reinforce the army with the 6th Guards Corps, then it must be withdrawn from the forests and swamps to the line of the Chudovo-Novgorod railway. He was listened to very politely.

On 8 June, Meretskov was summoned from the Western Front to GHQ. Stalin admitted that combining the Volkhov Front with the Leningrad command had been a very great mistake. Khozin had not carried out GHQ's order of 14 May to pull back the 2nd Shock Army and they had been cut off. Meretskov and Vasilevsky were sent to deal with the situation. On 10 June new attacks were ordered. After a week of heavy fighting, a new corridor, 400 metres wide, was cut from the 2nd Shock Army to the railway line at Myasnoy Bor and the wounded were taken out. The 2nd Shock Army troops, unable to widen the corridor, since their officers had lost control and could not prevent their retreat, fell back in great disorder. By 23 June the area occupied by the Soviet army had considerably diminished and was enfiladed by German artillery fire. A new attack was scheduled for the night of 23 June. German fire was very heavy and communications were cut yet again. On the morning of the 24th, a few troops extricated themselves from the encirclement but subsequently the Germans regained their control of the railway line. On the 24th Vlasov ordered his men to break up into small groups and find their own way out of the encirclement.

Meretskov made efforts at the end of June to find Vlasov and sent in a squadron of tanks to the area where the commander and his staff had last been seen, but neither the tanks nor the partisans could find any trace of him.

Strik-Strikfeldt states that at the last moment Stalin sent in an aeroplane for Vlasov, to get him out before the terrain was finally overrun by the enemy, but he refused to board it saying he preferred to share the fate of his men. This statement is probably incorrect: first, because the number of possible landing sites, frozen in the winter but swamp in summer, would have been substantially diminished;[26] second, Meretskov says that the last landing ground was already in German hands.[27]

This account of the operation of the 2nd Shock Army shows that it was inadequately trained, poorly supplied and was sent to deal with a situation beyond its capabilities. GHQ accepted none of the recommendations made by Meretskov which would have alleviated the situation and made the attainment of various objectives possible. Although in his memoirs Meretskov makes a number of opprobrious remarks concerning Vlasov's behaviour and indifference to the fate of the army, this is in conflict with the arguments propounded in an article in a military journal.[28] In the latter, Meretskov lays all the blame for the defeat of the 2nd Shock Army on GHQ which failed to appreciate the realities of the situation.[29] Meretskov's analysis consequently exonerates Vlasov from the standard accusation in Soviet publications that it was solely due to his cowardice and treachery that the 2nd Shock Army was defeated.[30]

Vlasov was captured on 12 July 1942. His military career in the Soviet Union had now come to an end. His subsequent life and actions in Germany, until the collapse of the Third Reich in May 1945, can only be understood within the context of Nazi ideology and war aims. The picture is further complicated by disagreements among German policy makers and by the radical divergence between Russian aspirations and German objectives.

2 OSTPOLITIK

The origins of *Ostpolitik*, German policy towards the Soviet Union and the occupied territories, can be found in *Mein Kampf*. Hitler maintained that the German nation needed *Lebensraum*[31] – living space – which could only be obtained in the East. In Russian Bolshevism he saw the embodiment of the aspirations of World Jewry to achieve global domination.[32] Furthermore, Hitler regarded the Slavs as an inferior race. He considered that all the achievements of the Russian state were owing to the influence of the Germanic minority.[33] The Slavs could, therefore, be used to serve the German interests, and Russia could be exploited to the same end. In the period leading up to war and after its outbreak Hitler developed these views further and his policies were expressed very clearly to Nazi personnel: the Russians were to become the tools of the Germans. Hitler intended to destroy Leningrad and Moscow completely,[34] to isolate and exploit the Russians, and to employ their natural resources for Germany. Such policies and views were supported by the Nazi hierarchy, and Himmler's publication *Der Untermensch*[35] was used to provide further propaganda evidence of the degeneration of the Slavs as a result of oriental influence. This, in its turn, led to the implementation of a very harsh policy in the occupied areas of the USSR by party fanatics, in particular by Erich Koch, the Gauleiter of the Ukraine.[36]

The Nazi leadership was divided in its approach to the East. Alfred Rosenberg, who was in charge of the Ostministerium, and who considered himself the ideologist and foreign affairs expert within the Nazi party, despite his loyalty to his Führer, could not agree with all of the latter's views on the Eastern problem. Rosenberg accepted the premise that Russia should be exploited for the benefit of Germany, but at the same time expressed an idea which was at variance with some assumptions of the *Untermensch* theory which applied to all Slavs without differentiation. Rosenberg wished to protect and free Germany from any future political or military pressure on her Eastern frontier and was therefore opposed to creating a united Russia. Rosenberg had been educated in Riga and had taken his final examinations in Moscow. He was, therefore, familiar with Russian culture and customs and considered that the Great Russians had been a vital force in the creation of Russian civilisation. Consequently, Rosenberg proposed the creation and isolation of a Great-Russian state, Muscovy, which would be surrounded by a ring of buffer states: Greater Finland, Baltica, Ukraine and Caucasus.[37] Rosenberg wished to provide a political programme for the nationalities of the Soviet Union, with the exception of the Great Russians, to enable them to develop into semi-independent states. The practical problems of creating and administering a truncated and subservient Russia, which was surrounded by a ring of semi-autonomous buffer states, were never solved. Although Rosenberg was made Reich Minister for the occupied territories in 1941, his theories and the fact that he was neither a practical nor a successful politician, meant that he clashed with and was overborne by the hardline Nazis such as Koch, of whose appointment as Gauleiter of the Ukraine he had been chary; and although Rosenberg continued to insist on his right and prerogative he was ignored, his directives evaded and questions of administration ostensibly under his jurisdiction were carried out by other agencies.

After the unprovoked attack by the armed forces of the Third Reich on the Soviet Union on 22 June 1941, German policy towards the USSR and the Russians in the occupied territories was to be conducted along the lines indicated by the basic assumptions of Nazi ideology. However, as the war progressed various Germans began to express their reservations about the conduct of the war and the attitudes adopted towards the inhabitants of the occupied territories. *Ostpolitik* found a critic, too, in Joseph Goebbels. In his diary for 25 April 1942 he noted that the inhabitants of the Ukraine had initially welcomed the Führer as a liberator, but that this attitude had changed as a result of the harsh treatment meted out to them.[38] Goebbels thought the Germans would lessen the threat from the partisans if they could win the confidence of the people. He considered that puppet governments in the occupied areas would serve the German interests better. These governments could carry out any harsh measures that were necessary and would serve as a screen for the Germans.[39] Later he was to say that he considered it would be wiser to wage the war against Bolshevism rather than against the Russian people.[40] Goebbels did, however, emphasise that these measures should have no political significance and were of propaganda value only.

Given Hitler's views, it can be argued that war with the Soviet Union was inevitable, even if in the short run resources to conduct such a war were insufficient or a suitable opportunity for the onslaught did not present itself. However, the inevitability of this course of action was not apparent at the time either to the diplomatic corps or to the military establishment, both of whom focused their attention on avoiding conflict, fearing the destruction and loss that it would bring in its train. The ambassadors in London and Moscow, Herbert Dirksen and Count Werner von der Schulenberg, whatever their early sympathies for some aspects of the Nazi regime, found it difficult, if not nearly impossible to believe that Hitler wanted war,[41] and to the last they endeavoured to promote peace, speaking in glowing terms of the Nazi-Soviet pact and the benefits to be gained from it. Von der Schulenberg, in particular, felt that it would be disastrous for Germany to wage war with the Soviet Union[42] and made repeated representations to his government on this subject. When war did eventually break out, he used his influence to mitigate the effects of Nazi administration in the occupied territories;[43] and even though the Foreign Office was precluded from influencing *Ostpolitik*, he supported attempts to find a political solution for the East, advocating a middle course on the nationality question, with all the nationalities being allowed self-determination.

The military establishment, like the diplomatic corps, included a large number of people who represented and were conditioned by the pre-Weimar regime; they remained relatively free from the influence of the Nazi party with the result that opposition arose from within these groups and dissenting policies could be hatched and harboured for a long period without being betrayed.[44] Hitler disliked and distrusted the diplomatic corps and the professional soldiers because of their adherence to standards other than his own. He was jealous of their professional expertise and because of their dislike for and lack of comprehension of politics.[45] He attempted to minimise their influence and power but complained that, unlike Stalin, who had been able to make a fresh start by sweeping away all the class enemies, he, Hitler, had to contend daily with elements hostile towards him.[46]

From November 1937 onwards, when Hitler announced[47] to the commanders-in-chief of the three services that he proposed to take Germany into war, because of the need for *Lebensraum*, individuals in the armed forces tried to dissuade him from this course of action, which would bring disastrous consequences for Germany. Hitler was not prepared to listen to political arguments from his senior commanders and under a variety of pretexts got rid of Field Marshal von Blomberg, the minister of war, Colonel-General Werner von Fritsch, commander-in-chief of the army, and Colonel-General Ludwig Beck, chief of staff of the army. He also replaced Freiherr von Neurath, the foreign minister and appointed von Ribbentrop in his place. Many senior officers disapproved of Hitler's attitudes and policies but no concerted action could be agreed upon by them to oppose him. Hitler effectively tied the hands of the military by changing the oath of allegiance sworn by the army. When the Nazis originally came to power the army had sworn loyalty to the people and the country: after President Hindenburg's death this was changed to allegiance to the Führer and many officers felt that they could not break this oath. Furthermore, Hitler had demonstrated to the professionals that they had been mistaken in their pessimistic forecasts on the outcome of his aggressive enterprises. Austria, Czechoslovakia and the Rhineland were all annexed and occupied without bloodshed and the blitzkrieg operations against the Western Allies were more successful than the military had anticipated. When war was declared on the Soviet Union, doubts that had been harboured were expressed more openly, and as the campaign did not draw to its victorious close within six weeks as the Führer had predicted, the voice of the opposition began to be heard and alternative policies were soon under discussion.

The initial march into Soviet territory made rapid progress. Despite warnings both from the British and from his own intelligence services, Stalin could not, or would not, believe that Hitler was going to declare war on the Soviet Union in the summer of 1941.[48] When the German forces did attack on 22 June 1941, Soviet forces were caught almost completely unawares. Despite requests from some commanders based on the border, no contingency plans or orders existed in case of an attack. Stalin was apparently thoroughly shaken by the course of events, and when all was in total confusion he retired, locking himself away in his own apartments, and leaving his commanders to cope by themselves. Not only was the Red Army unprepared for a surprise attack, but at that time it was also suffering from a number of 'structural' weaknesses. The army had not recovered from the effects of the purge, initiated after the Tukhachevsky affair, in which the high command echelons were very severely hit and three out of five marshals disappeared; of the field officers, about 35,000 were arrested, subsequently imprisoned or killed.[49] With the destruction of these cadres, plans for renovation, technical improvements or advances in the army had to be shelved. The new commanders lacked experience and expertise and this was reflected in the pitiful state in which the Red Army found itself when war broke out. Indeed, some of the former, purged commanders, for example Gorbatov (who before the purge had commanded the Parachute Troops Administration), were made to swear not to divulge what had happened to them and were then rushed from concentration camps to the front line as the lack of adequately trained and experienced commanders showed up in some of the early actions of the war. Marshal Rokossovsky is another example of a Soviet commander arrested during the Tukhachevsky purge, to be subsequently rehabilitated, who played a prominent part in the defence of the USSR during the Second World War.

In addition, the population in some of the areas under attack, particularly in western Russia, welcomed the German advance, assuming that the Germans came as liberators from a hated regime rather than as conquerors, and were classed as 'politically unreliable' by the Soviet order. Initially most of the Russians who were to become involved in the so-called Vlasov movement, or Russian Liberation Movement, thought, like so many of their German contemporaries, that Nazi ideology must be based on, and take into account, logical considerations; it took an appreciable amount of time for them to realise that this was not the case and the arbitrary whims of just one man could sweep all before them. Some of the troops were unreliable too, and the capitulation by a vast number of prisoners was a result not merely of the Red Army having been taken by surprise but because some units had voluntarily gone over to the Germans, refusing to fight for the Soviet regime. To counter this, in August 1941 a directive[50] was read out to formations saying that commanders who did not carry out their orders or who showed cowardice would be demoted to the ranks or, if necessary, shot on the spot. If commanding officers should surrender to the enemy then they would be deemed traitors and their families would be arrested and punished. If the rank and file surrendered to the enemy they would also be regarded as traitors and would be annihilated by all possible methods – the order specifies air attack – and their families would be deprived of all state aid and assistance. This attitude towards those taken prisoner, for whatever reason captivity had occurred, added to the fact that the Soviet Union had not ratified the Geneva Convention of 1929[51] which dealt with the status of prisoners-of-war, meant that prisoners captured in the first few months of the war endured appalling living conditions and treatment resulting in a very high proportion (in some camps 80% or 90%) dying in the winter 1941–2.[52]

The treatment meted out to the population of the occupied areas, however, as well as to the prisoners-of-war, slowly began to swing public opinion away from support for the Germans, who were not behaving as expected of the hoped-for liberators, and towards a renewed support for the Soviet authorities. Stalin declared that the war was a 'Patriotic War' in which Russia rather than the Soviet regime was to be defended, and various reforms, particularly in relation to the church, were instigated. State pressure against the church was relaxed, greater freedom of worship was allowed,[53] and many believed that this change indicated a modification in the nature of the regime which would continue after the war.

The extent of popular disaffection at the beginning of the war was something that was recognised by both Russians and Germans opposed to Nazi policies in the Soviet Union. Russians opposed to the regime argued that this disaffection could be used to overthrow the Soviet order and to establish a non-Stalinist system. Stalin, allegedly, also feared that this might have been possible[54] in the early stages when the German forces appeared to be achieving speedy victories and the true nature of Nazism was not yet apparent to the local population. It was the treatment of the Soviet population which preoccupied the majority of Germans who disagreed with Nazi policies. They did so not because they were concerned with the fate of Russia but because they felt that winning the war was made more difficult by mistaken assumptions on which the Nazi administrators were acting.

From the beginning of hostilities, Russian prisoners-of-war had been made use of by German forces. To begin with, volunteers were used in non-military positions, such as the commissariat or ambulance services, but this developed into their being given arms and serving in military formations. These individuals serving on the German side were known as *Hilfswillige* (*Hiwis*). At the same time, units of Russians were formed; these were mostly of battalion strength and were initially known as *Osttruppen*, a name which was changed to *Freiwillige Verbände*,[55] although the names *Osttruppen* and *Hiwis* stuck. Larger formations, legions, were recruited from the non-Russian nationalities of the Soviet Union, and were called the *Ostlegionen*, consisting of Turkestan, Armenian, North-Caucasian, Georgian, Azerbaidjan and Volga Tartar legions.[56] This enterprise was fostered by Rosenberg as a corollary to his plan of independent statehood for the national minorities of the Soviet Union, and it was frowned upon by Hitler who did not wish to have his Aryan troops contaminated by other races. The only grouping favoured by Hitler was the Cossacks. In his early days as a politician Hitler had been supported by some Cossack leaders, and furthermore, Hitler had accepted the theory which demonstrated that the Cossacks were descendants of the Goths and were therefore not Slavs but Aryans.[57] A Cossack division under General von Pannwitz was enlarged to the size of a corps.

Attempts were also made to set up semi-autonomous military units from Soviet nationals but the earliest experiments along these lines were created for purely military purposes without a political programme. The history of the Russian Liberation Movement (*Russkoe Osvoboditel'noe Dvizhenie*) ROD, is a vivid illustration of the particular problems encountered on the German Eastern Front. Further, the development of ROD, the policies of the various ministries and departments which became involved with ROD, their attitudes both

to ROD and to each other illuminate the contradictions and multiplicity of authority inherent in the Nazi system.

The Russian National Army of Liberation, RONA (*Russkaya
Osvoboditel'naya Narodnaya Armiya*) led by Bronislav Kaminsky, was
better known as the Kaminsky Brigade.[58] He held sway in the
Bryansk-Lokot region, as a kind of war-lord, was equipped by the
Germans and espoused, at least theoretically, a quasi-National
Socialist platform.[59] He engaged for the most part in partisan
activity; but the brigade was disbanded in 1944 after Kaminsky had
been shot by the SS, and part of the brigade had been employed in
suppressing the Warsaw rising. The Gil-Rodionov Brigade,[60] also
known as the SS Druzhina I, was another venture along similar lines.
It was led by a Soviet lieutenant-colonel, Vladimir Rodionov, and
ended in 1943 when Gil-Rodionov returned to the Soviet side. A third
experiment was the Russian People's National Army (*Russkaya
Narodnaya Natsional'naya Armiya*) RNNA, or Osintorf (the name of the
locality where it was formed) Brigade, which was initially led by old
émigrés, including Colonel K. G. Kromiadi, also known as Colonel
Sanin, who later was to be in charge of Vlasov's secretariat. In 1942,
Kromiadi was replaced by Zhilenkov and Colonel Boyarsky, both of
whom were also later to be closely associated with Vlasov. The
RNNA was sponsored by the German Army. Field Marshal von
Brauchitsch considered it could make a vital contribution to the
fighting on the Eastern Front, and Field Marshal von Kluge[61] gave
the go-ahead for its formation, but its German and Russian leaders
were not able to see eye-to-eye and the RNNA was dissolved in 1943.

Opponents of *Ostpolitik*, however, considered that these military
formations in themselves were insufficient. They advocated the
formulation of a political solution in the East which would give the
anti-Stalin opposition something positive for which to fight. They
also insisted that treating the Slavs as *Untermensch* had the effect of
increasing resistance as well as making the task of the Wehrmacht
and the German administration more difficult. This was clearly and
openly expressed in a memorandum written by Dr Otto Bräutigam,
deputy chief of the Political Department of the Ostministerium, who
said that a Russian 'de Gaulle'[62] should be found, in the person of a
rebellious Red Army general who could lead a Soviet opposition
movement. A number of people were approached to lead a positive
opposition movement, among them Yakov Djugashvili,[63] Stalin's
eldest son, who, despite being on bad terms with his father, refused to

co-operate and apparently died in a prisoner-of-war camp. General Lukin, commander of the 19th Army, who was taken prisoner in the Vyazma-Bryansk battles in October 1941, was also considered as a possible leader, in spite of being badly wounded and subsequently losing both legs. However, although Lukin could not be called a supporter of the Soviet regime, he did not trust the Germans and refused to collaborate unless given troops and equipment immediately.[64] Into these quicksands of politics, collaboration, treachery and anti-Stalinist opposition, Vlasov was now to tread.

3 DECISION TO LEAD

After his troops had dispersed, Vlasov spent more than two weeks, from 24 June to 12 July, wandering in the swamps and forests presumably analysing his position. This fact contradicts the Soviet assertion that he gave himself up to the Germans immediately,[65] and in one case that he had had contacts with the Germans ever since the battle for Kiev.[66]

The time spent in the forest appears to have been crucial for the evolution of Vlasov's state of mind from that of a prominent Soviet commander, to that of a collaborator with the enemy, and prepared the ground for his subsequent decision to try and form an anti-Stalin Russian Liberation Army; a decision which still gives rise to bitter debates over the morality of his action.

The period between the defeat of the 2nd Shock Army and Vlasov's capture by the Germans gave him a brief respite from the constant pressure to which, as a front line commander, he had been subjected, and allowed him to reflect both on the reasons for his present situation and on possible courses of action in the future.

It must have been evident to Vlasov that he could not easily return to Soviet jurisdiction. His military career was certainly finished. He had been the commander of the 2nd Shock Army which had been beaten. Regardless of where the blame lay, he would be made to pay for it. Other commanders in similar situations had been shot.[67] Undoubtedly he would be considered a failure and probably treated as a traitor.[68] Thus, Vlasov, who had been careful to keep out of political discussions and controversy and who had concentrated on practical matters, was finally forced into a position where he had to evaluate his situation and thereby make a political decision.

It seems quite plain that during his early career Vlasov did not concern himself with politics. His posting to China in the autumn of 1938 indicates that his work was viewed in a favourable light. It is most unlikely that he would have been sent abroad at this juncture, in spite of the need for his specialist knowledge, unless he was regarded as a totally reliable individual. It is said that while in China he was careful not to get involved in political discussion.[69]

The significance of Vlasov's relatively late entry into the Communist party in 1930 has been interpreted by his supporters to mean that he never had any real sympathy for the regime. His opponents argue that it indicates that he was always politically untrustworthy.[70] Both arguments appear to be over-tendentious. This delay in membership would seem to suggest that Vlasov had kept away from political discussion, had concentrated on the practical aspects of his profession and was finally made a member of the Communist party when his rank demanded it, and possibly in recognition of his military abilities.[71] Vlasov was untouched by any purge or by the consequences of the Tukhachevsky affair. Some supporters have argued that this was because he was in China at the time.[72] This argument is totally invalid. The Tukhachevsky affair erupted in June 1937 while Vlasov was still in European Russia. Secondly, the Far Eastern Command did not escape the repercussions of the affair. Marshal Blyukher, commander of the Far Eastern Forces, was shot in November 1938. Finally, the fact that Vlasov's posting to China must have been cleared at a very high level suggests that from a political point of view, his record was unblemished and that he was sufficiently trustworthy to be sent on a foreign mission.

Later Vlasov was to tell friends of various incidents throughout his life which had produced a strong impression on him and which reinforced his anti-Stalin feelings. He said that the implications of many such incidents had been thrust below his consciousness and were only rethought during this period in the forest.

Vlasov declared that he had fought in the Red Army during the Civil War because he believed it would give land and freedom to the people. Yet throughout his life he was witness to events which showed that the Bolsheviks were not keeping their promises and were denying the people basic justice. On one occasion Vlasov recounted how he had been reading a newspaper from which it was clear that the peasantry were being very harshly repressed. He was talking it over with his wife when his chief of staff entered, to whom Vlasov remarked that yes, indeed it was a marvellous article and what a wonderful government they had. When the chief of staff left, his wife looked at him and said: 'Andrey, can you really live like that?'[73] Another negative impression intruded itself when Vlasov saw the trains at Kushchevka, a station in the Caucasus, in which the peasantry, the so-called 'Kulaki', were being transported away from their villages to labour camps and exile. He was particularly distressed that he and his wife had helped his parents by giving them a cow and because of this, a year later, they had been classed as rich peasants and punished.[74] Epstein mentions that during the Civil War, when Vlasov was fighting in the 2nd Don Division, his eldest brother was executed because he was allegedly involved in an anti-Bolshevik conspiracy.[75] This fact is not mentioned anywhere else, which seems strange, as it would be a very telling argument. If it is true, this must have left an impression on Vlasov, particularly since his brother helped finance Andrey's education.

Although the Tukhachevsky affair bypassed Vlasov, it must have raised some questions in his mind. How could so many members of the armed forces be arrested as traitors and enemies of the regime? Memoirs of the 1930s[76] provide eloquent testimony that the enormous numbers of arrests could at that time only be understood as the product of some kind of disastrous mistake. If even educated party members could see no better explanation for government policy, it is more than likely that Vlasov would not try to dwell on the implications of the affair. Nevertheless, when he returned from China Vlasov could not but have been struck by the damage inflicted on the armed forces by the purge of the officer corps. Vlasov, according to one account, was much impressed by the relative freedom he had found in China.[77] Another account states that while in China Vlasov kept out of political discussions, but that it could be deduced from various remarks that he was not in total sympathy with the Soviet regime.[78] If Vlasov had formed an unfavourable impression of the Soviet Union by contrast with China, this impression must have been considerably strengthened by the outrage of a professional soldier when confronted by the emasculation of the armed forces so manifest in the Finnish campaign. Such doubts must have been augmented when Vlasov encountered brother officers who had been rehabilitated and sent to the front. Vlasov had fought alongside Rokossovsky, rehabilitated in 1939, in the successful defence of Moscow. Later Vlasov was to say that, could he but contact him, he could easily convert Kostya Rokossovsky to his – Vlasov's – way of thinking.[79]

Early in his captivity, Vlasov recounted an occurrence at the beginning of the war which brought home to him the unpopularity of the regime among the population as a whole. Vlasov was sent back to a recently evacuated town to collect some important papers which had been forgotten at headquarters. As he entered the town in his tank he saw the inhabitants preparing to greet the Germans, whose arrival in the town was imminent, with flowers and gifts of bread and salt.[80] Vlasov was taken aback by this display; nevertheless he stopped his machine gunner from shooting at the crowd.[81] Then while fighting on the Volkhov front, Vlasov received a letter from his wife which said: '*Gosti byli*' – we've had guests – i.e. the secret police had been to search his flat.[82] This incident cannot have strengthened his faith in the regime.

The outcome of the battle on the Volkhov and the fate of his army must be the decisive factor in explaining Vlasov's state of mind. Why had he been sent to deal with an impossible situation? Why had nothing been done to support the army? For what and for whom had his men died? Vlasov said that while he was in the forest he began to see the errors of the government. He reconsidered his own fate, but decided not to commit suicide. Apparently, he compared himself to General Samsonov who in August 1914, during the First World War, had also been commanding a 2nd Army. When Samsonov felt that he had let down his country, he shot himself. Vlasov said Samsonov had something for which the latter felt it was worthwhile to die, whereas Vlasov was not prepared to shoot himself for Stalin's sake.[83]

If he was no longer prepared to continue to fight for Stalin, Vlasov was automatically ranging himself against Stalin. Although he did not seek out the Germans, he did not resist when they found him. Vlasov had rested and reassessed his purely military life, and now was to move into the political sphere. His first steps were to reveal his naivety, lack of knowledge and inexperience in this area.

On 12 July 1942, Vlasov was found in a small hut in the village of Tukhovetchi, by the intelligence officer of the German 38th Corps, Captain von Schwerdtner, and the interpreter, Klaus Poelchau. They had already identified one body as that of Vlasov, and local officials suspected that partisans were in the hut. When he heard the Germans, Vlasov came out saying: 'Don't shoot, I'm Vlasov'. On 13 July, Vlasov was taken to General Lindemann, the commander of the 18th Army at their headquarters at Siverskiy (approximately 50 kilometres south-south-east of Leningrad). Vlasov was apparently struck by his courteous reception from General Lindemann and this first favourable impression may have supported his hope that he could work with the Germans. On 15 July he was taken to Lötzen, arriving there on 17 July, where he was interrogated by OKH (Oberkommando des Heeres). A few days later he was taken to Vinnitsa, in the Ukraine, where there was a camp for 'Prominente'.

There were about 80–100 prisoners here, who were well treated and given German rations. In the camp he met other high-ranking Soviet prisoners. With one of them, Colonel Vladimir Boyarsky,[84] Vlasov wrote a letter to the German authorities.[85] In it they advanced the idea that anti-Stalin sentiment in the population at large and among the captured prisoners-of-war in particular, should be utilised by the Germans. They advocated the formation of a Russian National Army.

Judging from the exclamation marks in the margin, the concepts put forward were completely incomprehensible to the German reading the letter. Nonetheless, it appears to have been the catalyst for a number of meetings betwen Vlasov and various individual Germans opposed to Nazi policies.

Four days after writing the letter, Vlasov was visited by Gustav Hilger,[86] a diplomat who had been with Ambassador von der Schulenberg in Moscow. After his meeting with Vlasov, Hilger submitted a report to von Etzdorf, the liaison officer between the Oberkommando des Heeres (OKH) and the Auswärtiges Amt[87] in which he emphasised that mistaken Nazi policy and attitudes towards the USSR and its people, that is to say the implementation of measures which would turn Russia into a German colony, were merely increasing Soviet resistance.

Another visitor at the Vinnitsa camp was Lieutenant Dürksen from the Propaganda Department of the Oberkommando der Wehrmacht (OKW). His chief, Captain Nikolas von Grote, was also active in the search for an anti-Stalinist Soviet general, who would sign propaganda leaflets designed to be dropped on the Red Army lines, thereby increasing desertion from the forces. Dürksen also suggested that Vlasov should move to Berlin to the OKW propaganda centre at 10 Viktoriastrasse, where other 'Prominente' were held. The officers in OKH and OKW hoped that the use of Vlasov, the attendant propaganda and the consequent rise in the number of Red Army deserters would be a powerful argument in favour of changing Nazi policy. Finally Vlasov met Captain Strik-Strikfeldt, who had been sent by Colonel Reinhard Gehlen and Colonel von Roenne from *Fremde Heere Ost*, a branch of the General Staff concerned with intelligence gathering on the Soviet Union. Captain Wilfried Strik-Strikfeldt was a Baltic German, who had been educated in St Petersburg and had served with the Russian Imperial Army during the First World War. After the war, he had run a business in Riga. In 1939, following the Molotov–Ribbentrop pact he was evacuated to Poznan and in 1941 he was invited to join the staff of Field Marshal von Bock. In 1942 he was transferred to *Fremde Heere Ost*. Strik-Strikfeldt and Vlasov made friends quickly and it appears that it was owing to Strik-Strikfeldt's persuasion that Vlasov agreed to lead the opposition movement. Strik-Strikfeldt believed passionately both in the possibility of the creation of and in the fruitful effect that the Liberation Movement could have, and he was anxious that Nazi policy towards Russia should be changed in the interests of Russia herself, and not merely because of the advantages it could bring to the German war effort. In this Strik-Strikfeldt was unusual. Among the many opponents of *Ostpolitik*, few cared about the fate of Russia, they were concerned only with the best interests of Germany.

Strik-Strikfeldt became the mainstay of the whole 'Wlassow-Aktion', encouraging and supporting Vlasov through all his doubts and throughout the periods when German policy was at its most inflexible. After the war, some of the Russian participants, when discussing the failure of the Vlasov enterprise, blamed it partly on Strik-Strikfeldt's rank – he never held a position higher than Captain. Because of his lower status, they alleged, he was denied personal contact with the upper echelons of the Nazi hierarchy; in any case, he was only interested in the German point of view.[88] This is a somewhat unfair accusation since without the constant support of Strik-Strikfeldt it is arguable that the Vlasov movement would have died away at a much earlier stage. On the other hand, initially Strik-Strikfeldt, like so many of his countrymen, failed to grasp the essence of Nazism. He had once said to Vlasov: 'The Führer is still surrounded by men who are blind',[89] a remark most revealing of Strik-Strikfeldt's attitude. For a long time Strik-Strikfeldt remained convinced that Hitler would be amenable to reason, once the true state of things had been clarified to him. Since neither Strik-Strikfeldt nor many of the other supporters of the idea of the Russian Liberation Movement moved in circles close to Hitler, which would have enabled them to understand more clearly the driving force of Nazism, the whole enterprise rested on hopes which were extremely unlikely to come to fruition.

It appears the officers of OKH and OKW were concerned as to how long Vlasov would agree to co-operate if they could not make progress towards the actual formation of Russian units. Part of Strik-Strikfeldt's role seems to have been to assure and persuade Vlasov that progress could be made. Vlasov could not have failed to be in an impressionable state of mind at this juncture and the practical, patriotic rather than orthodox Nazi sentiments of these Germans must have been communicated to him. Various incidents undoubtedly had created a bad impression: on his capture Vlasov was marched at the head of a column of prisoners-of-war with the obvious desire to humiliate him.[90] At a later stage Vlasov complained that German junior officers were not sufficiently respectful to a senior Soviet officer; a major had ordered him to stand up[91] which Vlasov had refused to do, and in another incident Vlasov had refused to participate in a roll-call for all prisoners-of-war, demanding that senior officers should be paraded separately. These, however, were all minor incidents and Vlasov's introductory experiences at German hands had been good, thereby mitigating, in some measure, reports of the barbaric treatment accorded to Soviet prisoners-of-war.

His initial impressions of the Germans and the conversations he held with fellow detainees of an anti-Stalin outlook must have had a considerable effect on Vlasov. His meetings with German officials and officers who understood to some extent the situation in the Soviet Union and who appeared to sympathise with Russian aspirations, probably strengthened his hopes that a solution which would improve the lot of Russians and their country was a possibility. This laid the foundation for Vlasov's decision to co-operate with attempts to create a Russian Liberation Movement. It is equally clear that Vlasov took this decision without being fully aware of the complexities of the Nazi machine. He failed to understand the illogicality inherent in the core of the Nazi system. Vlasov was used to the USSR where the system of control was so pervasive that it would have been very unwise to criticise official policy without higher authorisation. Consequently, when German officers were openly hostile to Nazi policy, Vlasov concluded that this must echo some directive and that policy could be altered. It seems very unlikely, however, that Vlasov, whose early career proves him to have been a practical man, and whose subsequent career shows him to have had the interests of

Russia and the Russians very close to his heart, would have taken such a decision without the conviction that this movement had a chance of success, both in terms of the support that Russians would give it, and because the Nazi authorities would sanction this venture.

At last the opponents of *Ostpolitik* found what they were looking for: a well-known Soviet general who had become disillusioned with the Soviet regime and was willing to lead a liberation movement. This would provide a focus both for those Russians in the occupied territories and for those serving in the Wehrmacht who desired a positive aim for which to fight; a new non-Stalinist order within the USSR, which also was prepared to combat the German goals of ultimate destruction of the Russian state and the subjugation of its inhabitants.

Opponents of *Ostpolitik* in Wehrmacht Propaganda hoped that if they provided proof of the support in the occupied territories of the Soviet Union for a political solution, this would induce the authorities to change their policy. Wehrmacht Propaganda produced a leaflet[92] which was designed to increase desertion from the Red Army, and Vlasov was asked to sign it. At first he refused, saying that as a soldier he could not ask other soldiers to stop doing their duty. Finally he was persuaded to sign a leaflet which did not include the request to desert. The leaflet was addressed to the Red Army commanders and the Soviet intelligentsia. It was signed by Vlasov at Vinnitsa and published on 10 September 1942.

Vlasov, perhaps, did not realise the duplicity of his captors. Having used him to produce a leaflet which would ring true to the average Red Army soldier, Wehrmacht Propaganda then produced a very similar publication[93] addressed to Russian soldiers, officers and political cadres, which said that it could be used as a safe conduct through the German front lines. This leaflet was not signed by Vlasov. Another appeal, however, did bear his name and Vlasov's supporters have claimed that this was a fabrication, which he did not sign, as it contained turns of phrase which linguistically would not have been used by a Soviet officer.[94] In September another leaflet was produced which put forward a political programme consisting of thirteen points.[95] The Russian version is supposedly signed by Vlasov but the German copy is unsigned. This was written by Captain von Grote of Wehrmacht Propaganda. Von Grote had suggested that a specific political programme should be formulated for the Russian Liberation Committee. He therefore composed the thirteen point programme which was dropped over enemy lines as a propaganda leaflet in September 1942.

On 17 September 1942 Vlasov was brought to the Wehrmacht Propaganda centre dealing with Soviet affairs (WPrIV) located at 10 Viktoriastrasse in Berlin. Here Vlasov met other Russian prisoners-of-war, among them M. A. Zykov who was to play a leading role in the establishment and development of the Russian Liberation Movement, and also G. N. Zhilenkov.[96] As well as having conversations with other high-ranking Soviet prisoners, Vlasov met members of the old emigration, most notably members of the NTS, and had the opportunity of seeing their draft programme,[97] all of which undoubtedly helped him to form a more coherent and independent outlook.

Von Grote's thirteen point programme was too pro-German in orientation and was expressed in very general terms. As a result, Zykov and Vlasov decided to write their own political platform which would be of greater relevance to Soviet readers. Their programme eventually became the Smolensk Declaration[98] and was ostensibly issued in the name of the 'Russian Committee' from Smolensk. The Committee, which consisted of Vlasov as chairman and Malyshkin[99] as secretary, was an attempt to provide a focus for Russian aspirations and to bring the idea of the Russian Liberation Movement out into the open. However, the project was not given official German approval. The Committee was not recognised, and its members were not allowed to travel to Smolensk. The Declaration was signed in Berlin, on 27 December 1942. It was published on 13 January 1943, when Rosenberg gave his permission for it to be dropped on the Soviet side of the front, as a propaganda manoeuvre. The pilot entrusted with the mission of dropping the Declaration made a 'mistake'. This error was arranged by Strik-Strikfeldt, so that the Declaration was dropped on the German side of the lines, thereby making it available to the population of the occupied territories. The German supporters of the 'Vlasov enterprise' hoped that they would get support for their venture from the Ostministerium. The Ostministerium, in its turn, was in search of allies, since its prerogatives and powers were being encroached upon by Koch, Martin Bormann and those who agreed with the *Untermensch* approach. Although the Ostministerium was theoretically in favour of a political solution in the East, it was not particularly inclined to support the Vlasov enterprise since it was a Great Russian initiative which did not fit in with Rosenberg's plans for a subservient Russia and a ring of satellite states. Rosenberg, however, was willing to support Vlasov so long as he confined his efforts only to the Great Russians and did not interfere with the committees of the national minorities. Vlasov, in his turn, was at first somewhat confused by the emphasis that the Germans laid on the nationality question, which for Russians of his generation was of minor importance, although policy on this modified in the course of time. Rosenberg still had strong reservations about supporting a Russian nationalist movement. Yet he gave permission for the publication of the Smolensk Declaration because he was given to understand – incorrectly – that if he was uninterested in the Declaration, the SS would become involved and Rosenberg did not wish his authority to be challenged on yet one more matter.

The publication of the Smolensk Declaration aroused great interest among both the population of the occupied territories, and the Russian troops in the Wehrmacht. Smolensk was inundated with letters and individuals seeking the fictional Committee.

Rosenberg in his turn wrote to Hitler,[100] expressing all the arguments of the military who wanted a change in Nazi policy, and added at the end his recipe for success, which was to create committees of all the nationalities side by side with the Russians. Hitler, apparently, saw Rosenberg but took no decision on this question of political propaganda, although the dropping of copies of the Smolensk Declaration had caused a number of army agencies to ask why it was not supported by articles in the German press.

After the attempts by Wehrmacht Propaganda, in the summer and autumn of 1942, to increase desertion from the Red Army[101] and thereby to demonstrate the positive effect of political propaganda, von Grote attempted to implement the next stage in his plan. His scheme was actually twofold – to obtain official approval for the use of Vlasov's name in propaganda and to form a Russian Liberation Army. Keitel returned all the proposals sent to him, minuting on them that politics were not the business of the army. Strik-Strikfeldt, who did not realise that Hitler was not prepared to change his plans for the subjugation of the USSR, was nonplussed by this negative reaction. Strik-Strikfeldt managed to retain Vlasov's trust and to persuade him that they should continue to work for a change in *Ostpolitik*, despite Vlasov's anxiety lest his name should be used without his sanction.

The creation of the Russian training school at Dabendorf[102] and the publication of the Smolensk Declaration were additional developments in the struggle to change *Ostpolitik*. It was decided that in order to exploit further the favourable response to the Smolensk Declaration, Vlasov should be sent, under the auspices of the army groups, on a tour of the occupied territories to talk to the population, and to the *Osttruppen*, now referred to as ROA in the propaganda leaflets, even though the units were still dispersed among the German forces and under German control. This idea was the brainchild of Wehrmacht Propaganda designed to illustrate the fervent desire among the population for a political solution in the East, and their desire to gain a political entity. The tour also clearly displayed Vlasov's personal attributes: his charisma and ability to appeal to a large variety of people, his forthrightness and honesty when dealing with them, as well as a certain lack of political guile.

The first trip was organised by Colonel Martin, a subordinate of Goebbels, whose jurisdiction covered Wehrmacht Propaganda, and by von Grote with whose work Martin did not interfere. Initially, Vlasov refused to go, saying that he could not give the population of the occupied territories any positive assurances while the whole enterprise still lacked approval at the highest level. He was, however, finally persuaded by the argument that if the Nazi authorities were presented with an accomplished fact, i.e. great support in the occupied territories for the supposed movement led by Vlasov, in other words support for a political solution, then, once confronted with this development, they would come to terms with the situation. Vlasov was invited to visit the Army Group Centre.

On 25 February 1943 Vlasov, accompanied by General von Schenkendorff's intelligence officer, Lieutenant-Colonel Wladimir Schubuth and Captain Peterson, the erstwhile commandant of the POW camp at Vinnitsa, travelled via Lötzen to Smolensk. He was met by von Schenkendorff, with whom he discussed the political aspects of the Russian Liberation Movement. In the evening he spoke with great success in the theatre to a large gathering of Russians. In his address Vlasov described his career in the Red Army and his reasons for turning against Stalin. He spoke of the aims of the Russian Liberation Movement and emphasised that the Russians themselves must overthrow Stalin. He said that although the Germans were allies, National Socialism could not be imposed on Russia. Using proverbs which seem to have been popular and suited his image as a true son of the people, he added: 'A foreign coat will not fit a Russian.' In answer to specific questions about German intentions and actual possibilities available to the Russian Liberation Army, Vlasov could only express the hope that there would be increased understanding in German policy-making circles of the need for change *vis-à-vis* Russia.

During the next three weeks Vlasov visited towns and villages in the area. In addition to Smolensk, he visited Mogilev and Bobruisk, where he spoke to volunteer formations, but was prevented from making a speech over the radio by high-ranking officials in the Propaganda Ministry. He created a good impression on the members of an anti-partisan detachment known as the Volga Battalion[103] in the town of Shklov. Its commander said that Vlasov's clarity, logic and simplicity delighted him.

In all his speeches Vlasov reiterated the same ideas. His constant insistence that Russia should be independent and his emphasis on Russian national feeling were very popular. These sentiments created a favourable impression on the population and gave them hope that Nazi policy would finally be altered. On his return to Berlin, Vlasov sent in a memorandum[104] to the Nazi authorities in which he emphasised repeatedly that because of their short-sighted policies towards the population of the occupied territories, a population which had initially viewed the Germans as liberators, the Germans were alienating the people and thereby only making their own task more difficult. He stressed that it was imperative for the Germans to change their policies. At that moment, Russians in the occupied territories could be mobilised and persuaded to join the anti-Stalin camp but soon it would be too late. He insisted that the anti-Stalin Russians needed a positive goal, which the Smolensk Declaration had provided, but without further developments in this direction, the Declaration appeared unconvincing. Vlasov put forward all the arguments used by the opponents of *Ostpolitik*. Unlike them, however, he did so not because he felt it was in the German interest to produce this change, but because he was concerned with the fate of Russians under German control in the occupied territories and in Germany. Needless to say, this memorandum had no effect on the course of Nazi *Ostpolitik*, although Goebbels read it and commented: 'One cannot but be astounded at the lack of political instinct in our Central Berlin Administration. If we were pursuing or had pursued a rather more skilful policy in the East, we would certainly be further advanced than we are.'[105]

Once again the hope that fuelled the entire enterprise is evident, i.e. that when the situation on the front became more difficult, events would ultimately force the policy makers to rethink policy so that a political solution favourable to Russian interests could be found which would also further German interests. Vlasov saw this logic clearly and had no hesitation in spelling it out to both Russians and Germans.

Since the first trip was successful in demonstrating that the population of the occupied territories wanted a political solution, a second trip was arranged. Vlasov was supposed to appear at the May Day celebrations at Pskov. He once again refused to co-operate. He said that he had nothing to offer troops or civilians in the occupied territories and was not prepared to deceive them. Vlasov was eventually persuaded to change his mind but not, apparently, without the use of threats.[106]

Vlasov was invited to visit Army Group North by Field Marshal von Küchler. He was accompanied by Eduard von Dellinghausen, who acted as interpreter and was a representative of the OKW and by Rostislav Antonov, Vlasov's aide-de-camp. The visit started off badly. They had to travel by train in a third-class compartment and ran out of food and tobacco. Vlasov was in a very bad mood and repeatedly said that he would go back to Berlin at the first opportunity. Moreover, he did not know von Dellinghausen and was suspicious of the latter's motives. They arrived in Riga late on 29 April and the warm reception given to them by members of the German Propaganda Department put Vlasov in better spirits. In the morning, Vlasov met journalists and then continued his journey to Pskov. Arriving in the evening, he met representatives of various Russian organisations including, once again, representatives of the Russian Orthodox Church.[107] The next day, 1 May, Vlasov spoke at a factory and later at a theatre, in each case to overflowing auditoriums. He was warmly greeted everywhere. After Pskov, Vlasov went on to visit various towns and villages including: Luga, Volosovo, Siverskiy, Tolmachevo, Krasnogvardeysk, Pozherevitsy and Dedovichi. At Luga, the crowds in their excitement broke through the police cordon. Everywhere Vlasov was greeted with great enthusiasm and his speeches were rapturously received. Those records of Vlasov's speeches which are still in existence show that his utterances dwelt on the same themes, and that he impressed many, even those who were critical of his actions.[108] He stressed again that

Russia would not permit any form of foreign domination.[109] The German nation, in alliance with the Russians, would help to overthrow the Stalinist dictatorship just as, he said, the Russians had helped the Germans to get rid of Napoleon. He explained that Stalin was using various methods to deceive the population as to his real intentions and Vlasov repeatedly made the point that they must not be taken in by this. Vlasov's nationalism was very blatant and he made little effort to camouflage it from the authorities. At one gathering he asked the crowd whether they wished to be slaves of the Germans, to which with a roar they replied: 'No!'[110] Although not an accomplished orator, he spoke with great firmness and his vocabulary was directed at and appealed to the man in the street rather than to the intellectuals, who nevertheless listened to him with interest.

The success of Vlasov's trip in the occupied territories was all that his supporters had anticipated, and provided incontrovertible evidence that the course of *Ostpolitik* should be changed. However, the outcome was a rebuff to all such hopes. In March 1943, Himmler sent Bormann a memorandum[111] in which he said that Wehrmacht publicity for the Russian Committee was clearly in contradiction to the Führer's will. Later, Himmler received a report of Vlasov's speech given at Gatchina (Krasnogvardeysk), during the second trip, in which he said that the anti-Stalinist Russians were guests of the Germans at present, but when they had won the struggle and were in power, then the Germans would be their honoured guests. Himmler was enraged by the suggestion that 'subhumans' should dare to invite Germans anywhere, and reported this remark to Hitler. Immediately an order was issued by Field Marshal Keitel[112] that Vlasov must be returned to prisoner-of-war camp and that his name henceforth should be used only for propaganda purposes.

At the same time Rosenberg was unhappy about the sponsorship of a Russian national movement. As Goebbels noted in his diary for 29 April 1943: 'The Russian General Vlasov, who is fighting on our side in a separatist Army, has been pretty much shelved by the Ostministerium.'[113] Vlasov, it appeared, had lost all support within the Nazi hierarchy.

Vlasov's conduct during these visits shows him to have been a single-minded individual. He had decided on a course of action and was not prepared to compromise to any great extent. Once again there is little indication of political subtlety on his part. His rationale was that his duty to his country demanded that he should be open and honest with his compatriots even when this led to conflict with the German authorities.

Conjointly with his visit to the occupied territories, Vlasov's Open Letter: 'Why I decided to fight against Bolshevism'[114] appeared. This publication was designed to strengthen the effect created by Vlasov's visits to the occupied territories. It gave an explanation of Vlasov's own change of attitude towards the Soviet regime, a change which he called upon his countrymen to copy. At the same time the Letter was a call to arms. Vlasov stressed that he was a typical product of the regime, but that gradually he had become aware that many of the hardships endured by the Russian people were the result of policies carried out by the state. Vlasov declared that during the war he had realised that the interests of the people were not those of the government. This interpretation of his actions, and Vlasov's speeches during his two tours, with the accent placed on patriotism, evoked a very favourable response from the local population. However, the strongly critical reaction of the Nazi hierarchy to this initiative precluded the supporters of the Vlasov enterprise from capitalising on this response, and from developing their ideas any further.

The threat of sending Vlasov back to the prisoner-of-war camp was not carried out, but he was placed under virtual house arrest in Dahlem, a suburb of Berlin. He was, however, able to visit the training camp at Dabendorf, whenever he wished, which was less than twenty miles south of Berlin. In November 1942, Gehlen and Count Claus von Stauffenberg had authorised the setting-up of this training camp for Russians at Dabendorf.[115] It became and remained a centre of activity for the Russian Liberation Movement. Dabendorf was under the control of the Propaganda Department of OKW. Baron Georg von der Ropp, who had organised propaganda courses at the Wulheide prisoner-of-war camp, near Berlin, under the auspices of the Propaganda Ministry and the OKW, directed the training programme at Dabendorf.[116] Strik-Strikfeldt headed the propaganda section with Captain von Dellinghausen as his deputy. Strik-Strikfeldt was responsible to the OKW, the Propaganda Ministry, the Ostministerium and the SS; he used this multiplicity of authority to his own advantage by playing one department off against another. The Russians picked volunteers, mostly from among the *Hilfswillige*, who were sent to the camp where, in addition to physical and military instruction, they listened to lectures, took part in discussions and were trained to disseminate the ideas of the Russian Liberation Movement. The assumption underlying the organisation of the camp at Dabendorf was that the Russian POWs and the *Ostarbeiter* should be taught to think in a different way from that which had been inculcated in Stalinist Russia. They would then work within the system of military formations in order to explain these new ideas to their fellow soldiers. Thus, their job was, in some respects, a parallel to the political proselytising role of the commissars in the Red Army, except that the Russian Liberation Movement was expressing different ideas. These Dabendorf 'graduates' were supposed to encourage discussion which would be free from the limitations imposed by Soviet ideology. They were taught to see the faults in the Soviet approach, and thereby were to encourage their 'students' to think along less stereotyped lines.

Despite the efforts of the top Nazi hierarchy to try and impede the development of the 'Wlassow-Aktion', the success of Vlasov's trips in the occupied territories seemed to the Germans to confirm the hypothesis that *Ostpolitik* should acquire a political flavour. An idea put forward by Gehlen and Colonel Heinz Danko Herre of *Fremde Heere Ost* was developed, and on 6 May 1943 the *Silberstreif*[117] propaganda campaign was launched. This campaign was aimed at Red Army soldiers in an attempt to get them to desert. The propaganda of earlier attempts to increase desertion, a mixture of crude anti-semitism and material inducements, had been dropped and was replaced in the *Silberstreif* campaign by the appeal of the 'Russian Committee', the Russian Liberation Army and a pledge to treat deserters separately and better than other prisoners-of-war. Apparently, desertion did increase during this period, but this might well have been attributable to other factors and the impact of the *Silberstreif* campaign is neither clear-cut nor easy to assess. The Soviet authorities, however, seem to have taken note both of this propaganda campaign and of Vlasov's visits to the occupied territories and saw in these events an indication heralding a change in Nazi policy.[118] In 1942, Soviet propaganda had either remained silent on the subject of Vlasov's capture, or made out that he was being used against his will by the Propaganda Ministry. By 1943, however, the position changed, and much more systematic propaganda, to counter the injunctions of the Russian Liberation Movement, was issued.

This campaign even included an agent, Major S. N. Kapustin,[119] who had orders to join the Liberation Movement, kill Vlasov, and set up subversive cells within the Movement.[120]

Notwithstanding the disappointment shared by Vlasov and his staff at Keitel's 'detention' order after the second trip, it was agreed that the fight could still be continued despite the obstacles in its path. In July 1943, Major-General Malyshkin travelled to Paris to give an address at the Salle Wagram. This speech informed the older generation of Russian émigrés in Paris – the centre of post-1917 émigré life – of the existence and aims of the Russian Liberation Movement. Both Zherebkov[121] (who had initiated this meeting) and Malyshkin were reprimanded for their part in the event.[122] While it seemed that the Russian enterprise was at last getting off the ground, with a centre forming at Dabendorf, and the population of the occupied territories showing interest in the idea of a Russian Liberation Army, Hitler made it quite clear that he was absolutely against all such developments and took steps to prevent further action. On 8 June 1943, Hitler met Field Marshal Keitel, chief of the High Command of the German forces, and Colonel-General Zeitzler, chief of the General Staff of the German army, for a conference at Berghof.[123] Keitel had wished to hold the conference to discuss the *Silberstreif* propaganda campaign. He was worried about the wording of the leaflets used in this campaign. Hitler, as the protocol of the conference shows, was not alarmed by this aspect, but he was angry at the political conclusions being drawn by some of the military. Hitler emphasised that the Vlasov enterprise was to be confined purely to the realm of propaganda which was to be directed at the Soviet side of the front. Hitler did not wish Vlasov to travel in the occupied territories, encouraging the growth of aspirations to national independence and the creation of a Russian Army. Hitler stated: 'We will never build up a Russian Army, that is a phantom of the first order.' During the conference, Keitel and Zeitzler were at pains to conceal the extent to which military formations composed of the national minorities of the Soviet Union and of Great Russians already existed, and alleged that most of the Vlasov propaganda had been linked to the *Silberstreif* campaign.

Hitler also seems to have sensed the fact that the conflict between Nazi and Russian aims was such that there could not be real co-operation between them, and that eventually the Russian Liberation Movement might turn against its protectors. As a result of the

Berghof conference, a special talk was given to commanders of army groups on 1 July 1943.[124] Since Hitler was anxious that the value of auxiliary troops should not be overrated, it was stated that Eastern battalions could be formed but that no political developments should follow. At the same time, Keitel wrote to Rosenberg[125] to say that the National Committees should not be used to recruit volunteers, that Vlasov was not to travel in the occupied territories, and that, although propaganda mentioning Vlasov's name might be used, none of his programme was to be taken seriously. This was a severe blow for the advocates of a Russian Liberation Army, and members of Vlasov's entourage were to have considerable difficulty in persuading him that he had to continue to promote his ideas.

Despite all these initiatives, the publication of the Smolensk Declaration, Vlasov's visits to the occupied territories, his Open Letter and then the inauguration of the *Silberstreif* propaganda campaign, all of which had proved that there was overwhelming support for a political solution to the Eastern question, no change materialised in *Ostpolitik*. The reaction of the authorities to Vlasov's first trip was an eloquent pointer to their attitudes. Vlasov was deeply disappointed and depressed by Keitel's first order that meant he was to be kept under virtual house arrest, prevented from making any further trips and from expounding his programme, but the *coup de grâce* and Vlasov's final awakening to the realities of Nazism came when he heard the results of Hitler's conference on 8 June 1943. Hitler's adamant reiteration of the fact that a Russian army would never be created was kept from Vlasov for as long as possible by Strik-Strikfeldt.

When Vlasov did learn of Hitler's conference, he completely lost heart. He said that he would return to prisoner-of-war camp. Malyshkin is said to have evoked the memory of the Decembrists who likewise suffered because of their desire for freedom. The Vlasovites certainly considered the Decembrists as their precursors in the struggle for liberty. Zykov and Major-General Trukhin, Vlasov's chief of staff, tried to persuade Vlasov to continue with the struggle and remain as leader of the Movement. They were afraid that if he gave up, his place would be taken by opportunists and reactionaries. Vlasov replied that he would consider it. Strik-Strikfeldt mentions a meeting with an unnamed general, who said to Vlasov that all was not yet lost and that even the appointment of a new supreme commander was possible. This man was, presumably, involved in the conspiracy to assassinate Hitler. According to Strik-Strikfeldt, after this meeting, Vlasov decided to continue to head the Liberation Movement.

But the news of Hitler's decision had shocked Vlasov profoundly. He must now have realised that there was little possibility for the development of any initiative on his part since the Führer's opposition to ROA was adamantine. He had hoped that Hitler would see reason but these hopes had been in vain. It had now been made obvious to him that the Russian Liberation Movement rested on very fragile hopes. It would only continue underground, as a conspiracy. This realisation was certainly a watershed in Vlasov's development as the leader of ROD. It does seem that after this Vlasov's determination to succeed gradually withered away.

After the summer of 1943, all attempts to reopen and encourage the Vlasov enterprise were in vain. Wehrmacht Propaganda's belief in the efficiency of the enterprise waned. The Wehrmacht had never been trusted wholeheartedly by Hitler. The Ostministerium was losing most of its power, and in any case Rosenberg had never really approved of this policy. The Abwehr, which had always been an advocate of a political approach to the Eastern question, was being swept increasingly into the orbit of the SS. In August 1943, Otto Bräutigam reiterated the idea[126] that some hope must be given to the Russians, that the population of the occupied territories needed to know that the Germans did not regard them merely as a colony fit for exploitation. Once again, this appeal fell on deaf ears. A few individuals, such as Edwin Erich Dwinger, an author and erstwhile SS officer, who originally had agreed with the *Untermensch* idea, but had been converted to a different way of thinking – and then had been attacked for his heretical views – still agitated on behalf of the Vlasov enterprise. So did Melitta Wiedemann,[127] a journalist who edited the anti-communist periodical *Die Aktion*, and who supported Vlasov and tried to introduce high-ranking officers of the Russian Liberation Movement to Nazi dignitaries. This also had no effect and although activity at Dabendorf continued, the whole project effectively went into abeyance.

This period of forced inactivity for Vlasov was filled by visits to Dabendorf, and travel in Germany accompanied by Strik-Strikfeldt; Vlasov visited Magdeburg, met Baldur von Schirach in Vienna, toured Frankfurt, Mainz, Cologne and took a trip along the Rhine. He also had meetings with the older generation of émigrés such as

General Biskupsky,[128] a member of the ROVS, and head of the Russian émigré community in Germany, and with S. L. Woyciechowsky,[129] head of the émigré community in Warsaw. Vlasov, on the whole, created a favourable impression on many who had been inclined to be sceptical of his motives and aims. Vlasov's persuasive explanation of why and how he had decided to turn against the Soviet regime also seems to have had an impressive effect. Vlasov's meeting with Dr Robert Ley, the head of the Deutsche Arbeitsfront, however, was not a success. Ley failed to understand any of his patriotic motivation and thought that Vlasov had been personally offended by Stalin.

In September 1943, a further blow was dealt to the idea of developing a Russian Liberation Movement. Reports reached Hitler of defections among the *Osttruppen* to the Soviet partisans. Apparently, these reports so enraged him he demanded that all the units be disbanded, and the men sent to the mines and factories.[130] Objections were raised by the High Command since this order would have involved between 800,000 and 1 million men, which would have been an enormous loss in manpower. All the German elements in favour of the *Ost* formations had to intervene to get this order reversed. General Heinz Hellmich, GOC *Osttruppen* under the OKH, ascertained from all the division commanders the exact number of desertions. Finally, a compromise was reached. The units were not disbanded but were transferred to the Western Front. This decision was unacceptable to Vlasov and his associates as it negated the essential feature of the Liberation Movement, that these Russian troops wished to fight Stalin. Indeed, on hearing of this decision, Vlasov again suggested that he should withdraw from the whole enterprise and return to prisoner-of-war camp; he was dissuaded from doing so. Wehrmacht Propaganda was keenly aware of the effect of this order on morale and von Grote drafted a letter which he wished Vlasov to sign, a move unexpectedly approved by Jodl. Vlasov refused to sign the letter[131] unless changes were made, but OKW published the letter without making the alterations. The text of the letter appeared in the German-controlled Russian press with the opening sentence: 'By order of the High Command of the German Army ...'[132] a form of words often used to indicate items in *Zarya* or *Dobrovolets* which appeared as a result of German insistence and not because the Russian staff of the newspapers agreed with the given article. Steenberg suggests a different interpretation of Vlasov's reaction to the transfer, and says that Jodl's approval of the idea of the letter cheered Vlasov as it was an indication that he realised Vlasov's moral authority with the Russian troops, and, therefore, was giving some indication of official approval for a Russian Liberation Army. This interpretation does not seem to fit in with Vlasov's growing pessimism about the possibility of a successful outcome to the proposed Liberation Movement, a pessimism brought on by his increased experience of the Nazi machine. If Vlasov was encouraged by Jodl's approval of the letter, then it seems that he was clutching at straws precisely because he was depressed at the impasse reached, rather than because he considered it to be a genuine indicator of a change in direction of *Ostpolitik*.

By January 1944, most units had been tranferred to the Western Front. Vlasov was not allowed to visit them, although General Malyshkin reviewed the units in France, and General Trukhin inspected others in Italy.[133] Both emphasised to the troops that the transfer would be of short duration. However, although this may have satisfied the demands of the OKW in terms of maintaining levels of manpower, it did not satisfy the units concerned in terms of their political aspirations. And although Jodl's letter helped to curb and contain displeasure in the ranks, it was clear to them that there was less chance of forming a Russian Army of Liberation than ever before.

The impetus for further development came from an unexpected quarter: the SS. Himmler had been one of the most fanatical exponents of the *Untermensch* idea, and in 1943, when many people were beginning to reject the concept of a Slav as a subhuman being, had said: 'How the Russians or the Czechs are doing is a matter of total indifference to me ... Whether these peoples live in prosperity or starve to death interests me only in so far as we need them as slaves for our *Kultur*. Whether 10,000 Russian females drop dead from exhaustion while digging an anti-tank ditch interests me only in so far as the anti-tank ditch is finished for Germany.'[134] Himmler had also inveighed against Vlasov and had nothing but scorn for those who supported him. Despite such blood-curdling utterances and the policies consequent upon them, it was the SS and Himmler who were instrumental in creating a reality – limited though it was – out of the myth of the Russian Liberation Army.

This apparent volte-face was less sudden than it might appear. Although Himmler had envisaged that the SS were to be the Nazi elite, composed of individuals who were 'racially pure', and who were in the forefront of the struggle to spread Nazi ideology, in reality this purity and single-mindedness demanded by Himmler was not maintained. The Waffen SS, the elite of Nazi troops, began to lose some of its racial and ideological purity.[135] SS Brigadeführer Gottlob Berger was responsible for recruitment into the SS, which was in any case regarded with great disapproval by the regular soldiers in the Wehrmacht. Berger recruited 'racial Germans', for instance those in Rumania, into the Waffen SS. By the spring of 1941 the 'Viking' SS Division had been formed from recruits from Denmark, Holland, Belgium and Norway, all countries which could be considered ethnically Germanic, or which had a Germanic element. From this Berger went on to persuade Himmler that even the Eastern peoples could be recruited, and divisions were formed from the Baltic nationalities, the Ukrainians and the Balkan Muslims. Russians, such as those in the Kaminsky Brigade, also came under the control of the SS at this time.

Himmler had been unwilling to disagree with his Führer on the question of the Vlasov enterprise. In 1943, Himmler is supposed to have called Vlasov 'a Bolshevik butcher's apprentice'[136] and had forbidden Colonel Gunther d'Alquen to have anything to do with the Vlasov enterprise. Yet, early in the summer of 1944, under pressure from d'Alquen,[137] Himmler was forced to reconsider his position and finally agreed to meet Vlasov. D'Alquen was an SS officer who had been editor of *Das Schwarze Korps*, the SS paper known for its fanaticism but also for its occasional deviation from Nazi orthodoxy. His experience on the Eastern Front gradually convinced him that the Nazi approach towards the population was a mistake. After mid-1943, with the phasing out of the *Silberstreif* campaign, desertion from the Red Army had decreased. D'Alquen organised another similar campaign, code-named *Skorpion*.[138] He persuaded Himmler that two of Vlasov's colleagues, Zykov and Zhilenkov, might be used in the *Skorpion* propaganda operation. D'Alquen even proposed that Zhilenkov might head the Liberation Movement in place of Vlasov,[139] but Zhilenkov declined. Himmler agreed to meet Vlasov on 21 July 1944, but the assassination attempt on Hitler on the previous day caused an indefinite postponement of the meeting.

Strik-Strikfeldt took Vlasov off for a holiday to a convalescent home for SS officers in Ruhpolding, Bavaria. This home was run by a widow, Frau Heidi Bielenberg,[140] whom Vlasov was eventually to marry. This marriage has been a matter of some debate among

Vlasov's staff and supporters. Frau Bielenberg spoke no Russian and knew next to nothing about the Soviet Union; Vlasov spoke next to no German. Furthermore, it seems probable that Vlasov knew that his wife was still alive in the Soviet Union. Colonel Kroeger, later to become the liaison officer between Vlasov and the SS, considered that much of the initiative for the marriage came from Frau Bielenberg. She was attracted by the idea of marriage to someone who was intending to overthrow Stalin, and she imagined that she would become First Lady of the New Russian State. According to Kroeger, Frau Bielenberg's mother insisted that her daughter must marry Vlasov, that the relationship should be legal.[141] It is also possible that the SS encouraged this marriage in order to keep Vlasov's mind off politics. If he knew that his first wife was alive,[142] and simply submitted to pressure from the SS to contract this second marriage, this could be a further indication that Vlasov, normally strongminded, had lost much of his will to resist and most of his faith in the possibility of creating a Russian Liberation Army. It was also a bad tactical move to marry a German, especially the widow of an SS officer. Vlasov was leading a Russian movement, a movement opposed both to the Soviet regime and to Nazism. A German wife, a non-Russian speaker, was not likely to be the helpmate needed to encourage the patriotic impulse necessary in such a movement. The Vlasov enterprise suffered yet one more blow at this juncture because many of those who had encouraged a change in *Ostpolitik*, including von Stauffenberg, von der Schulenberg, General von Tresckow and Colonel von Freytag-Loringhoven perished for their part in the 20 July plot.[143]

However, various individuals continued to press for the SS to take over the operation, arguing that otherwise the Ostministerium would do so. Finally, Himmler met Vlasov on 16 September 1944, and it appears that Hitler gave his blessing to the meeting. No transcript remains of this meeting.[144] Strik-Strikfeldt was not allowed in, and Vlasov spoke to Himmler in the presence of d'Alquen, and SS-Oberführer Dr E. Kroeger, who had been head of the Russian desk under Dr Fritz Arlt in Berger's department at the Ostministerium. Kroeger was of Baltic origin and spoke Russian, and ostensibly because of this Strik-Strikfeldt was excluded. Standartenführer Ehlich of Amt III (SD) was also present at the meeting. One account[145] has it that Colonel Sakharov, a Russian émigré and one of Vlasov's aides-de-camp was also there, but others maintain that Vlasov was the only Russian present at the meeting.

Vlasov seems to have regained some of his old energy, and Himmler[146] was apparently favourably impressed by his direct and fearless speaking, and seemingly strong personality. Vlasov put his case resolutely, pointing out all the errors of the German administration. For his part, Himmler, when asked why the SS had produced the *Untermensch* publication which had done so much harm, replied that every race had its subhumans.

At this meeting Himmler gave the go-ahead for the official formation of the KONR (*Komitet Osvobozhdeniya Narodov Rossii*), for the publication of their Manifesto, and for the formation of divisions to be commanded by Vlasov. There seems to be some discrepancy over the number of divisions promised. Vlasov apparently considered that he had been promised ten divisions, and was bitterly disappointed[147] when it was made clear that the Germans would only countenance the formation of two, with the third as a possibility. In addition there is an undated memorandum,[148] possibly the draft of a formal agreement produced by Berger's office, in which the Russian Liberation Movement renounced the territory of the Crimea and promised self-government to the Cossacks and extensive cultural autonomy to the national minorities within Russia. To what extent this can be regarded as a true expression of the views of the parties concerned is arguable, since by the autumn of 1944 the German forces no longer held the Crimea. Also, since Vlasov always promised that the national minorities would be allowed to determine their own future, it would not appear that Vlasov was agreeing to anything very significant.

The formation of the Committee and the divisions, as well as the composition of the Manifesto involved Vlasov in a great deal of work. He was chairman of KONR, and also became commander-in-chief of the KONR troops. It seems probable that Vlasov occupied himself with the various details to avoid contemplating the wider implications. It was clear that KONR had been launched too late, especially since the population of the occupied territories, whose support would have been so valuable, and on which Vlasov had placed such great hopes, had now returned to Soviet jurisdiction.

After the meeting with Himmler, work went ahead in choosing members of KONR and in writing the Manifesto. The date set for making the Manifesto public was 14 November 1944, and the venue chosen was Prague, the last major Slav city still in German hands. From the point of view of the Russians, the official opening was somewhat of an anticlimax,[149] in that no one from the highest echelons of the Nazi party attended. The publication of the Manifesto, consequently, was not the triumph that the Russians had hoped that their official recognition by the German authorities would prove to be. Himmler sent a telegram, Hitler was silent. The ceremony[150] itself was attended instead by Frank, the protector of Bohemia and Moravia, and by Lorenz, von Ribbentrop's deputy. Initially, Himmler had been expected to attend. But in order not to provoke Rosenberg any further and to lessen the chances of the latter fomenting discord over the advisability of promoting the Vlasov enterprise, Himmler changed his mind.[151] It is possible that Lorenz was sent in order to give the whole project a wider appeal. If Himmler had attended the ceremony it would have appeared that Vlasov was merely a tool of the SS, but with the arrival of a representative of the Foreign Ministry, KONR appeared to have some vestige of international significance. In his speech, Lorenz conveyed greetings from the German government. He acknowledged the Committee as the mouthpiece and representative of the peoples of Russia, he affirmed the German determination to fight Bolshevism and said that Germany would provide aid for her ally, Vlasov and his forces.[152]

The fact that the German authorities were now referring to the Russian Liberation Movement as their ally, vividly illustrates German weakness at this stage of the war. But although Himmler had been anxious to appropriate this last 'weapon' and to consolidate his power *vis-à-vis* the Ostministerium and the Foreign Office, once he had achieved his goal he seemed in no hurry to champion the enterprise further. Although every minute was supposedly of value, and the Russians were impatient at the delay, Vlasov was only given command of two incomplete and ill-equipped divisions on 28 January 1945.[153]

At the Prague meeting, the Germans had referred to Vlasov and KONR as their ally and after the meeting implied that KONR was now acknowledged as an autonomous group on an equal footing with the Germans. But the practice remained rather different from theory, and relations between the German authorities and the Russian opposition movement were not good, with each side distrusting the other.

4 KONR AND THE FINAL STAGES

A record of the discussions of KONR and the activities of its various sections and sub-committees has not been preserved for posterity.

The haste with which the Russians were trying to bring the organisation into being, the confusion of the last few months of the war, and particularly the effects of Allied bombing, did not facilitate the preservation of records, while the minutes of the KONR meetings and the lists of names of those involved were deliberately destroyed by Vlasov's secretariat before the evacuation of KONR from Berlin so that this information should not fall into the hands of the Soviet authorities.

KONR was intended to represent the peoples of Russia and consequently its members were to be a cross-section of Soviet society and representatives of the various nationalities of the USSR. Of the thirty-seven full members who signed the Manifesto,[154] thirteen were members of the Red Army, nine were Soviet professors or lecturers, and seven were members of the old emigration, in addition to a peasant woman and seven others; the associate members included two factory workers. Of the non-Russian nationalities of the USSR there were representatives of the Ukrainians, the Kalmyks, Belorussians, Cossacks, the nationalities of the Caucasus and of Turkestan. After the Prague meeting, KONR grew in size to 102 members[155] but no record remains of the names of all the individuals concerned. Although the appointment of the members of KONR was theoretically purely a matter for the *Wlassow-Aktion*, in fact the German authorities had to give their consent. It was intended that the full Committee of KONR should meet each month to ratify the decisions taken by its various sub-committees. After the original meeting in Prague, and a similar meeting to publish the Manifesto in Berlin on 18 November,[156] the second KONR meeting occurred on 17 December 1944[157] and the third and last meeting took place on 27 February 1945, after the evacuation of KONR from Berlin, at the Richmond Hotel, Karlovy Vary, Czechoslovakia. There was no full meeting of KONR in March and April, only the Praesidium met[158] and discussed, for the most part, the difficulties in equipping and deploying the KONR forces.

A number of sections were established:[159] the Military Section, headed by Vlasov himself, and with General Trukhin as chief of staff; Central Administration was organised by General Malyshkin with D. A. Levitsky, an émigré from Riga, as secretary; the department dealing with civilian affairs, for the most part with problems connected with the *Ostarbeiter*, was under General Zakutny, with Y. K. Meyer, an émigré, as secretary. The Propaganda Section was headed by General Zhilenkov and the Security Section by Colonel Tenzerov. Further sections were: the Financial Department headed by Professor S. Andreyev, the Academic Committee under Professor Moskvitinov, and the Red Cross under Professor F. P. Bogatyrchuk. Because there were difficulties in setting this up at an international level,[160] owing to the already existing Soviet Red Cross, a new name was coined, 'National Aid' (*Narodnaya pomoshch*). This acted, in effect, as a department of social services, collecting donations and distributing them to those in need, and was organised by G. A. Alekseev. The KONR newspaper *Volya naroda* was edited by an émigré, A. S. Kazantsev,[161] although final responsibility rested with Zhilenkov. The central Cossack HQ was commanded by General Tatarkin; the Foreign Department was run by Y. S. Zherebkov; a legal department was set up, the adviser was Professor I. D. Grimm; a youth section was also established, which after the war became the basis of the post-war émigré Vlasovite organisations. Some of the departments were little more than notional, for example the Cultural Department, which would account for some minor discrepancies in the memoir literature. Others were in existence and active even before the Prague meeting. For some time before the official formation of KONR, members of the Russian Liberation Movement had tried to improve the position of the *Ostarbeiter*. They wanted the *Ostarbeiter* to be treated on an equal footing with all other groups of workers,[162] and to have the *Ost* sign – worn by all *Ostarbeiter* to distinguish them – removed. The Department of Civilian Affairs dealt with complaints about the treatment of *Ostarbeiter* and was involved in negotiations to improve their conditions. Finally, on 26 January 1945, Himmler issued an order that *Ostarbeiter* were not liable to corporal punishment. The *Ost* badge, however, was not removed, and KONR and the KONR forces continued to receive complaints from *Ostarbeiter* about the treatment which they received at German hands. An apparent success was scored by the Financial Department: on 18 January 1945 the government of the Third Reich concluded a credit agreement with KONR.[163] It stated that the government of the Third Reich would advance an unspecified sum to KONR for use in the struggle against Bolshevism which would be paid back to the German government once the Committee was in a position to do so. This credit agreement has been used by a number of supporters of ROD as proof[164] that KONR was on an equal basis with the German forces: they were allies and not hirelings.

Between the beginning of December 1944 and March 1945, in order to create a united anti-Stalin front, there was an attempt to initiate negotiations between General Vlasov and General P. N. Krasnov, who had been Ataman of the Don Cossacks in 1918 and was still an important Cossack leader in Germany, but personal relations between the two generals were not good and their political views differed too much to agree upon a common platform.[165] The creation of the KONR military units was hampered by lack of supplies, especially military equipment, as well as by German officialdom. All this, however, was far too late either for a revival of German fortunes, or for the establishment of an effective Russian political centre. Furthermore, since the tide of victory clearly lay with the Red Army, not with the Wehrmacht, the victors automatically acquired a propagandistic and moral superiority.

Discussions were going on in both German and Russian circles as to the best course of action. What should be done both to preserve the Russian units and to utilise them for an effective stand against the Red Army, and how were they to get in touch with the Allies, explain their position *vis-à-vis* both the Third Reich and Stalin, and prevent their own repatriation to the Soviet Union? Various solutions were put forward and a number of individuals attempted to achieve a satisfactory conclusion by different means.

Various plans were put forward for the utilisation of the Russian units. A plan for the fortification of an area in Central Europe was suggested, primarily by a number of Germans, including General Aschenbrenner, Erich Dwinger and Theodore Oberländer.[166] They hoped to unite the KONR units with the Cossack divisions, and anticipated that Field-Marshal Schörner would also take part, although when he was asked to participate, he declined to do so. Together these units would form a 'free European Resistance Movement', and would fight against the Red Army, until the advancing American forces arrived. A German-Russian staff was created in which General Aschenbrenner and Major-General Maltsev, the head of Vlasov's air squadron, took part, but the collapse of the Third Reich and the end of hostilities, came faster than they anticipated. Furthermore, the formations designated for this resistance force were widely scattered. Although Vlasov's 1st Division was approaching Czechoslovakia, the 2nd Division was still incomplete. The Cossack formations were in Austria and in Italy, and the 1st Ukrainian Division was in southern Germany while the

2nd Ukrainian Division, still not entirely complete, was fighting the Red Army in Saxony.

The SS, meanwhile, had their own plans for the Russian formations. At the beginning of April 1945, plans were made to evacuate KONR from Karlovy Vary to Füssen on the German-Austrian border, as part of the plan to concentrate all political organisations and military units in the Alps. Ordered to Füssen in advance of the main party of Vlasov's staff, for whom he was to arrange billets, Colonel Kromiadi entrained for Füssen together with the major part of Vlasov's documents and records. American bombers on their way to Pilsen scored a direct hit on the train, severely wounding Kromiadi and destroying the papers. On 19 and 20 April, the staff of KONR were evacuated from Karlovy Vary to Füssen, although accommodation was insufficient to house everyone. Dr Kroeger went into the Tyrol to find out more about the construction of the redoubt in the Alps and whether it would be possible for all the Russian formations to gather there. Kromiadi, unhappy with this plan, wished to open negotiations with the Americans, and wanted Vlasov to hide in the Alps until the initial wave of reprisals against the Germans had passed. However, Kromiadi's wounds and the swift pace of the final stages of the war meant that none of these plans ever went beyond preliminary proposals.

A number of individuals did realise that the position was already critical, that the Allies must be contacted and the position of the anti-Stalin Russians explained in order to prevent their repatriation to the USSR. Various methods were essayed, but once again it was too late. Ostensibly, General Zhilenkov was in charge of KONR propaganda and director of the Department of Foreign Relations, but he did nothing. It appears that Zhilenkov understood very little of the workings of the Western world, and like so many of the members of the Russian Liberation Movement was inclined to think that the Allies would instinctively understand the position of the Vlasovites, without any further explanation. Yuri Sergeevich Zherebkov, a member of the 'first' emigration, who had been made answerable by the Germans for the Russian emigration in Paris, was very critical of Zhilenkov's attitudes.[167] Zherebkov had supported Vlasov whom he viewed as a Russian patriot and an anti-communist. On his own initiative, Zherebkov had given publicity to Vlasov in the pages of *Parizhskiy vestnik*. In July 1943, he had been instrumental in explaining the genesis and aims of the Russian Liberation Movement to the Russian émigrés in Paris by inviting General Malyshkin to speak at the Salle Wagram.[168]

Zherebkov thought it necessary to get in touch with the Allies and also would have liked to explain to the world at large the position of the Liberation Movement. To achieve this latter aim, he hoped to be able to publish information about the Russian Liberation Movement in the newspapers of neutral countries, possibly by using contacts within the first emigration to get access to these newspapers. In particular, Zherebkov hoped to write a series of articles for the *Neue Züricher Zeitung*, but the Swiss constitution and Swiss neutrality prevented the publication of articles of this nature.

When KONR was formed, Zherebkov was one of its members. Shortly after the official ceremony in Prague, Zherebkov suggested to Vlasov the need to contact the Allies and the necessity of publishing abroad the particular circumstances and attitudes of the Russian Liberation Movement. Vlasov, apparently, paid little heed to this, since he, too, failed to understand the role of public opinion in the West and felt sure that the politicians would know about the Russian Liberation Movement and would support its struggle against Stalin. In January 1945, Zherebkov, with Vlasov's permission, started to negotiate with Dr Kroeger and the German Foreign Office to obtain permission to get in touch with the International Committee of the Red Cross.[169] Zherebkov wished the Red Cross to intervene on behalf of Russians who had been serving in the Wehrmacht and had now fallen into Allied hands; it was believed that the intervention of the Red Cross would prevent the repatriation of these troops to the USSR. It was also hoped that Zherebkov might be allowed to travel to Geneva to put the case for the Russian troops and at the same time to contact the British and American embassies in Switzerland. On 26 February 1945, Zherebkov wrote to Dr Lehnich in Berlin. He was informed that the International Red Cross would be willing to help Russians captured while serving in German formations but because of their peculiar status and the anomalous position of KONR, as an ally of Germany, it would be easier for the Red Cross to do something for the Russians if Vlasov could do something in return. It transpired that the Red Cross were very worried that at the last moment, with defeat on the doorstep, the SS might massacre all the inmates of the concentration camps. The Red Cross hoped that Vlasov might intervene with the SS to stop any such eventuality. Zherebkov promised that Vlasov and

KONR would do all in their power to help. Zherebkov then travelled to Prague.

It had been envisaged that Vlasov would be given permission to make a radio broadcast from Prague to the first meeting of the United Nations Organisation in San Francisco.[170] It seemed that here was an excellent opportunity to explain the position of KONR to the Allies. This speech was due to be broadcast on 19 April 1945. Frank, though the protector of Bohemia and Moravia, said that he was unwilling to take the responsibility for such a speech, since this would be a political action. He was unable to contact his superiors in Berlin for their sanction.

On 27 April, Zherebkov met Vlasov for the last time and suggested that since it was unlikely that Switzerland would let him in, Vlasov should take an aeroplane to Spain and there continue his work as the focal point for the Liberation Movement. Vlasov turned down this offer, saying that he had to share the fate of his men. However, Vlasov gave Zherebkov full permission to negotiate with the Swiss authorities and with the Allies. Yet this was to no purpose; when Zherebkov reached the Swiss border on 30 April, he was refused permission to cross it. Zherebkov tried three times to cross the border illegally, and on the third attempt he was successful, but was expelled from Switzerland a few hours later, and so direct negotiations on a personal level with the International Red Cross never took place. Zherebkov also tried to get in touch with Gustav Nobel, through the Swedish military attaché in Berlin, Colonel von Danenfeld, but this was also unsuccessful.

Another Russian, B. V. Pryanishnikov, who worked in an advisory capacity for the Department of Civilian Affairs and was a member of the first emigration, hoped that through contact with the Poles, it might be possible to get in touch with the Allies, but once again this proved to be a forlorn hope.[171]

S. B. Fröhlich, another Baltic German of Russian culture, and a friend of Strik-Strikfeldt, who was a liaison officer with KONR, went to see General Klecanda[172] to discuss the plan to unite all Russian units in Central Europe, in the region of Czechoslovakia. Klecanda, a Czech, who was a veteran of the Russian Civil War, was well known both in Czech military circles and abroad. His views of the KONR forces and possible further developments were realistic. He said that, in the first place, the Czechs were waiting to be freed by the Red Army, and were therefore not likely to support KONR troops for very long. He did not think, therefore, that if he added his support to KONR his example would be particularly helpful. People would merely think that he had gone mad or that he had sold himself to the Germans. Secondly, he was of the opinion that the only possible safety for the KONR forces lay with the Americans, but even here he had his doubts because of his experience during negotiations with the West when Hitler invaded Czechoslovakia. At that time, he had argued that occupied Czechoslovakia must be allowed to keep her officers, 20,000 of them, and not allow them to be murdered, as they would be very necessary in the coming conflict. The Western powers, however, would not believe in the inevitability of the coming conflict and were uninterested in the plight of the Czech officers. Thus, Klecanda believed that similar considerations of short term expediency would prevail in the attempts of KONR to persuade the Allies as to the justice of their cause.

While these attempts to decide on a plan for the utilisation of the KONR forces were taking place, and the debate was continuing as to how to preserve them after the cessation of hostilities, the formations finally took shape and played their part in an effort by the Russians to demonstrate their independence from the German authorities.

The Russians' own plans were nebulous; various plans had been mooted, including Aschenbrenner's idea of defending an area of Central Europe and forming a European resistance movement. An even more tentative plan was that of uniting with the forces of Draze Mihailjovic[173] and with General von Pannwitz's Cossack Division, in order to retreat into the mountain strongholds of Yugoslavia. In addition to the fear of reprisals and repatriation by the Soviet authorities, there was also the realisation that the KONR troops must link up with the Allies. There was a widespread and deeply held – but unfounded – belief that the Allies[174] despite their alliance with the Soviet Union, would welcome the stand taken by the Russian Liberation Movement against the oppressive regime in the USSR, and that once Nazi Germany had been defeated, the Allies would attack the Soviet Union and destroy the totalitarian system there.[175]

The accounts which are available on this last period of the Vlasov enterprise differ somewhat in emphasis.[176] The Russians believed the German authorities had, once again, broken the promises made to them. The Russians wished to be used as a unified Russian command under Vlasov and wanted to preserve their divisions in the face of what they saw as the German policy to use them as cannon fodder in

Figure 2 KONR and the last stages of the war

the last ditch stands. The German interpretation does not accept this accusation that even at this last juncture they were tricking their Russian allies. German officers connected with the 1st Division assert that, with Himmler's agreement, and he was now commander-in-chief of the Weichsel Army Group, all obstacles in the path of creating an actual combat force of the 1st Division had been overcome. Colonel Herre, of the General Staff, was apparently anxious that the 1st Division should be used in action so that when it had proved itself, this would provide a further impetus for the formation of Russian units. However, the order[177] instigated by him in March 1945, making the 1st Division part of Himmler's Army Group and ordering the division to Stettin, became the first in a series of disagreements between the German and Russian commanders on the disposition of the 1st Division.

The 1st Division (600th Panzer Grenadier Division) was formed in November 1944 at Munsingen, in the Württemberg Province. Commanded by Major-General Sergei Kuz'mich Bunyachenko, its ranks were made up of Russian units which had previously been serving in the Wehrmacht. To the 1st Division were also drafted men from the Kaminsky Brigade. After the shooting of Kaminsky (see p. 36) and the utilisation of some of his men in the suppression of the Warsaw rising, other members of the brigade, apparently not those used by the SS, were also assigned to Vlasov. These soldiers were ill-disciplined, their morale was low, and consequently the 1st Division commanders met with difficulty in training them to become part of an efficient and integrated fighting force.

The 1st Division was initially 10,000 strong, but later increased to 20,000. On 16 February 1945 the division held its passing-out parade[178] attended by Vlasov and by Major-General Köstring. Köstring had been appointed in 1943, in succession to General Hellmich, general in command of *Osttruppen*, a position renamed general of volunteer formations on 1 January 1944. Two weeks later, the order from the General Staff dispatching the 1st Division north to Stettin in Pomerania arrived. The division was to be moved by rail. Bunyachenko was outraged at the order which he considered broke the promise made to the Russians that they would operate as a unified command under General Vlasov. It also appeared to the Russians that the German authorities were ignoring Vlasov's position as an independent commander of the KONR force. Bunyachenko immediately got in touch with Vlasov who was with the 2nd

Division (650th Division) at Heuberg, 60 kilometres to the south-west. Meanwhile, Bunyachenko carried out negotiations with Colonel Herre, trying to impress upon him that all orders had to proceed via Vlasov. When Vlasov finally arrived, it transpired that he knew nothing of the order. However, Vlasov was not prepared to support Bunyachenko's intention to disobey German orders totally and to move with his army as quickly as possible to the mountains near the Swiss border, where Bunyachenko could then try and get in touch with the Allies. Vlasov left for German headquarters and returned a couple of days later with amended orders. The division was to proceed to the Cottbus area, south of Berlin. The division would not entrain immediately since the line was under bombardment, but would march to Nuremberg and board there. During the march to Nuremberg, the division was joined by escaped Russian prisoners-of-war, escaped *Ostarbeiter*, and even by Russians serving in the Wehrmacht formations stationed in the vicinity of the route. The numbers became so large that in order to provide rations for them, they were formed into a reserve regiment 5,000 strong, for which the German authorities were willing to allocate supplies, although they could not provide arms. On 26 March, the division reached its destination and on the 27th was ordered to form part of the command of General Busse of the 9th Army. The Russians were concerned about the position of Vlasov, his relationship with the 9th Army Command, and also about the location of the other Russian formations. They were told that Vlasov's position as commander would be respected and that other Russian formations (the KONR 2nd Division, the reserve brigade, the air squadron, the officers' training school commanded by General Meandrov, and the Cossack formations) were all on the way and would form a unified command under Vlasov. On 6 April 1945, however, the division was ordered to liquidate a Soviet bridgehead on the Oder, a task which German troops had been unable to carry out. Bunyachenko once again questioned the validity of this order, saying that he would only accept orders from General Vlasov. Vlasov in fact arrived the next day, with an escort of German officers, and he gave the impression that he had only heard of the order on the previous day. However, he confirmed that the division was to take part in the proposed attack. Apparently, Himmler had insisted that the division participate in this operation as a precondition for creating more units. Vlasov told his commanders that the attack must be undertaken regardless of the risk of failure and then he conferred with Bunyachenko alone. It is not known what was said at the meeting although it has been surmised that Vlasov told Bunyachenko to withdraw from the front once the attack had failed, to march south, and to use the argument to the German command that nothing would be done without Vlasov's sanction. Vlasov then left.

On 13 April, Bunyachenko mounted the attack but heavy machine gun and automatic fire from the flanks made it impossible to continue the assault. The German command would not allow a retreat and merely repeated that the position must be held. Bunyachenko called his commanders together and ordered a withdrawal. To German requests to explain his behaviour, Bunyachenko replied that the orders he had received from the German command contradicted those from Vlasov and also contravened the aims of the 1st Division. Finally, Bunyachenko was informed that he and Vlasov would be shot, a statement that only served to strengthen Russian suspicion of the motives of the German command. The next day the division was refused rations. The Russians then decided on a further course of action. They warned the German command that if Vlasov did not arrive within three days, then the division would march south in order to meet up with other Russian formations and, if force was used against them, they would retaliate in kind. Bunyachenko was asked to discuss his ultimatum with General Busse but was not prepared to change his point of view, and on 16 April when Vlasov had not arrived, the division began to march south. When Klettwitz was reached, German officers arrived with orders that the division should go to the front. Bunyachenko refused on the grounds that he only accepted orders from Vlasov. When told that Vlasov was occupied with important matters to do with the Russian Liberation Movement, Bunyachenko expressed disbelief and said that this was merely another ruse to trick the Russians. The division continued its march south and near Senftenberg was joined by a separate volunteer regiment under Colonel Sakharov, which had been at the front. The 1st Division, now over 20,000 strong, reached Dresden and came under the command of Field Marshal Schörner of Army Group Centre. Bunyachenko was invited to meet Schörner, but his distrust of the Germans was reawakened and negotiations were not carried out by him in person. The division moved towards the Elbe but despite the insubordination of its commanders, no measures were taken against it, even in those areas where it would have been possible to stage an attack or an ambush. Schörner later explained that German troops were facing difficulties because of the situation on the front and could not, therefore, spare the time to deal with the recalcitrant Russian division. Secondly, they feared retaliation from Russian units in the Wehrmacht if the 1st Division was attacked, and thirdly, they did not wish the High Command to hear of a clash of this nature for, up to this point, Schörner had not informed OKW of the various difficulties encountered by the German command with the 1st Division.[179]

The division crossed the Elbe, once more disobeying German orders to the contrary, and had to employ a subterfuge to do so, sending ambulances over first and, when a narrow path across the bridge had been cleared of mines, the rest of the force followed, thus bypassing the German barriers. Bunyachenko refused another invitation to visit Schörner, using the invented excuse that he had been hurt in a car accident. There were also fears that the KONR Division might be attacked by an SS division, whereupon the KONR Division evacuated the area. On 26 April, the chief of staff of Schörner's Army Group arrived once more, this time with the request that the division go to the front. As supplies were very low, Bunyachenko reluctantly agreed to fight Soviet troops in the vicinity of Brno. Having obtained the necessary supplies, Bunyachenko called his commanders together to discuss their course of action. Once again they agreed that in the interests of the division and of the cause of the ROD their strength should be conserved and not decimated to no purpose. The commanders decided not to obey German orders. On 27 April the division continued its march south. The German liaison officer, Major Schwenniger, was horrified and, after contacting his superior officers, returned to tell Bunyachenko that Schörner would send a tank detachment if they would not obey the order. The division merely continued its march, advancing in combat formation against a possible attack. A letter from General Aschenbrenner had equally little effect.

In Czechoslovakia, Schörner and Vlasov arrived to meet Bunyachenko. The meeting was short and Vlasov, behaving somewhat unnaturally, criticised the action of the commanders in not obeying German orders. Later, when he had got rid of his German entourage, Vlasov explained that he did not disapprove of the division's action, it was just that he had been placed in a position where he had to appear to be on the German side, because if the Germans felt that they could no longer rely on his influence, then he feared that there would be reprisals against Russian troops in the Wehrmacht.[180] This remark again betrayed the deep distrust with which the Russians regarded the actions of the German authorities. Vlasov went on to say that he was quite happy for Bunyachenko to operate as he saw fit and that he, Vlasov, would not remain with them since he was concerned about the other Russian formations which were in far worse shape than the 1st Division.[181]

On Czech territory, German commanders were somewhat alarmed by the mutinous division and its intentions, but the Czech population now welcomed the Russian division which was assumed to have disobeyed the Germans. Various Czech partisan units came to the division to ask for supplies and the partisans were prepared not only to co-operate with Vlasov's troops, but apparently even offered Vlasov the leadership of all the nationalist, as opposed to the communist, partisan units in Czechoslovakia.[182] This great friendliness, based on a common hatred of their German oppressors, changed very rapidly when it became evident that it was no longer politically expedient or wise to support the Vlasovites.[183]

Hatred of the Germans led to a number of clashes between KONR troops and German soldiers even before what was, to quote George Fischer's words: 'the most dramatic single episode of the entire history of wartime Soviet opposition'.[184] On 2 May the 1st Division halted 50 kilometres south-west of Prague, where a delegation of officers from the Czech Army arrived from the Czech capital. They introduced themselves as the staff of the Prague rising and had come to ask for support.[185] Initially, Bunyachenko was unwilling to get involved in Czech affairs and did not give any definite answer. However, anti-German feeling was running high amongst both officers and men and this, combined with the friendly reception afforded by the Czech population to the division, made it seem likely that if Bunyachenko did not accede to the request of the Czech insurgents for help, members of the division, as individuals, would become involved in the rising against the Germans. Therefore, in order not to lose command of the troops and also to prevent the division from falling apart, Bunyachenko decided to support the Prague insurgents. By 5 May the uprising was under way, the insurgents appealing over the radio for help.[186] The decision to fight the Germans in Prague was also influenced by the need felt by the Vlasovites to demonstrate to the Allies the fact that they were not

Nazi hirelings and that they were opponents of Nazism. On the evening of 5 May the division reached the outskirts of Prague, and on 6 May took part in the attack on the German troops, including part of an SS division which had been sent to put down the rising.[187]

However, Russian aspirations were destined to be disappointed. On the afternoon of 6 May, Colonel Arkhipov, the colonel of the 1st Regiment, was called to a meeting. There he found an American captain in charge of an armoured scout column, which had been sent ahead to discover what was happening in Prague.[188] The Americans wished to know whether the population needed help. Eisenhower had already conducted talks with the Soviet general Antonov and demarcation lines had been agreed upon, but the question still remained of a possible initial occupation of the city by the American forces before withdrawing and leaving it in Soviet hands. The KONR 1st Division naturally knew nothing of such agreements and negotiations. However, Arkhipov was summoned with the other leaders of the Prague insurgents to clarify the situation. The Americans were very surprised to see the German uniforms of the 1st Division, and then asked whether the insurgents needed help or whether they could manage by themselves. The American captain explained that his armoured column was not the vanguard of approaching American forces, and they were not intending to enter Prague; he had been sent on ahead to see whether the insurgents could hold the city by themselves until it could be handed over to the ally of the USA, the Soviet Union. Arkhipov then realised that one of the chief reasons for taking part in the rising, to make contact with the American forces, was illusory; he told the captain that, although in the purely military sense, the KONR division could hold the city, it would be politically inexpedient for them to do so (i.e. that the Americans should enter Prague). How much of all this was understood by the American was not clear, and after the meeting Arkhipov told the insurgents that the division would have to leave the city, since Soviet forces would shortly enter it. That evening he told Bunyachenko and Vlasov what had occurred. On the same day, representatives of the KONR forces met representatives of a newly formed 'Czech government', who declared that they had not asked the Vlasovites for help and did not sympathise with the KONR cause.[189] In reply to the protestations of the KONR officers, they said that the organisers of the insurrection represented neither the Czech people, nor the government, that two-thirds of the government were communist and that their advice to the KONR Division was to surrender to the advancing Soviet armies.

On 7 May, the KONR troops left Prague and began a march south in order to make contact with the Americans and to come within their zone of occupation. On the way south they found that Major-General Trukhin, Major-General Boyarsky, Major-General Shapovalov and General Blagoveschensky had been captured by partisans. Boyarsky had been shot, Shapovalov hanged, while Trukhin and Blagoveschensky had been handed over to the Red Army. Trukhin had come into contact with the Americans on 5 May and had been ordered to surrender the 2nd Division within 36 hours.[190] When Shapovalov arrived with Vlasov's order to march into Czechoslovakia – the 2nd Division was then in Austria – Trukhin sent Boyarsky to Vlasov in order to persuade him to surrender the 1st Division as well. When Boyarsky did not return, Trukhin set off with Shapovalov and they were captured, as was Blagoveschensky when he went in search of his colleagues. In the evening of 9 May, still on Czech territory, the 1st Division came across tank detachments of the US 3rd Army. On 10 May, negotiations began, and by the 11th, the division was disarmed and was in the Schlusselburg region, whither Vlasov drove as well. The Soviet 162nd Division was encamped not far from the KONR Division. Bunyachenko tried to get permission to cross to the American zone immediately but was unsuccessful. At the same time the Soviet division was sending emissaries over to the KONR Division in order to encourage desertion back to the Soviet side. There was a fear that the Soviet division might advance before the Americans gave permission for the KONR Division to cross over to their zone. Time was gained on this question, when the commander of the 2nd Regiment, Colonel Artem'ev, accidentally encountered Soviet officers, and pretended to have been sent to negotiate terms for the KONR division. It was agreed that at 12 a.m. on 12 May the KONR Division would cross to the Soviet side. Some time had thereby been gained. At 10 a.m. on 12 May, Bunyachenko, with his chief-of-staff, Lieutenant-Colonel Nikolayev, went to the castle at Schlusselburg, the American HQ, where they were informed that, although the American commander sympathised with the position of Vlasov and his men, he had to refuse permission for them to cross the demarcation line. To this announcement was added the information that the Americans were due to evacuate Schlusselburg, and that the town was to be handed over to their Soviet ally. This news was the death blow for the division. The order was given for the men to dismiss and to fend for themselves.

Steenberg estimated that about half of the division, 10,000 men, either fell into the hands of the Red Army straightaway, or were captured by Czech partisans and then handed over to Soviet forces, and that approximately half of the division got through to the Americans, but many of those who did so were repatriated at a later date.[191] Bunyachenko asked to be allowed to join Vlasov in the castle, where they both fell into Soviet hands.

There are four published accounts, by his followers, of Vlasov's capture,[192] which differ slightly in detail: the number of vehicles in the column, and the individuals accompanying Vlasov. However, it seems clear that the column left the castle at Schlusselburg in the afternoon, hoping to enter the American zone. In the event, they were met by a Soviet column, Vlasov was identified and taken captive. The Soviet account[193] of Vlasov's capture states that he was found wrapped in a carpet on the floor of a jeep. However, it seems unlikely that Vlasov, who had already turned down a variety of suggestions as to how he should escape and go into hiding, should suddenly start concealing himself at this late date. He was not heard of again until 2 August 1946 when *Izvestiya*[194] announced that Vlasov and eleven others had been tried for treason by the Military Tribunal of the Supreme Court of the USSR. They had been found guilty of being agents of German intelligence, and had carried out active espionage and terrorist activity against the USSR. They had been hanged.

The fate of the other KONR formations was no better. The 2nd Division now under the command of General Meandrov – Trukhin having been captured by partisans – surrendered to the Americans on 6 May. The government of the Third Reich agreed to surrender on 8 May and Colonel Neryanin and General Meandrov, without waiting for further permission from the Americans, decided to move into the American zone.[195] However, these troops were later interned and, after a number of moves to different camps, were repatriated to the Soviet Union.[196]

Very little is known of the details of the imprisonment and interrogation of the leaders of the opposition movement. Vlasov's interpreter, Resler, thought that he may have seen General Trukhin in the corridors of a prison in Moscow, where Resler was being interrogated.[197] Leopold Trepper, who was involved in collecting military intelligence in Europe during the war for the Soviet Union, and then was arrested after he arrived in Russia in 1945, met someone whom he describes as 'Vlasov's number two man' while in prison. Trepper could not recall the man's name and the description of this man fits neither Malyshkin nor Zhilenkov.[197] It appears that at the trial this individual, although remaining a convinced opponent of the Soviet regime, regretted his involvement in the Vlasov enterprise.[198]

The most interesting testimony[199] is that of an officer who was sent to the cells of the leading Vlasovites to persuade them to admit that they had betrayed their country, and to stop criticising Stalin. They were promised that if they recanted, their lives would be spared. Some wavered, but the majority of the leadership, amongst them Vlasov and Trukhin, refused to make such confessions. Trukhin continued to reiterate his position: 'I was not a traitor and will not confess to treachery. I loathe Stalin, I consider that he is a tyrant and will say so at the trial.' Apparently when Vlasov was told that if he would not confess, then he would be tortured to death and there would not be a trial, he replied: 'I know that. And I am very frightened. But it would be even worse to have to vilify myself. But our sufferings will not be in vain. In time the [Russian] people will remember us with warmth.' As a result of this determined resistance to the threats and torture of the interrogators, the trial of Vlasov and other leaders of the Russian Liberation Movement was not held in public, but *in camera*.

The four available accounts of the trial,[200] which began on 30 July 1946, are by no means a transcript of the proceedings. All four articles are designed to prove that Vlasov willingly collaborated with the Nazi authorities. Short passages of Vlasov's 'confession' are quoted in support of this accusation. It appears that in the trial Vlasov may have been trying to take the blame on to himself. In two of the accounts he is quoted as saying: 'Undoubtedly, I carried out the most active struggle against Soviet power and carry the full responsibility for this.' It is possible that Vlasov hoped that by claiming full responsibility, his subordinates would be punished less severely. This would be in line with the opinion expressed by him earlier, when it was suggested that he should escape, possibly to Spain, and he replied that he had to share the fate of his men.

In another passage Vlasov describes his activities as 'counter-revolutionary' and 'anti-Soviet' and his colleagues as 'scum and dregs'. However, such terms are common to this type of trial, and since the context of the remarks is not provided, it is difficult to ascertain the implications of such phrases. Further, since such confessions were induced by the NKVD, it is unlikely that a confession of guilt reflected the truth.

In the case of Vlasov's trial, it has not been possible to verify any part of the proceedings. The accounts of the trial are written in such a way that it is difficult to disentangle objective evidence from the political message. All the accounts stress that Vlasov had very close links with the Nazi authorities, that he had no independent ideology whatsoever, and that there was very little support for him. If that was indeed the case, then it is difficult to understand why the details of the trial were not published. It is also not clear, in the light of these accusations, why it took the Soviet authorities so long to bring Vlasov and eleven close associates to trial. The Nuremberg war crime trials, which were a far more complex and lengthy procedure, began in November 1945.

Sentence was passed on 1 August 1946, and the accused were all hanged on 2 August.[202] Rumour asserts that Vlasov and his entourage were hanged on piano wire, with the hook inserted at the base of the skull. One witness states that the method of execution was so horrible that he could not repeat the details.[203]

NOTES

1 Vlassov, A. A., *Les confidences du General Vlasov, 'J'ai choisi la potence'*, Paris (1947) is supposedly Vlasov's reminiscences, but is clearly a forgery containing factual errors, e.g. an account of Vlasov's meeting with Hitler, an event which never occurred. This publication was designed to discredit Vlasov by misrepresenting the extent of his link with the Nazis.

2 The fullest account of Vlasov's life is in a short biography published by one of the lecturers at Dabendorf: Osokin, V., *Andrey Andreyevich Vlasov (Kratkaya Biografiya)*, izdatel'stvo shkoly propagandistov Russkoy Osvoboditel'noy Armii (August 1944). This must be regarded as an official biography and is the main source of information for Vlasov's origins and for his career in the Soviet Union. The biography is little more than a curriculum vitae with some indication of what might be termed 'watersheds' in Vlasov's evaluation of the Soviet regime. The conditions in which this biography appeared undoubtedly influenced its presentation and contents. In the summer of 1944 the position of the Russian Liberation Movement was not easy; their freedom of action was being very considerably restricted by the German authorities. In these circumstances the biography of Vlasov presented an opportunity to stress all

possible commendable points of both the Movement and its leader. The biography aimed at demonstrating that Vlasov was a genuine son of the Russian people, who was devoted to their interests and not to those of their German 'allies' or to anyone else. At the same time this biography cannot be regarded purely as a piece of propaganda. Any factual distortion would not only have occasioned strictures from Vlasov's contemporaries and colleagues but also would have provided an opportunity for adverse publicity from the opponents of the Russian Liberation Movement. Osokin was the pseudonym of V. Arseniev, see Steenberg, S., *Vlasov*, p. 5.

3 For a programme of study at a seminary see Brokhaus, F. A. and Efron, I. A., 'Dukhovno-uchebnie zavedeniya', *Entsiklopedicheskiy slovar'*, St Petersburg, vol. 11 (1893).

4 See North, R. C., *Moscow and the Chinese Communists*, Stanford (1953), pp. 183, 186; Dallin, D. J., *Soviet Russia and the Far East*, London (1949), pp. 70–3, 129–35, 139–43.

5 Steenberg, S., *Vlasov*, pp. 9, 11; ROA Archives BAR 7663, Columbia University, Solomonovsky MS.

6 *Krasnaya zvezda* (28 September 1940).

7 *Izvestiya* (23 February 1941).

8 *Krasnaya zvezda* (29 September 1940, 2 October 1940).

9 Vlasov, A., 'Novye metody boevoy ucheby' in *Krasnaya zvezda* (3 October 1940), and reprinted in *Novoe v podgotovke voisk*, izd. Krasnaya Armiya, Kiev (1940), pp. 95–6. In another, shorter article, 'Krasnoe znamya', *Krasnaya zvezda* (23 February 1941), Vlasov again lays great emphasis on the need for constant training, practice and the need for effort in order to achieve a high standard.

10 Alexander Vasil'evich Suvorov (1730–1800) (General, later Field Marshal) is considered to be one of the founders of Russian military tactics. During the Second World War he was one of the Russian national heroes used to emphasise the patriotic nature of the conflict. Stalin mentioned Suvorov in his speech of 7 November 1941, the Suvorov military decoration was instituted in 1942, and in 1943 the Suvorov military academies were created.

11 Ogin, P. and Korol', B., 'Komandir peredovoy divisii', *Krasnaya zvezda* (9 October 1940) and *Novoe v podgotovke voisk*, pp. 97–8.

12 Erickson, J., *The Road to Stalingrad*, London (1975), pp. 131, 165, 166.

13 *IVOVSS*, 2, p. 109.

14 A. A. Vlasov v besede s N. Ya. Galaem, BA-MA collection: Steenberg III and Erickson, J., *The Road to Stalingrad*, p. 222.

15 Lesueur, L., *Twelve Months that Changed the World*, London (1944), pp. 87, 89.

16 Curie, E., *Journey Among Warriors*, London (1943), p. 184.

17 *Krasnaya zvezda* (13 December 1941). The other generals cited were: Zhukov, Rokossovsky, Kuznetsov, Lelyushenko, Govorov, Belov, Boldin and Golikov.

18 *Izvestiya* (3 January 1942 and 25 January 1942).

19 Meretskov, K. A., *Na sluzhbe narodu*, p. 275. On the other hand, Ehrenburg, I., 'Lyudi, gody, zhizn', *Novy mir* no. 1, (1963) p. 91, recalls that

when he heard of Vlasov's appointment, his first reaction was that it was not a bad choice.

20 Osokin, V., *Andrey Andreyevich Vlasov*, p. 22, mentions that Meretskov did not come to the aid of Vlasov's beleaguered army. This criticism could only have originated from Vlasov since none of his staff were captured with him.

21 Stalin had been furious with Meretskov's performance as chief of the General Staff during war games in December 1940 and January 1941. Meretskov had been dismissed. See Erickson, J., *The Road to Stalingrad*, pp. 8–9. It is possible, even though Meretskov had survived temporary disgrace, that he and Stalin did not see eye-to-eye, and therefore Stalin did not respond to his appeals for reinforcements.

22 Meretskov, K. A., *Na sluzhbe narodu*, Moscow (1968), p. 268.

23 Ibid., p. 281.

24 Vasilevsky, A., *Delo vsey zhizni*, Moscow (1976), p. 184. Khozin, M. S., in his article 'Ob odnoy maloissledovannoy operatsii.' *Voenno-istoricheskiy zhurnal*, 2, (1966) pp. 39–40 writes that he asked for greater co-ordination between the Volkhov and Leningrad Fronts but that the suggestion actually to unite the two Fronts came from Stalin.

25 Meretskov, K. A., *Na sluzhbe narodu*, p. 282.

26 Recollections of A. Svetlanin, a major in the 2nd Shock Army, as recalled by N. E. Andreyev.

27 Meretskov, K. A., 'Na Volkovskikh rubezhakh', *Voenno-istoricheskiy zhurnal*, 1 (1965), p. 68.

28 Ibid., pp. 54–70.

29 Meretskov claims that 16,000 broke out of the final encirclement, 6,000 were killed in action, 8,000 were missing. Carell, P., *Hitler's War in Russia*, London (1964), p. 410, says that 32,000 were taken prisoner.

30 See, for example: *IVOVSS*, 2, p. 470, *Bitva za Leningrad*, Moscow (1964), p. 159. *IVMV*, 5, p. 240.

31 Hitler, A., *Mein Kampf*, translated by Manheim, R., London (1972), p. 128.

32 Ibid., p. 604.

33 Ibid., p. 598.

34 *Hitler's Table Talk 1941–1944*, 2nd edn, London (1973), p. 5: 5–6 July 1941 and p. 617: 6 August 1942.

35 Himmler, H., *Der Untermensch*, SS-Hauptamt-Schulungsamt, Berlin (1942).

36 *TMWC*, 38, p. 90.

37 Ibid., 26, p. 616.

38 Lochner, L. (ed.), *Goebbels' Diaries*, London (1948), p. 135: 25 April 1942.

39 Ibid., p. 169. 22 May 1942.

40 Ibid., p. 254. 14 April 1943.

41 Craig, G. A., and Gilbert, F. (eds.), *The Diplomats 1919–1939*, Princeton (1953), p. 511.

42 von Herwarth, J. *Against Two Evils*, London (1981), p. 188.

43 Hilger, G. and Meyer, A. G., *The Incompatible Allies*, New York (1953), p. 275.

44 Hoffmann, P., *The History of the German Resistance 1933–1945*, translated by Barry R., revised edn, London (1977), p. 350.

45 Wheeler-Bennet, J., *The Nemesis of Power*, London (1953), p. 354–5.
46 Bullock, A., *Hitler: A Study in Tyranny*, London (1972), p. 666.
47 *TMWC*, 25, pp. 402–13, and *Akten zur deutschen auswärtigen Politik 1918–45*, Series D.1., Göttingen (1969), pp. 25–32.
48 Geller, M. and Nekrich, A., *Utopiya u vlasti*, vol. 2, p. 76.
49 Conquest, R., *The Great Terror*, Harmondsworth (1971), p. 645, gives the following figures for the effect of the purge on the armed forces:
    3 of the 5 Marshals
    14 of the 16 Army Commanders Class I and II
    8 of the 8 Admirals ('Flagman') Class I and II
    60 of the 67 Corps Commanders
    136 of the 199 Divisional Commanders
    221 of the 397 Brigade Commissars
    All 11 Vice-Commissars of Defence
    75 of the 80 members of the Supreme Military Soviet
    Half the officer corps, about 35,000, were shot or imprisoned.
50 Kagan, V., 'Postscriptum k prikazu', *Kontinent*, 14 (1977), pp. 301–5, and Buchbender, O., *Das tönende Erz* (1978), pp. 96, 295–6.
51 *TMWC*, 11, p. 501.
52 Streit, C., *Keine Kamaraden*, p. 224.
53 Fletcher, W. C., *The Russian Orthodox Church Underground 1917–70*, London (1971), p. 155, and Alexeev, W., and Stavrou, T. G. *The Great Revival: the Russian Orthodox Church under German Occupation*, Minneapolis (1976), pp. 41–66.
54 B. A. NS 19/ neu 1246, Baetr. Kapitan Boris Russanow.
55 *Kriegstagebuch des Oberkommando der Wehrmacht*, Frankfurt am Main (1965), vol. 3/2, pp. 1483–4.
56 Hoffmann, J., *Die Ostlegionen 1941–1943*, p. 12.
57 Longworth, P., *The Cossacks*, London (1969), p. 332.
58 Dallin, A., *The Kaminsky Brigade*, Harvard Russian Research Centre (1952) and Nikolaevsky, B. I., 'Porazhenchestvo 1941–5 godov i gen. A. A., Vlasov', *Novy zhurnal*, 18 (1948), pp. 218–23.
59 Interview: Redlich, R. N.
60 Dallin, A. and Mavrogordato, R. S., 'Rodionov, a case study in wartime redefection', *American Slavic and East European Review*, 18 (1959), pp. 25–33. 'Gil' was a *nom de guerre*.
61 Kromiadi, K. G.,*Za zemlyu, za volyu . . .*, p. 58.
62 *TMWC*, 25, pp. 332–42, von Bräutigam, O., 'Aufzeichnung' 25 (October 1942), Doc. 294, PS.
63 Strik-Strikfeldt, W., *Against Stalin and Hitler*, pp. 32–3.
64 B. A. Vernehmung General Lukin, 14 December 1941 R 6 77. *Ogonek* No. 47 (1964), pp. 26–30, and Strik-Strikfeldt, W., *Against Stalin and Hitler*, pp. 35–6, 93–4.
65 *IVMV*, 5, pp. 139–40.
66 Korol'kov, Y., *Cherez sorok smertey*, Moscow (1960), p. 124.
67 Svetlanin, A., *Dal' nevostochny zagovor*, pp. 105–6. Svetlanin, a major in the 2nd Shock Army, mentions commanders who had been shot: Rychagov, Klimovsky, Korobkov, Loktinov, brigade commissars and others. If a

major was thinking of this it seems more than likely that Vlasov must also have had in mind the fate of those who had been put to death as a result of their military failures. In any case Vlasov probably knew of those commanders who had been shot for 'panic-mongering', 'dereliction of duty' in the summer of 1941. See Erickson, J., *The Road to Stalingrad*, pp. 175–6.

68 Kagan, V., 'Postskriptum k prikazu', *Kontinent*, 14 (1977), pp. 301–5.
69 Steenberg, S., *Vlasov*, p. 10.
70 Tishkov, A., '"Predatel" pered sovetskim sudom,' *Sovetskoe gosudarstvo i pravo*, no. 2 (1973), p. 91. Tishkov states that Vlasov was kept out of the Communist party because he had been educated in a seminary. Meretskov, K. A., *Na sluzhbe narodu*, p. 297, says that Vlasov became a member of the Communist party merely for the sake of advancement.
71 Fischer, G., *Soviet Opposition to Stalin*, pp. 27–8. Fischer considers that Vlasov's commitment to the regime was never maximal, it was a question of necessity and promotion that made him join the party.
72 Kiselev, A., *Oblik generala Vlasova*, p. 43.
73 Ibid., p. 43.
74 Novosiltsev, I. L., 'A. A. Vlasov', *Novy zhurnal*, 129 (December 1977), pp. 183–90.
75 Epstein, J., *Operation Keelhaul*, Old Greenwich, Connecticut (1973), p. 53.
76 See, for example: Ginzburg, E., *Krutoy marshrut*, Frankfurt am Main (1967), pp. 7, 29.
77 Kazantsev, A., *Tret'ya sila*, p. 149.
78 Steenberg, S., *Vlasov*, p. 24.
79 Interview: I. L. Novosiltsev.
80 Buchbender, O., *Das tönende Erz*, p. 265, has photographs of similar incidents.
81 Novosiltsev, I. L., 'A. A. Vlasov', *Novy zhurnal*, 129 (December 1977), p. 188.
82 Steenberg, S., *Vlasov*, p. 24.
83 Recollection of N. E. Andreyev of article in *Zarya*. It proved impossible to find this issue.
84 Dneprov, R., 'Vlasovskie li?' *Kontinent*, 23, p. 302 says that Boyarsky was commander of 41st Guards Division and was taken prisoner when wounded.
85 Vlasov and Boyarsky letter. Vinnitsa, 3 August 1942 German translation: Armee Oberkommando 16.1c.Dc. 12 September 1942. Captured German records, US National Archives, Reichsführer SS, TI 175 66 EAP 161-b-12/195 298 2721. Translation back into Russian from the German text in Pozdnyakov, V. V., *A. A. Vlasov*, pp. 36–41.
86 Captured German records. FCO Auswärtiges Amt 997/305 144, 147.
87 F.C.O. Hilger to von Etzdorf, OKH O Qu 4 G 15 Auswärtiges Amt 997 305 144, 147.
88 Interviews: I. L. Novosiltsev, N. G. Shtifanov.
89 Strik-Strikfeldt, W., *Against Stalin and Hitler*, p. 75. The impression gained from Strik-Strikfeldt's memoirs is of an idealist of unwavering honesty and great integrity, but whose political judgement is not without error. This impression is confirmed by von Herwarth, J., *Against Two Evils*,

p. 289.

90 Strik-Strikfeldt, W., *Against Stalin and Hitler*, pp. 70–1.
91 Kromiadi, K. G., *Za zemlyu, za volyu* ... pp. 118–19.
92 YIVO, German document 480/RAB/IX.42.
93 YIVO, German document, 481/RAB/IX.42.
94 Pozdnyakov, V. V., *A. A. Vlasov*, pp. 44–6.
95 YIVO, 482/RAB/IX.42. Pozdnyakov, V. V., *A. A. Vlasov*, pp. 47–50.
96 G. N. Zhilenkov had been the secretary of the Communist party of the Rostokinsky district in Moscow. When war broke out he became a commissar and was captured in the autumn of 1941. He survived by hiding the fact that he had been a commissar and drove supply vehicles. He was involved in the Osintorf Brigade before joining Vlasov. He was editor of *Dobrovolets* and during the composition of the Prague Manifesto was one of the chief intermediaries between the German authorities and the Russians. He was made head of the KONR propaganda section and was ostensibly editor of the KONR newspaper, *Volya naroda*. He was able but with a rather flamboyant personality and not very popular in the Movement. He was hanged with Vlasov.
97 Interview: I. L. Novosiltsev.
98 See discussion of the Smolensk Declaration, pp. 97–100.
99 General V. F. Malyshkin became Vlasov's second-in-command. He was a professional soldier who had been arrested during the Tukhachevsky affair and was subsequently rehabilitated. He was a bitter opponent of Stalin but a convinced Russian patriot. In June 1943 he made a speech in Paris which made the existence of the Russian Liberation Movement known to the Russian emigration.
100 Dallin, A., *German Rule in Russia*, p. 562.
101 Buchbender, O., *Das tönende Erz*, pp. 207–18. It appears that, although in the autumn of 1942 desertion, in numerical terms, dropped, as a percentage of the total captured, it increased.
102 See p. 51.
103 Demsky, A., 'A. A. Vlasov v batal'ione Volga' in Pozdnyakov, V. V., *A. A. Vlasov*, pp. 72–84.
104 Pozdnyakov, V. V., *A. A. Vlasov*, pp. 67–71.
105 Lochner, L. (ed.), *Goebbels' Diaries*, p. 271: 29 April 1943.
106 von Dellinghausen, E., 'Poezdka A. A. Vlasova v severo-zapadnye raiony okkupirovannoy chasti SSSR' in Pozdnyakov, V. V., *A. A. Vlasov*, pp. 85–94.
107 Svobodin, I., 'Beseda s generalom Vlasovym', *Novy put'*, Riga (10 May 1943) in Pozdnyakov, V. V., *A. A. Vlasov*, pp. 108–11.
108 Hromenko, G. D., 'Dnevnik', in Pozdnyakov, V. V., *A. A. Vlasov*, pp. 99–108.
109 '"General Vlasov v Rige." Vospominaniya morskogo ofitsera. Aprel' 1943', *Russkoe vozrozhdenie*, no. 10, New York (1980).
110 Tel'nov, Y., 'A. A. Vlasov na severo-zapade okkupirovannoy Rossii', *Novy zhurnal*, 157 (December 1984), pp. 268–71.
111 Dallin, A., *German Rule in Russia*, p. 572.

112 Keitel, 18 April 1943, in Heiber, H., *Hitler's Lagebesprechungen*, Stuttgart (1962), p. 266, n. 1.

113 Lochner, L. (ed.), *Goebbels' Diaries*, p. 271.

114 '"Pochemu ya stal na put' bor'by s bolshevizmom." Otkrytoe pis'mo generala Vlasova', *Zarya* (3 March 1943) and in *Dobrovolets* (7 March 1943); see Appendix B.

115 Pozdnyakov, V. V., *Rozhdenie ROA*, pp. 44–96, 99–138; Pozdnyakov, V. V., *A. A. Vlasov*, pp. 276–300; Shtifanov, N., 'Dabendorf' *Novoe Russkoe Slovo*, New York (18 February 1974).

116 For a discussion of the courses at Dabendorf, see Chapter 2 on the programme, pp. 153–5.

117 Buchbender, O., *Das tönende Erz*, pp. 232–44.

118 Dallin, A. and Mavrogordato, R. S., 'The Soviet Reaction to Vlasov', *World Politics*, 8 (April 1956), pp. 307–22; Armstrong, J. A., *Soviet Partisans in World War II*, Madison (1964), pp. 243–6.

119 Perhaps the choice of the name Kapustin, almost certainly a false one, is evidence of black humour to be found within the security service? 'Kapustin' was the pseudonym used by Gershuni at the SR congress in 1907. He had chosen this name to commemorate the barrel of pickled cabbage in which he had hidden and so escaped from Siberia! Niko-laevsky, B., *Istoriya odnogo predatelya*, New York (1980), pp. 256–7.

120 'Aufzeichnung: Betr. Vernehmung des Spions Kapustin der unter anderen mit dem Auftrag herüberkam, terroristische Gruppen zum Zwecke der Ermordung von Vlassov zu bilden'. Captured German files. FCO 997/305 056-058, 997/305 067-071; Armstrong, J., *Soviet Partisans in World War II*, pp. 246–8. See later discussion, Chapter 2, pp. 120–2.

121 See Chapter 2, p. 134.

122 Interview: Y. S. Zherebkov.

123 Fischer, G., 'Besprechung des Führers mit Generalfeldmarschall Keitel und General Zeitzler am 8.6.1943 auf dem Berghof', *Journal of Modern History*, 23, no. 1 (March 1951), pp. 58–71. For an English translation, see Fischer, G., *Soviet Opposition to Stalin*, pp. 176–87.

124 'Auszug aus der Ansprache des Führers an die Heeresgruppenführer pp. am 1.7.43 abends', *Vierteljahrshefte für Zeitgeschichte*, 2 (1954), pp. 305–12.

125 Keitel to Rosenberg. Abschrift, Juni 1943. FCO 997 3 305 202.

126 Dallin, A., *German Rule in Russia*, p. 584.

127 U.S. National Archives Vlassow Documents (Nuremberg War Crimes Trials) No. 5899, 5900.

128 ROA Archives BAR 0661, Y. K. Meyer manuscript.

129 Interview: S. L. Woyciechowsky.

130 Steenberg, S., *Vlasov*, pp. 114–15.

131 Strik-Strikfeldt, W., *Against Stalin and Hitler*, pp. 176–9.

132 Text of letter in *Dobrovolets*, 56 (17 November 1943) and *Parizhskiy vestnik*, 76 (27 November 1943).

133 'General Malyshkin v chastyakh ROA na zapade', *Dobrovolets*, 17 (1944).

134 *TMWC*, vol. 29, pp. 11–73. Doc. 1919 PS.

135 Hohne, H., *The Order of the Death's Head*, London (1969), pp. 436–59.

136 Dallin, A., *German Rule in Russia*, p. 606.

137 US National Archives, No. 3125. Vermerk betr. General Wlassow (Labs).

138 Buchbender, O., *Das tönende Erz*, pp. 255–6.

139 Interview: N. G. Shtifanov.

140 Frau Wlassow, 'Die Tragödie eines Generales', *Schweitzer illustrierte Zeitung*, Zurich (10 January 1951) and 'Mein Mann wurde gehenkt', *Die 7 Tage*, Konstanz (2 November 1951, 9 November 1951, 10 November 1951).

141 Kroeger letter to Steenberg, 6 May 1967, BA-MA Steenberg III.

142 It appears that Vlasov's first, Russian, wife was still alive in 1948, in a labour camp. BA-MA collection Steenberg III. Die Rede Koslows.

143 Hoffmann, P., *The History of the German Resistance*, pp. 507–34.

144 The only record that remains of this meeting was written down by d'Alquen in 1947. Russian translation in Kiselev, A., *Oblik generala Vlasova*, pp. 163–76.

145 Dallin, A., *German Rule in Russia*, p. 617.

146 Letter of Kroeger to author, 24 March, 1979.

147 Artem'ev, V. P., *Pervaya Diviziya ROA*, p. 26.

148 BA R6 35.

149 Bogatyrchuk, F. P., *Moy zhiznenny put' k Vlasovu i Prazhskomu Manifestu*, p. 191.

150 Pozdnyakov, V. V., *A. A. Vlasov*, pp. 113–41.

151 Dallin, A., *German Rule in Russia*, p. 635.

152 Pozdnyakov, V. V., *A. A. Vlasov*, pp. 117–20.

153 Prikaz, no. 1 (28 January 1945); *Volya naroda* (31 January 1945).

154 Text of Manifesto *Volya naroda*, no. 1 (15 November 1944) and reproduced in many publications, e.g. Pozdnyakov, V. V., *A. A. Vlasov*, pp. 125–33.

155 Kromiadi, K. G., *Za zemlyu, za volyu ...*, p. 205.

156 Pozdnyakov, V. V., *A. A. Vlasov*, pp. 142–65.

157 *Volya naroda* (20 December 1944).

158 Bogatyrchuk, F. P., *Moy zhiznenny put' k Vlasovu i Prazhskomu Manifestu*, p. 205.

159 Pozdnyakov, V. V., *A. A. Vlasov*, p. 301; interviews: D. A. Levitsky, I. L. Novosiltsev.

160 Bogatyrchuk, F. P., *Moy zhiznenny put' k Vlasovu i Prazhskomu Manifestu*, p. 185.

161 Kazantsev, A. S., *Tret'ya sila*, pp. 293–325.

162 Interview: Y. K. Meyer; *Bor'ba*, no. 14 (1948), pp. 25–7.

163 FCO Captured German Files, 5822/E 424 133–8; *Volya naroda* (24 January 1945).

164 Orlov, S., 'Na ch'i den'gi sozdavalos' Russkoe Osvoboditel'noe Dvizhenie?', *Zarubezh'e*, no. 53–5, Munich (February–April 1977), p. 21.

165 Polyakov, I. A., *Krasnov-Vlasov, vospominaniya*, New York (1959), pp. 14, 28; 'Pis'mo generala Krasnova', *Kazachiya zemlya*, no. 12 (16 March

1945); 'Otvet gen. A. A. Vlasova' and 'Otvet Kazach'ego Upravleniya pri KONR', *Put' na rodinu*, 2 (3 April 1945). Reprinted in *Bor'ba*, 29/30 (1950).

166 Ausky, S. A., *Predatel'stvo i izmena*, pp. 129–34.

167 Interview: Y. S. Zherebkov.

168 For a discussion of Malyshkin's speech, see discussion of anti-semitism in Chapter 2 on the programme, pp. 133–5.

169 Zherebkov typescript 1947. Nikolaevsky Archive no. 201, box 1, 3; 'Popytki KONR ustanovit' kontakt s zapadnymi soyuznikami', *Zarubezh'e*, no. 61/62/63 (1979), pp. 16–22.

170 Interview: Y. S. Zherebkov; 'Nesostoyavsheesya vystuplenie gen. Vlasova', *Bor'ba*, 13 (1948).

171 Interview: B. V. Pryanishnikov.

172 Ausky, S. A., *Predatel'stvo i izmena*, pp. 130–1.

173 Kazantsev, A. S., *Tret'ya sila*, p. 181; interviews: P. I. Kruzhin, N. G. Shtifanov.

174 The British, in fact, via the British Ambassador in Moscow, asked Molotov about Vlasov and his forces. PRO. FO 371 36960. XIN 067 46 – Sir Archibald Clark Kerr to Sir Orme Sergeant, 4 August 1943.

175 U.S. National Archives SHAEF Documents G-2 Div. Record Group 331 NND 760210. A.C. of S., G-2 Headquarters XXI Corps. Interview with representative of White Russian Army – 24 April 1945.

176 The most detailed eye-witness account is Artem'ev, V. P., *Pervaya Diviziya ROA*. His account provides much of the material available on the actions of the 1st Division, although occasionally the author was not privy to the events described and mistakes and discrepancies occur. This account is an excellent illustration of the state of mind of the Russians and their attitude to the Germans. His account of this final period leaves the reader with the impression that the movements of the KONR forces were similar to those of a caged animal. They knew that they had to escape, but it was not clear how they should do so. Ausky, S. A., *Predatel'stvo i izmena* provides the fullest interpretation of events using Russian, German and Czech sources.

177 *Kriegstagebuch des Oberkommando der Wehrmacht 1940–45*, vol. 4/2, p. 1150. Lagebuch (7 March 1945), 600 Inf. Div. (Russ.).

178 *Volya naroda* (21 February 1945).

179 Artem'ev, V. P., *Pervaya Diviziya ROA*, p. 83, n.

180 Ibid., p. 99.

181 Ausky, S. A., *Predatel'stvo i izmena*, pp. 202–4 and 222, considers that discipline and training were poor in the 1st Division and that the 2nd Division was, in fact, in much better order.

182 Artem'ev, V. P., *Pervaya Diviziya ROA*, p. 107.

183 Interview: N. E. Andreyev.

184 Fischer, G., *Soviet Opposition to Stalin*, p. 100.

185 Artem'ev, V. P., *Pervaya Diviziya ROA*, pp. 111–12.

186 *New York Times* (6 May 1945).

187 Ausky, S. A., *Predatel'stvo i izmena*, pp. 156–205.

188 Ibid., pp. 140–1.

189 Artem'ev, V. P., *Pervaya Diviziya ROA*, p. 120.

190 Steenberg, S., *Vlasov*, p. 202.

191 Steenberg, S., *Vlasov*, p. 208.

192 Pekarsky, I., 'Kak byl zakhvachen general Vlasov' in Pozdnyakov, V. V., *A. A. Vlasov*, pp. 416–18. Resler, V., written down by Kruzhin, P. I. in *S narodom za narod* (5 December 1965). Antonov, R., two versions, one to Yakovlev, B. the other to Pozdnyakov, V. V. in Pozdnyakov, V. V., *A. A. Vlasov*, pp. 423–27. 'Poslednie dni generala Vlasova. (svidetel'stvo ochevidtsa) 8 July 1945', *Rossiskiy demokrat*, I (1948) pp. 23–7.

193 'Vospominaniya byvshego komandira 25go tankovogo korpusa, geroya Sovetskogo Soyuza general-lieutenanta zapasa Ye. Fominykh.' *Izvestiya* (7 October 1962).

194 'Announcement of the Military Collegium of the Supreme Court of the USSR. Within the last days the Military Collegium of the Supreme Court of the USSR has been examining charges against: Vlasov, A. A., Malyshkin, V. F., Zhilenkov, N. G., Trukhin, F. I., Zakutny, D. E., Blagoveschchensky, I. A., Meandrov, M. A., Maltsev, V. I., Bunya-chenko, S. K., Zverev, G. A., Karbukov, V. D., Shatov, I. S. They were accused of treason and that as agents of the German espionage service, they carried out espionage, diversionary and terrorist activity against the USSR, that is crimes under Section 58, paragraphs 8, 9, 10, 11, 16 of the criminal code of the USSR.
'All the accused admitted their guilt, and were condemned to death under Article 11 of the order of the Supreme Soviet of August 19 1943. The sentences have been carried out.' *Izvestiya* (2 August 1946).

195 Aldan, A. G., *Armiya obrechennykh*, pp. 25–39.

196 Aldan, A. G. and Kuznetsov, B. M., *V ugodu Stalinu*, London, Ontario (1968), pp. 42–5, 56–7.

197 Resler, V., written down by Kruzhin, P. I. in *S narodom za narod* (5 December 1965).

198 Ausky, S. A., *Predatel'stvo i izmena*, pp. 265–6, assumes that this individual was Zhilenkov, and that his behaviour was consistent with his earlier actions.

199 Trepper, L., *The Great Game*, London (1977), pp. 379–80.

200 Grigorenko, P. G., *V podpol'e mozhno vstretit' tol'ko krys*, New York (1981), p. 216.

201 See p. 18, n. 38.

202 See above, n. 194

203 Grigorenko, P. G., *V podpol'e mozhno vstretit' tol'ko krys*, p. 216.

2

Ideals

I HIGH HOPES

After his capture and preliminary interrogations, Vlasov was sent to a special prisoner-of-war camp, at Vinnitsa in the Ukraine, which held other Soviet commanders.[1] Here, Vlasov immediately became involved in political activity.

The Vlasov-Boyarsky Memorandum

As a result of discussions with captured compatriots on the possibility of change within the Soviet Union, Vlasov and Colonel Boyarsky, who had been involved in the Osintorf Brigade and was later to become one of Vlasov's commanders in the Russian Liberation Movement, wrote a memorandum[2] to the German High Command. The Memorandum discussed the situation within the USSR and German attitudes towards the Soviet Union and proposed the formation of a National Russian Army. Dated 3 August 1942, it was written a bare two weeks after Vlasov's arrival at Vinnitsa. The speed of composition undoubtedly reflects the urgency with which the Russians viewed the situation. Every minute was of importance. The letter appears to have taken a further five-and-a-half weeks to pass through the wheels of the German military bureaucracy. This document consists of two pages, approximately 600 words altogether. Its particular interest lies in its being the only extant record containing an accurate, as far as can be ascertained, reflection of Vlasov's own views. All later leaflets, proclamations and appeals were larded[3] with the ideas and advice of others. Since Vlasov was the senior officer, it is more likely that he composed the greater part of the letter.

89

The advice proffered to the German High Command in this communication was the product of attitudes found among members of the Soviet intelligentsia in the latter half of the 1930s,[4] when it was considered that the Soviet regime would only collapse if subjected to external attack. The system was considered to be too monolithic for any one individual to weaken the structure from within. Vlasov and other high ranking officers must have been greatly upset by the condition of the armed forces at the outbreak of war, and by the initial prosecution of the war. As commanders they were well aware of the disaffection within the Soviet Union. They considered that the Germans must be made to appreciate that they could not hope to conquer the USSR without internal support from the population; the size of the country alone presented insuperable problems for an invader. Hence, it seemed only sensible that the Germans should harness internal Soviet disaffection by permitting the formation of a Russian national group or government, which would, the officers considered, greatly facilitate the overthrow of the Soviet regime.[5]

The Vlasov-Boyarsky Memorandum indicates some of the problems which would have to be faced by a Russian Liberation Movement, and how the leaders of such a movement envisaged tackling these questions. It betrays the authors' lack of knowledge of Nazism.[6] The writers were completely unaware of any need for circumspection and failed to leave themselves room for further political manoeuvring.

The first paragraph of the Memorandum stated that Stalin's government had lost popularity. This was ascribed to the government's inability to organise the war, both at the front and in the rear where the civilian population was experiencing famine and economic disruption. Furthermore, the authors considered that the government was only able to maintain power through terror. This criticism of the Stalinist government and emphasis on the sufferings of the population was a theme which was to be repeated in all later proclamations of the Russian Liberation Movement and was the starting point for all developments of the opposition. The second paragraph described the situation of the Soviet military commanders. To them, as to the civilian leaders, 'the futility of continuing the war is becoming increasingly obvious'. The war was destroying millions of lives and enormous amounts of capital quite needlessly. The military leaders were faced with the alternative either of dying on the front, or at the hands of NKVD. The army commanders were held responsible for military defeat, but it was in fact not their fault. In addition, their actions were impeded by the commissars. This had resulted in more of the higher ranking leaders surrendering to the Germans. Vlasov's comment was a product of the poor relationship between the political and military command in the Red Army. Lack of experience on the part of the political commissars and their equal responsibility with the military commanders had disastrous consequences in the Finnish campaign. This dual command was subsequently abolished only to be introduced again on 16 July 1941. However, it was so unpopular that on 9 October 1942 it was abolished.[7] The third paragraph explained that these captured commanders exchanged ideas as to how the Stalinist government could be overthrown, and how a 'New Russia' should be built. The Memorandum then included a sentence in which the authors naively posed the question as to whether it would be best for 'the anti-Stalinist Russians to ally with Germany or with Britain and the United States'. The Memorandum explained that given the nature of the task – the overthrow of the Soviet government – the opposition to Stalin should ally itself with Germany, since one of the German avowed war aims was to overthrow the Soviet regime.

This was the crux of the matter. These two sentences betray the dilemma of the opposition movement. For, whereas the captured Soviet officers considered that without outside support it would be difficult to defeat the Soviet government, these Soviet citizens opposed to Stalin undoubtedly would have preferred an alliance with a democratic regime had not Britain and the United States already been allies of the Soviet Union.[8] Only the Third Reich had openly declared its hostility towards the Soviet Union and communism. Yet, as the captured Russians would shortly discover, the hostility of the Third Reich towards the USSR was based not so much on political grounds, despite statements to this effect, but on racial theories first elaborated in *Mein Kampf*.

These assertions by the authors of the Memorandum, with their tacit avowal of the difficulties faced by an opposition movement, showed that the nature of Nazism was, as yet, far from clear to them. No Nazi official reading such a letter would have been moved to do anything about it. Anyone sympathetic to the *Untermensch* theory would consider the views of the Russians to be unworthy of serious consideration. Still less would such a reader be tolerant of an exposition of the problems faced by Soviet citizens opposed to the Stalinist regime. It is clear from the underscoring of certain key words and question marks in the margin on the original copy of the Memorandum, that the sentiments expressed by Vlasov and Boyarsky were incomprehensible to the reader of this document.

The fourth paragraph expressed the conviction that Stalin would continue the war to the bitter end. The fifth paragraph advanced the idea that the formation of a Russian army would serve a need. The authors of the letter considered that the hostility of the prisoners-of-war towards Stalin's government should be utilised by the German command. This sizeable Russian military force would provide the kernel for the creation of a new social and political system in Russia. The authors of the letter also considered that the formation of a Russian army would give voice to the disaffection amongst the prisoners-of-war, and that official recognition would do away with the feeling current among the prisoners-of-war that otherwise their collaboration was treasonable. In other words, Vlasov and Boyarsky, in this very confused phrase, intimated that the Russians were not willing merely to become German mercenaries, but would fight if their actions were motivated by patriotism. These ideas of patriotic motivation counter-balancing treachery also drew forth underlining and queries from the reader.

The Memorandum exemplifies many of the problems which were to occur as the Russian Liberation Movement developed. Two strategies had to be considered in order to overthrow the Stalinist regime. One was a short-term aim, the need to develop sufficient force to destroy the Soviet government; the second was a long-term programme for the construction of a new social and political system within the territories of the USSR. The immediate methods to be used in forming a Russian Liberation Army were much clearer and more easily put into practice than the long-term aspirations, and consequently more attention was devoted to short-term requirements. It was not, of course, easy to discuss plans for a non-Stalinist Russian state given the attitudes of Nazi ideology towards this question, but, nevertheless, even in this first letter, where political guile is non-existent, more emphasis is laid on the need to create an army than on the need to create a new system within Russia. Admittedly, the aim of Vlasov and Boyarsky was to prompt the German High Command into swift action to alleviate the situation of the Russian prisoners-of-war and to find positive use for them, rather than to argue the political alternatives to Stalinism. Yet this constant concern with the immediate military issues obscured, to a large extent, the broader question of the future complexion of a new regime inside the Soviet Union. This shortcoming can be found in much of the subsequent history of the Russian Liberation Movement.

The Memorandum also illustrates the approach of the leaders of this enterprise. They advanced strictly factual evidence in support of their contention that there was a need for change in the Soviet Union, i.e. evidence of recent events and experiences; especially the state's use of terror, and the poor condition of the Soviet armed forces during the war. Such arguments would easily be understood by the Soviet audience the Russian Liberation Movement hoped to attract. These Soviet citizens were not used to dealing with political abstractions; neither were the leaders of the Liberation Movement. Furthermore, the Memorandum illustrates a common misunderstanding prevalent in Soviet circles: the assumption that the West was generally well-informed about conditions within the Soviet Union.[9]

At the outbreak of war, the Germans had been considered by many to be liberators.[10] It was thought that they would be aware of conditions in the Soviet Union in the late 1930s and would understand the attitude of the population to the regime. Although the letter might have been intelligible to a Russian opposed to the Stalinist regime, it presupposed a greater comprehension on the part of a German reading it than was in fact likely to be the case.

Leaflet addressed to Red Army commanders and the Soviet intelligentsia

Vlasov's next political act was to sign a leaflet[11] which was addressed to Red Army commanders and the Soviet intelligentsia. Vlasov had refused to sign the initial leaflet presented to him by Wehrmacht Propaganda,[12] and though the text was subsequently rewritten, this new leaflet bears evidence of further Nazi interference and of compromise on the part of the Russians opposed to Stalin with their German captors. The leaflet, about 600 words long, was signed at Vinnitsa on 10 September 1942. Since Vlasov had refused to sign a request to his fellow countrymen in the Red Army to desert, the leaflet, written in the first person ostensibly by Vlasov, consisted for the most part of criticism of 'the Stalinist clique'; a form of words which was to be repeated in all the declarations of the Russian Liberation Movement. The leaflet started off with a brief description of Vlasov's career, particularly his war service, adding that he had risen through the ranks to the position of lieutenant-general. It quoted him as saying that as commander of the besieged 2nd Shock Army he continued to fight to the last possible moment and then was taken prisoner. After this introduction, the leaflet explained that having witnessed the people's sufferings during the war, and having been greatly distressed by the constant military setbacks, Vlasov had been forced to ask himself the question: whose fault was it? The leaflet did not confine its criticism of 'the Stalinist clique' merely to military incompetence and inefficient prosecution of the war.

The leaflet explained that when Vlasov looked back at the last twelve to fifteen years, he had come to the conclusion that all the hardships endured by the people had been the result of the policies of the government. The country had been ruined by the *kolkhoz* system. Millions of the finest individuals had been destroyed, the best military cadres had been decimated and a completely incorrect system of training had corrupted both the country at large and the army. All unfettered thought in the country had been stifled, and the growth of mutual suspicion had been encouraged.

Throughout this recital of the wrongs suffered by Russia the blame was laid at the door of Stalin and his close advisers. There was no intimation here that anything in the nature of communism or Bolshevism *per se* was the root cause of these sufferings. Also, although traces of the effect of Nazi influence can be seen in references to the progress of the war and the stylisation of German success and Soviet defeats, no mention was made of the Nazi catch-phrase 'judaeo-Bolshevik'.

The regime was also blamed for involving the country in a war which was not in the latter's interest. Now, having lost support among the mass of the population, shattered the apparatus of government, and undermined the economy, the government was leading the country to defeat. This section seems to have been influenced somewhat more by the demands of German propaganda. The Third Reich, not the USSR, had initiated hostilities between the two powers.[13] Further, given Nazi aims in the USSR, it was clearly not in the Soviet interest to submit tamely to this aggression.

This emphasis on the progress of the war was undoubtedly aimed at the military audience for whom this leaflet was intended. The content of this leaflet also supports the hypothesis that it was in fact the military situation, and in particular the fate of the 2nd Shock

Army, which had provided the impetus for Vlasov's change of attitude towards the Soviet regime.

The next paragraph contained more particulars of the war. German successes in the South and in the Crimea were mentioned; presumably referring to the capture of Kiev and to the advances in the Ukraine in September 1941 and in the Crimea in October 1941. It said that the attacking forces had met with poor resistance, and soldiers, who were not willing to fight for the interests of others, were surrendering in 'crowds'. The 'Stalinist clique', it was averred, knowing that it was unable to organise the defence of the country any more, was determined to hold on to power by means of the needless sacrifice of untrained troops.

This paragraph is a good example of the effect of Nazi ideology. The authors were forced to depart from a strictly factual description and the analysis of the situation became more stylised in response to the Nazi ideological demands. By the latter half of 1942, Stalin had been able to rectify some of the defects in the Soviet war economy. As hostile Nazi attitudes to the civilian population of the occupied areas had become more self-evident, so correspondingly, Stalin more easily was able to generate a greater patriotic wish to resist the aggressors. The more volatile situation prevalent in the early stages of the war, caused by large-scale disaffection within the country, no longer existed to the same extent.

The next section of the leaflet, however, gave vent to the feelings of frustration and hopelessness experienced by Red Army commanders when confronted by the party political apparatus. For, as the author explained, although the commanders were usually saddled with the brunt of the blame for any setbacks, they were obstructed at every turn by the commissars, the political department (*politotdel*) and the NKVD, none of whom had military training or expertise. The author of the leaflet considered that the result of this harassment by the political sector led to honest individuals being left with no alternative but to commit suicide. Although the leaflet did not give any names, this was indeed a way out of the situation taken by some individuals, for example, General Kirponos.[14]

The next sentence was obviously aimed at servicemen at the front who were worried about their families. The chaos in the country, it stated, resulted in hunger, which was being experienced by families of soldiers who were not getting any help from the government.

Further, the leaflet stated that 'the Stalinist clique placed great hopes on Anglo-American aid and on the opening of a "second front"'. This theme then developed into an attack on the British and American state systems known to exploit others for their own ends, and who would fight 'until the last Russian soldier'. It was explained that it was not the first time that Russians had had to pay for Anglo-American interests. This section is very much at odds with the remarks made in Vlasov and Boyarsky's Memorandum to the High Command which did not express hostility towards the Allies. The attack on Allied motives springs, almost certainly, from the insistence of the Nazi propaganda machine. Also, it may have been designed to appeal to anti-Allied sentiment still extant in the Red Army, which had originated as a result of Allied intervention in the Civil War. The leaflet was addressed to those who were critical of the Stalinist regime. Of course, these same people could equally be critical of the Western regime which, they had constantly been told, had imperialistic designs against them. Consequently, such a remark could well have struck an emotive chord in Red Army men and amongst individuals.

The next part of this appeal was clearly a product of Nazi propaganda: 'Lying propaganda frightens you with tales of fascism, firing squads and bestial cruelties in German captivity.' Vlasov did not experience these conditions for himself, but he must have been aware that the condition of the Soviet prisoners-of-war was pitiful. However, the leaflet maintained that Soviet prisoners-of-war saw conditions in Germany and in the Wehrmacht where they experienced better supplies and better quality of uniform than the Red Army troops, and relatively frequent home leave. The passage goes on to praise German culture, organisation and discipline, and is concluded in very vague terms.

What way is there out of the blind alley into which the Stalinist clique has led the country? There is only one way out. History does not provide any other. For those of you to whom their country is dear and who would like to see their fellow countrymen happy, they must struggle with all their might and main to overthrow the loathsome Stalinist clique. They must struggle to bring an end to a criminal war fought in the interests of England and America, and to obtain an honourable peace with Germany. The best people in the country, both within Stalin-held territory and in prisoner of war camps, are already thinking along these lines, some of them are working towards this goal – the rest is up to you!

Vlasov would not ask his fellow countrymen to desert to the Germans, nor did he specify what action was being taken where or by whom. This would seem to agree with the stand he is known to have taken at a later date, that he was unwilling to make promises to anyone, unless he could be sure that these had a chance of becoming a reality.

The Smolensk Declaration

The publication which marked a new departure and the start of a concerted effort to form a Russian Liberation Army, was the Smolensk Declaration[15] signed on 27 December 1942 in Berlin. Vlasov was chairman and Malyshkin secretary of the Russian Committee, which was ostensibly based in Smolensk, and in whose name the Declaration was issued. The Declaration, made public on January 1943,[16] covered two sheets of paper and was some 800 words long. The Russian Committee addressed 'men and officers of the Red Army, the Russian nation and other nations of the Soviet Union'. It started with the words 'Friends and brothers', a designation which marked a divergence from the more official 'comrades' of Vlasov's earlier leaflet. This term may also indicate that the 'Russian Committee' realised that the forms of address used by the Communist party were not popular.[17] The heading of the Declaration reflects the nationalistic flavour which the opposition movement exhibited from its inception, and which, although modified somewhat, was retained until the end.[18] Then came an introductory passage after which were listed the thirteen points, the principles on which the new social and political system in Russia should be founded; a concluding passage then rounded off the Declaration.

The document began with the assertion that Bolshevism was the enemy of the Russian people and went on to describe and enumerate the various hardships undergone as the result of the war. Once again, the aspirations of the British and Americans were viewed in a very poor light since they were allied with the Soviet Union and wished to profit from the exertions of the Russians. Description of the sufferings of the civilian population was succeeded by a depiction of the disastrous predicament of the Red Army. The root cause of all these misfortunes was the 'rottenness of the whole of the Bolshevik system, the incompetence of Stalin and the General Staff'. Stalin, it was alleged, retained power only through the use of terror. The allies of Stalin, the British and Americans, now mentioned as capitalists and plutocrats, were only interested in enriching themselves at the expense of Russia and had entered into secret agreements with Stalin.

The reference to the Allied capitalists was the first time that they were so defined, but was a phrase which recurred in later pronouncements. It would appear to denote a number of developments. First, the phrase was one which was used as a result of the insistence in the Nazi propaganda machine that the Allies should always be qualified by a negative epithet. Second, it is striking that only the capitalists and plutocrats were referred to, no mention was made of the nation. Vlasov and his entourage were always careful to make distinctions between a nation and its government. This distinction was usually applied to the Soviet Union and the Third Reich, but in this instance, it appeared to apply to the Allies as well. The reference to a secret agreement seems to have been the result of propaganda. It had been rumoured in the German press[19] that a crashed Soviet aeroplane had been found in northern Norway, and that the text of an agreement had been found by which, in return for aid, Stalin had agreed to give the Americans the Baku oil fields and bases at Murmansk. This agreement was once again referred to in the twelfth point of the political programme.

The next section of the preamble was obviously untrue and was also the product of pure propaganda. It stated that Germany was not fighting the war against the Russian people and their homeland but merely against Bolshevism. The authors of the Smolensk Declaration undoubtedly knew that this was a lie, but were prepared, nonetheless, to include it. They believed that by compromising over this issue and including this kind of statement, they could present a political programme to their compatriots, who in any case, it was thought, were sufficiently versed in methods of publication under a totalitarian regime, to be able to read between the lines. This passage also included the idea that the new system in Europe which was to be created would be without 'Bolsheviks and capitalists', a phrase which expressed the position of the Russian Committee on the type of social and political order which they would like to see in the Soviet Union.

The Committee proceeded to formulate its objectives, beginning with the assertion that the struggle against Bolshevism and the destruction of Stalin and his clique, in the first instance, were solely the business of the Russian people. This implies that the interference of other powers in this question would not be welcome. The aims of the Committee were to overthrow Stalin and his clique, to sign an honourable peace with Germany and to create a New Russia 'without Bolsheviks and capitalists'. Then the principles on which the new state would be based were listed. The first six points of the programme dealt with social and economic measures. Direction of labour and the collective farm system (*kolkhoz*) were to be done away with. The industrial worker would be guaranteed the right to work and the peasant would own land as a private individual. Trade and crafts would be re-established and private enterprise would play a part in the economy. Intellectuals would be allowed to work as they wished in the interests of their country, social justice would be guaranteed and the workers would be protected from exploitation. All working people would be guaranteed the right to education, leisure and old age pensions.

The next three points were more concerned with the political order. First, the system of terror and force would be abolished and freedom of religion, conscience, speech, assembly and the press would be established. The individual and his home would be inviolable. National freedom would be guaranteed. Those affected by the repressive system of Bolshevism would be freed.

The last four points were concerned with the effects of the present war. The government would pay for war damage, both industrial and civilian. The supposed agreements entered into with the Anglo-American capitalists would not be honoured (see above) and were void, and war invalids and their families would be paid an indemnity.

The thirteen points ended with an exhortation to all Russians concerned about the future of their country to unite in the struggle against the arch-enemy Bolshevism. The Declaration concluded with a call to arms and to Russian patriotism. The Russian Liberation Army was referred to as an ally of Germany, and the Russians who wished to respond to the call of duty and to destroy the cause of their country's misfortunes were urged to join this force. Such defectors were guaranteed safe conduct regardless of their past.

The publication of the Declaration achieved some of the goals that the authors had set. The term Russian Liberation Army became widely known amongst Soviet citizens who found themselves within the orbit of the Third Reich. Although this force was, as yet, a fiction, it indicated that attempts were being made to provide a focus for their political aspirations and to change the course of Nazi policy in the territories of the Soviet Union.

The preamble and conclusion of the document contained a

number of phrases which reached a compromise with Nazi ideology and the demands of Nazi propaganda, but the whole tone was quite different from the crude, anti-semitic, Nazi propaganda of the '*Bey Zhida Politruka, Morda Prosit Kirpicha*' (Beat up the Yid, the political instructor, his mug asks for a brick) variety.[20] This very crude approach did not provide an answer to any of the questions troubling Soviet citizens about the future of their country. Even if Nazi propaganda produced more meaningful slogans than the one above, they were, for the most part, negative in content. Although the economic and social order prevalent in the Soviet Union was not universally popular, as the existence of members of the Russian Liberation Movement proved, unless Russians were given some indication of what was to replace the Soviet state, German propaganda was unlikely to have much success. The intimation of a more positive approach was to be found in the Smolensk Declaration. The thirteen points of the programme were, overall, 'liberal' in spirit.

The Smolensk Declaration created a demand for information about the Russian Committee and the Russian Liberation Army. Since the Russian Liberation Army was non-existent and the Russian Committee was never allowed to go to Smolensk, such enquiries were made in vain. Nevertheless, it can be affirmed that, at this point, Soviet citizens within the Third Reich began to consider themselves members of a Russian Liberation Movement, and individuals serving in the Wehrmacht sewed insignia on to their uniforms to indicate their unity of purpose with the Russian Liberation Army. However, the enthusiasm expressed by the Russians for such a venture did not produce the desired modification in Nazi attitudes.

Plans for an organisation

A fragment of another memorandum[21] signed by Vlasov, in the capacity of chairman, Malyshkin as secretary and Zhilenkov as member of the Russian Committee, exists in Russian. The first two pages of five-and-a-half pages of typescript are missing. It appears from the remainder of the typescript that these two pages set out the principles on which a Russian Committee should be founded. The memorandum was submitted to the Ostministerium, and it was probably written between the formation of the Russian Committee, in December 1942, and March 1943.[22] The memorandum urged the official use of the term ROA for all Russian units, as this would then provide a unity of purpose. The aims of this force should be the same as those of the Russian National Committee: to fight Stalin and to form a new Russia. Only when armed with this idea would these troops cease to consider themselves as traitors and German hirelings. The authors also urged that a merger of all the anti-Stalinist groups and the inclusion of all the nationalist groups in the ROA should be effected. They emphasised, too, the necessity of having their own insignia and uniforms, since the wearing of German uniform created adverse propaganda and was bad for the morale of both the population of the occupied territories and the troops themselves. The need for Russian staff officers and troop commanders was also strongly emphasised. The memorandum ended with a brief description of those involved in the Russian Committee. They reaffirmed their conviction that the creation of a Russian Committee would be popular and would be supported by those opposed to the Stalinist regime. The Russian Committee was in the process of developing a political programme but it considered that the question of frontier boundaries and future forms of government should be decided only after Stalin's defeat. Similarly, they considered that the formation of independent committees for each national minority was unwise.

This memorandum may well reflect Vlasov's own personal views fairly accurately. The phrase referring to the state of morale amongst prisoners-of-war seems to echo his first memorandum written in conjunction with Boyarsky. This second memorandum was written in the blunt style favoured by Vlasov and once again, since he was the senior officer, his views must have carried weight in its composition.

Presumably, the object of this memorandum was to enlist the Ostministerium in the cause of the Russian Committee and the Russian Liberation Army. However, the authors of this memorandum do not seem to have been particularly diplomatic in dealing with the nationality question. The memorandum stresses that the anti-Stalinist opposition, including all the national minorities, should be united under Russian command. After Stalin had been defeated, then the nationalities would have the right to choose independence if that was what they wanted.

This documentary fragment reveals that the members of the Russian Committee were still not completely *au fait* with the intricacies of the Nazi regime, and possibly in the urgency of attempting to clarify their own point of view did not pay sufficient attention to the prejudices of the Germans with whom they had to deal. It also appears that much more attention was being paid to the details of a future Russian Liberation Army than to the far more complex matters of Soviet internal politics. However, possibly this was omitted since the expression and discussion of such questions would have been out of place in a document addressed to German policy makers.

The Open Letter

In March 1943, Vlasov's Open Letter 'Why I decided to fight Bolshevism' (*Pochemu ya stal na put' bor'by s bolshevizmom*) was published.[23] The appearance in the newspapers *Dobrovolets* and *Zarya* of this explanation of his views and actions was timed to coincide with Vlasov's visits and speeches in the occupied territories and to provide further evidence of genuine efforts to try and change the course of German policy. The Open Letter was the most sophisticated document to appear so far, in the campaign to promote the Russian Liberation Movement. The Letter demonstrates a greater awareness of the need for subtlety towards the demands and pressures of the Third Reich, an enhanced appreciation of the mentality and attitudes of those likely to read this text and also of the best way to present Vlasov's cause. Equally, the Open Letter sheds further light on some of the ideas held by the Movement.

The Letter, 1,800 words long, started off with the sentence that Vlasov, when exhorting his fellow countrymen to rise up against 'Stalin and his clique' and to build a 'New Russia without Bolsheviks and capitalists', found it necessary to explain his position. This was then followed by the remark 'the Soviet authorities have not harmed me in any way'. This phrase was intended to create the impression that the opinions expressed in the Letter were objective and persuasive, whereas if this passage had begun with criticism of the Soviet regime, then the impression created would have been much more that the enterprise was merely a product of Vlasov's personal feelings, that he felt personally let down and overlooked.

The paragraph goes on to show that Vlasov was a typical product of Soviet society; that he had shared their way of life and understood what Soviet citizens had undergone. The Letter explained that Vlasov was the son of a peasant and that he had accepted the 'national revolution' (*narodnaya revolyutsiya*), had entered the ranks of the Red Army in order to fight for land ownership for the peasantry, for a better life for the worker, for a brighter future for the Russian people. Then followed a brief résumé of Vlasov's Red Army career. The fact that he worked his way up to the position of general from the ranks was mentioned, as were his decorations, the Order of Lenin and the Order of the Red Banner. His membership of the Communist party was also noted.

The Letter then posed the question as to why Vlasov, a typical 'Son' of the Russian people, should engage in a struggle with Bolshevism and call on all other Russians to join him. The Letter had remarked that he had fought in the Civil War as a member of the Red Army because he believed that the Revolution would give the Russian people land, liberty and happiness. However, the Letter explained, his army career meant that he was in constant contact with the whole spectrum of Soviet society, soldiers were merely peasants, workers and intellectuals in uniform. He knew their opinions and worries, and he realised that none of the things for which the Russian people had struggled during the Civil War had been achieved as a result of Bolshevik victory. He saw the difficulties experienced by the worker, the way in which the peasant had been forcibly collectivised and how millions of people had disappeared, imprisoned without trial or judicial examination. The Letter said that Vlasov realised that everything Russian was being destroyed, and that the command of the Red Army was being taken over by time-servers who were not concerned with the real interests of the Russian people. There followed a short passage on the deleterious effects of the commissar system in the Red Army. When Vlasov returned from China he found that the best leadership cadres of the Red Army had been destroyed. The reign of terror was not confined to the army but embraced the whole population. This last statement seems to be in line with the development of Vlasov's evaluation of the Soviet system. Vlasov must have been aware of what was going on before he left for China in the autumn of 1938, but it is quite possible that he did not really realise the full implications of the purge initiated by the Tukhachevsky affair until he returned from China.

In the Letter, Vlasov said he felt that his duty was to strengthen the Red Army to meet the challenges of the coming conflict. This idea was in accordance with official Soviet thinking. Conflict with the capitalist world, despite the temporary respite provided by the Molotov-Ribbentrop pact, was seen as inevitable by both the political and military establishment. Vlasov affirmed that consequently he felt impelled to do his best to improve his division.

The Open Letter goes on to describe Vlasov's war service and each stage of the description was accompanied by severe criticism of the High Command. When war broke out, Vlasov was in the Ukraine. The Letter stated that his suggestions for counter-attack were rejected. Indecisive commissars and confused command of the front led to heavy casualties. During Vlasov's command in the Kiev region, he observed that the war was being lost for two reasons: first, that the population was unwilling to fight for Bolshevik power and the system of terror that the latter had instigated; second, the irresponsible command of the army, and the perpetual interference of the commissars. After defending Kiev for two months, Vlasov had to fight his way out of the encirclement. Next, Vlasov was transferred to aid in the defence of Moscow and did all in his power to ensure that this was successful. He led his troops in a victorious attack. Vlasov said that he observed how people in both civilian and military capacities co-operated in this counterthrust to safeguard the mother country. The text then stated that more than once he ignored the questions as to whether Bolshevism was camouflaging itself under the guise of patriotism. Here again, the authors of the Open Letter showed great dexterity in their phrasing. The reader is led gradually, through a recital of the ills of the regime, to the central problem: the true nature of Bolshevism.

From here, Vlasov went on to describe the position of the 2nd Shock Army. GHQ were not interested in the army's plight and issued contradictory orders. The rations received by the troops were grossly inadequate and yet many people still died selflessly. The question 'For what did they die?' is asked once again. Vlasov recounts how he continued to carry out his duty as a soldier until the last possible minute. He tells how he managed to get out of the encirclement and hide in the forest and swamps for about a month. It was at this point, according to the text, that Vlasov began to question more forcefully the reasons for the war and the resulting Russian suffering. He said that he realised that the Russian people were involved in the conflict because of the interests of the Anglo-American capitalists. He realised that Britain had always been the enemy of Russia, trying to weaken her whenever possible. Stalin considered that by co-operating with the British and Americans he could more easily achieve his plan of world hegemony. Consequently, the Russian people had become involved in the war and had to suffer countless hardships. Once again this passage is a product of Nazi propaganda rather than an objective view of the facts.

However, it serves to emphasise the deviousness of Stalin's 'Ruling Clique' and thereby provides a clear lead up to the answer of the next question to be found in the Open Letter. Was not Bolshevism, and Stalin in particular, the main enemy of the Russian people? Was it not the sacred duty of every Russian to fight Stalin and his clique? During the time between the collapse of the 2nd Shock Army and Vlasov's capture by the Germans, he apparently came to the conclusion that his duty lay in summoning the Russian people to take part in the struggle for a new Russia where happiness would be the universal prerogative. The Letter continued by saying that he, Vlasov, believed that the problems facing the Russian people could be solved by co-operation 'with the German people'. He considered that the interests of the Russian people were closely associated with those of all the people of Europe. Bolshevism had cut the Russians off from the rest of Europe behind a 'wall of hate and suspicion'. It was the duty of the Russian and German peoples to destroy this wall. Vlasov stated that he had not changed his views upon becoming a captive, on the contrary, imprisonment merely strengthened his resolve to serve his country and his compatriots by striving to create a new Russia.

The complexion of the 'New Russia' was to be described at some later date. However, it was not possible to go backwards and Vlasov called upon his compatriots to go forward to a brighter future, to a struggle to 'complete the National Revolution'. Vlasov stated that he had encountered great support for this appeal among both prisoners-of-war and in the USSR. The support evinced by Russians and their willingness to enrol in the Russian Liberation Army, had convinced him that what he was doing was correct.

Vlasov went on to sound a warning. Stalin, realising that the Russians would not fight for the Stalinist regime, had instituted various changes in internal policy both in the church and in the army. But this was merely a cover for his real aims; Bolshevism itself had not evolved in any significant respect. Neither Stalin nor Bolshevism were concerned with the true interests of Russia, whereas the Liberation Movement was securing that which was in the interest of all Russians.

The Open Letter is supposed to have been greatly influenced by

M. A. Zykov, and showed a greater appreciation of the implications of the position taken by the Russian Liberation Movement. It is clear that in this letter the appeal was being made to the patriotic emotions of Great Russians. As in the Smolensk Declaration, no allowance was made for the aspirations of the national minorities, and therefore this aspect of German policy had not been taken into account when the Open Letter was composed. Other aspects of German propaganda did make their mark on the content of the Letter. Enmity towards the Allies was emphasised, as was the need for an alliance with Germany. However, the authors were careful to make a distinction between the regime and the people. It is significant that the Open Letter spoke of co-operation with the German people, never of co-operation with the Third Reich.

The Open Letter also showed a noteworthy advance in the understanding of the problems which faced the Russian Liberation Movement. Thus the immediate concern of the authors of this appeal was to find a *modus vivendi* with the Nazi authorities. This would permit them to put forward the point of view of the Russian Liberation Movement, and remain independent of Nazism. The long-term aim was to create a viable alternative to the Stalinism of the immediate pre-war and wartime years. In the Open Letter, one gets the first indication that in order to produce a programme, the leaders of the opposition movement had begun to realise that a solution to their problems involved a more complex exploration of the question why communism in the USSR had the negative attributes of the Stalinist system. This inevitably leads back to the Bolshevik seizure of power in Russia. The nature of the February and October Revolutions of 1917 and their moral, legal and political justification have provoked disagreement and have been the touchstone of Russian social thought in the twentieth century. In one paragraph of the Letter the authors stated that the opposition to Stalin must aim at 'completing the Revolution' and that there could be no way back to restoration and reaction.

The Russian Liberation Movement has tended to be considered by historians merely as a strange by-product of the 1941–45 conflict between the Third Reich and the Soviet Union. Further, the development of the Russian Liberation Movement has been seen as an illustration of the peculiarities and anomalies of the war between these two powers. Vlasov's Open Letter, however, marks a new stage in the evolution of the attitudes of the leaders of the Movement and reveals another of its dimensions. In the Open Letter the leaders of the Russian Liberation Movement do not limit themselves to denigrating Stalinism and recapitulating the pernicious results of the policies of the regime. Here, for the first time, albeit in a very general manner, the question of the genesis of the Stalinist system is posed. It is by reference to the Revolution that the Russian Liberation Movement begins, tentatively, to adumbrate its own position in the continuing Russian debate on the possibilities facing their country.

The 'left wing' – Zykov

Meletii Aleksandrovich Zykov is acknowledged to have been a central figure of the Russian Liberation Movement and was widely regarded by his contemporaries as the spokesman and focal point of the 'left wing of the Russian Liberation Movement'. His influence in persuading the German authorities to develop a political approach towards the anti-Stalinist Russians and his role in the composition of some of the key pronouncements of the Russian Liberation Movement is held to be considerable. He is acknowledged to have been a very able individual, whom Vlasov held in high regard. Vlasov is alleged to have said that few people of such a high intellectual calibre were to be found inside the USSR since Stalin had destroyed the majority of them. Yet Zykov remains an enigmatic figure.[24] He seems to have been very secretive, and exceptionally careful what he said about his past, even when he was under the influence of alcohol.

Zykov claimed to be aged about 40 during the war, although a number of his colleagues considered that he looked younger. His father was said either to have been a merchant of modest means from Odessa or a minor literary critic of Menshevik views, living in Ekaterinoslav. Another testimony states that initially Zykov gave his name and patronymic as Meletii Evlampovich, and later changed Evlampovich to Aleksandrovich.[25] Since Evlampiy is a name which was common in church circles, Zykov's original patronymic could imply that his family was connected with the clergy. Zykov's own story was that as a young man he had been a political commissar in the army during the Civil War. Later, he became a literary critic, teaching at the Herzen Institute in Moscow and collaborating in various publications on eighteenth-century Russian literature. Some of his colleagues bear witness to the fact that he was very well read.

Zykov also claimed that he was a journalist who had worked under Bukharin on *Izvestiya*. He is said to have married the daughter of the commissar of education, A. S. Bubnov, and to have moved in the highest party circles. In 1937, when Bukharin was expelled from the party, Zykov alleged that he was arrested and sent to a labour camp in Magadan. At the outbreak of war he was sent to the front.

Not a great deal is known about the precise details of Zykov's capture by the Germans. Apparently, he surrendered to the Germans near Bataysk, in the Rostov area in 1942. Zykov alleged that he had been a political commissar at battalion level, although some of his colleagues were not convinced as to the accuracy of that statement.[26] He gave the impression of someone used to giving commands, and it is possible that he had been in a position of greater authority. It is not clear what happened to him after his capture. One version states that he wrote a memorandum on political warfare, which resulted in his being sent for immediately by Goebbels.[27] Another version states that he impressed von Freytag-Loringhoven, the intelligence officer of Army Group South, who assigned him to Wehrmacht Propaganda.[28] On arrival he wrote a detailed technical report on the condition of the Soviet economy, which caused a number of people to conjecture that he might have been a specialist in this field. Zykov was then employed in the Wehrmacht Propaganda Department, in part under Colonel Martin, the liaison officer with the Propaganda Ministry, and also under Captain von Grote, the head of the Russian section.

Zykov met Vlasov at Viktoriastrasse in Berlin, and appears to have been concerned with the development of the Vlasov enterprise from its inception. In December 1942, in conversation with another future Vlasovite, Colonel Pozdnyakov, Zykov appears to have been unwilling to reveal the name of the proposed leader of the Russian Liberation Movement. This might indicate either that Zykov did not trust Pozdnyakov, or that generals other than Vlasov were being considered as potential leaders, and that Zykov was privy to the discussion and in a position of considerable responsibility. Subsequently, Zykov is credited with rewriting the German's draft of what was to become the Smolensk Declaration. Zykov is said to have played a major part in the composition of Vlasov's Open Letter. Both documents suggest that the authors exhibited greater political acumen and subtlety than can be discerned in some of the other proclamations of the Russian Liberation Movement. In order to further the idea that *Ostpolitik* must be radically altered, it was not only necessary to produce a programme which was acceptable to the Soviet populace, it was also necessary to be circumspect *vis-à-vis* Nazi censorship. These two considerations do not seem to have been borne in mind by Vlasov when he toured the occupied areas. Some of his speeches were very nationalistic in tone, whereas Zykov, in his approach to the text of the Smolensk Declaration and the Open Letter, displayed an awareness of methods by which the demands of Nazi ideology could be circumvented. Zykov's approach to politics appears to have been pragmatic. He appears to have had an understanding of Nazi ideology rare among his contemporaries, and was scathing of the Nazi outlook.[29] Nevertheless, he was prepared to compromise slightly with the Nazi authorities in order to get the Russian enterprise off the ground. He hoped that common sense might prevail to the extent that when the German authorities were presented with the evidence of the substantial popular support for a political approach to *Ostpolitik*, they would have to allow the enterprise to develop.

He encouraged the publication of the Smolensk Declaration by whatever means possible, apparently saying: 'Let the devil out of the bottle and he will do the work himself.'[30] At the same time, Zykov was not particularly optimistic as to the chances of success, saying he considered that there was a 30% chance of being betrayed by the German authorities, a 30% chance of falling foul of the Soviet authorities, a 30% probability of being let down by the Allies, and only a 10% chance of survival.[31]

Zykov became editor of *Zarya*, the newspaper published for civilians. He tried to turn this paper into one which would be of genuine interest to Russians and not merely a translation of German propaganda. It is alleged that Zykov thought up the policy of quoting verbatim from the *Völkischer Beobachter* whenever the Nazi censors demanded that the paper should produce articles which reflected their ideology. Zykov appears to have been a very talented journalist and his colleagues recall him dictating a whole issue of *Zarya*, beginning with the editorial and ending with 'letters from readers', in a few hours. Zykov's undoubted journalistic ability and experience give credence to his claim that he was a journalist before the war.

Zykov was unusually able and talented, his supporters recall his gifts as an orator. Vlasov appears to have respected and liked Zykov, whose rather authoritative and brusque manner was disliked by many of Vlasov's subordinates. He is supposed to have mourned the loss of Zykov, especially when the Prague Manifesto was being composed, as Vlasov felt that they needed Zykov's skill and expertise. During the war years Zykov married a Russian émigré from Yugoslavia. Through her he met representatives of Drazhe Mihailjovic. This was the genesis of the plan by which, at the end of the war, the KONR forces hoped to link up with the forces of Mihailjovic and make a stand in the mountainous region of Yugoslavia after the fall of the Third Reich.

The rather nebulous information available about Zykov's past has led to a great deal of speculation as to his real identity.[32] B. I. Nikolaevsky considered that his real name was N. Mosivich, but Nikolaevsky's papers reveal nothing further about the origin of this information, or any further details about Mosivich. Another theory postulates that Zykov was in fact the literary critic, T. S. Vol'pe.[33] The entry for Vol'pe in the *Literary Encyclopedia* gives 1941 as the date of his death, but is vague about the location; this could fit in with Zykov's desertion to the Germans. However, it would seem likely that an academic with a name which indicates German origin, would have known German, yet Zykov did not understand the language. Another aspect of Zykov's identity which has aroused much discussion, is the question as to whether Zykov was of Jewish origin. Some claim that Zykov looked Jewish, another account states that at Dabendorf Zykov never used the communal washing facilities, only a private bathroom, and that this was done in order to hide his Jewish identity.[34] If Zykov was Jewish, it is a matter of speculation how he survived for so long under the Germans, and may well be the reason for his sudden disappearance in 1944.

Zykov's disappearance is shrouded in almost as much mystery as his past. In the summer of 1944, d'Alquen, the SS officer who became convinced that the Vlasov enterprise should be developed with all possible speed, was planning a propaganda campaign on the Eastern Front designed to increase desertion from the Red Army. Zykov was to be one of the key figures in this project. On the evening before he was due to leave for the front, Zykov was called to the telephone. Zykov was staying in a village outside Berlin. There was only one telephone in the village. Zykov, with his secretary Nozhin, left the building in order to answer the telepone. Neither Zykov nor Nozhin returned. It was said that Zykov was met by two men in civilian clothing. After what appeared to be a rather heated conversation, all four got into a car and drove away. They were never seen again. D'Alquen and Dellinghausen made enquiries, but the security services were not particularly helpful and no trace was ever found of either Zykov or Nozhin. Although some consider that Zykov was abducted by the NKVD, or was even a Soviet agent,[35] these theories seem to be the product of fanciful conjecture. The most plausible explanation is that the SD decided to eliminate Zykov as a Jew and a Marxist. Once again, this incident serves to highlight the contradictions within the Nazi machine. While one section of the SS wished to use Zykov for propaganda warfare, another branch of the security services considered him to be an undesirable and corrupting influence.

Unfortunately, as far as historians are concerned, he left no written record of his views and does not seem to have elaborated on his opinions to any great extent. The most detailed accounts of Zykov's views have been provided by Mikhail Kitaev,[36] who was one of Zykov's subordinates on the newspaper *Zarya*. Kitaev's views on Zykov do not seem to have been shared by all his colleagues and contemporaries. Kitaev states in one work[37] that Vlasov loathed Zykov. This assertion does not seem to be substantiated in any other of Kitaev's descriptions of the Russian Liberation Movement, and is contradicted by other testimonies of friendship between the two men.[38] Nonetheless, Kitaev does seem to have been in agreement with the views of the left wing of the Russian Liberation Movement, as exemplified by Zykov, consequently his assessment of Zykov's opinions is of particular importance since most other members of this outlook have left no detailed record of their position.

The 'left wing' of the Russian Liberation Movement is broadly defined as those who accepted the Bolshevik seizure of power, and fought for policies put forward during the Civil War. This 'left wing' may have had similar views to those held by the Bukharinist right wing opposition. This can be considered as an acceptance of many aspects of Soviet society which at the same time included criticism of specific policies. In particular, their indictment of the speed of industrialisation, which inflicted much suffering on the population, is a point of view which had obvious similarities to Bukharin's position.

Kazantsev, an émigré and member of the NTS, saw the left wing Vlasovites as the finest representatives of Russian Bolshevism and he considered, on the basis of what they said, that they were probably a rarity even among the Soviet intelligentsia.[39] They retained strong links with the early years of the Revolution and considered Leninism, and its expression prior to and during the Civil War, as the true face of communism.

There is disagreement over the question as to where Zykov stood as regards the February and October Revolutions. References to him as a Bukharinist Marxist[40] would seem to imply that he saw October 1917 as the real starting point for change and progress. He has also been classed as a Menshevik, and if this was the case then it would appear that his acceptance of the Bolshevik seizure of power would have been less than wholehearted. Kitaev considers that Zykov was prepared to accept that in certain respects, February 1917 inaugurated the process of change.[41]

On the basis of the evidence which shows Zykov to have had a realistic appraisal of the situation, it seems likely that Zykov would have been prepared to compromise on this question which, despite its theoretical nature, was prone to have a very divisive effect amongst Russians. Kitaev avers that *both* February and October 1917 had to be considered as parts of a national revolution which had yet to fulfil all the promises made to the people. Despite this compromise over the question of the moral justification of the Revolution, Zykov was not prepared to compromise with émigré desires for restoration whether of a monarchical order or of something akin to the Provisional Government.[42] Zykov was a product of Soviet society and understood that it was impossible to return to the past.

Zykov seems to have laid far more emphasis on the need to develop short-term tactics than on long term ideological goals. He saw the first priority as the need to establish the Russian Liberation Movement as a viable concern. To this end he was prepared to proceed gradually. He encouraged the formation of a Russian Committee and the publication of the Smolensk Declaration before the German authorities had given any official sanction. He hoped that once the existence of a co-ordinating centre of anti-Stalinist opposition became known, then the whole enterprise would create its own momentum and the Germans would have to give it the go-ahead since they would be unable to put a stop to this activity. Similarly, Zykov was prepared to compromise to some extent with Nazi propaganda, as can be seen in the text of the Smolensk Declaration, if this would allow the Russian Liberation Movement to grow. In this policy of gradual developments, Zykov was unlike many of his colleagues who were more concerned with the question of ethics and the grand design. Strik-Strikfeldt saw him as untypical in this respect and more westernised than some of his colleagues. According to Kitaev, Zykov considered the Russian Liberation Movement as the successor to a series of attempts to achieve democratic freedom.[43] In his search for historical analogies Zykov included not only the Decembrists and the revolutionary theorists of the nineteenth century but harked back to the rule of the Veche in Novgorod the Great,[44] Stenka Razin,[45] Bogdan Khmelnitsky[46] and Pugachev.[47] Zykov also cited examples going back as far as Ivan Kalita,[48] of individuals who made use of the prevailing political situation in order to further their own ends. While the historical interpretation is questionable if Zykov did, in fact, produce these examples, under the circumstances it was an acute piece of political psychology. Thus, it placed the Movement in a Russian historical perspective and made the participants feel – an idea which was essential for them – that not only were they not alone but they were also part of the mainstream of the continuing search for progress within Russian society. This, too, served to emphasise the nationalistic aspect of the Russian Liberation Movement and to demonstrate to its adherents that it was not merely a product of the German propaganda machine.

Zykov's strong personality and many talents alone would have made him a person of considerable interest in the Russian Liberation Movement. Added to this was the fact that he expressed the view that although many of the later policies carried out by the Soviet authorities had disastrous effects, the Soviet system as a whole had positive aspects and should not be condemned completely. This analysis of the situation was used to counter the émigré contention that everything that had happened in Russia after 1917 was without redeeming features, a view which was unlikely to please those who had fought for this state or were a product of that system. Zykov seems to have had a powerful effect on his supporters, and even though he had disappeared before the composition of the KONR Manifesto, his deputy, N. Kovalchuk, the pseudonym for N. Granin, seems to have expressed the so-called 'Zykov line'. Kovalchuk is thought to have been, with G. N. Zhilenkov, one of the editors of the text of the Prague Manifesto.[49]

Visits to the occupied territories

Few texts of Vlasov's speeches during his tour of the occupied territories are on record. What little available information there is on their content indicates that they were met with warm appreciation by the populace, an indication that change was in the air and that the desires of the local people would be taken into account. The potential for a mass opposition movement was stressed. In answer to questions, Vlasov seems always to have replied that the Russian Liberation Army was not yet a reality but he considered that it was in the best German interest to make it one. When Vlasov went on to suggest a solution to the question as to what form the Russian state should take, he couched his answer within the terms of the framework provided by the Smolensk Declaration and the Open Letter. He said that the aim of the Liberation Movement was to return to the people of Russia the rights for which they had fought in 1917 and which had been usurped by the Bolsheviks.[50] Bolshevik tyranny would be overthrown and the population would be able to live without fear of repression, and in better material circumstances. There are a number of witnesses to the fact that Vlasov, in his addresses, constantly stressed that there was no question of Russia becoming a German colony – the future of Russia had to be decided by Russians.[51] The Russians would co-operate with the Germans, but only as equals. In speaking of a reformed social and political order in Europe, not just in Russia, Vlasov continued to reiterate his conviction that Russians and Germans were equals, and to say that no nation could enslave another.

The Anti-Bolshevik Conference, April 1943

Following Vlasov's visit to the occupied territories, the 'First Anti-Bolshevik Conference of captured commanders and soldiers of the Red Army, now members of the Russian Liberation Army' was held. George Fischer describes this as 'the constituent assembly of the Vlasov Movement'.[52] Since the audience consisted of committed participants of the Movement, it was unlike any of the mass meetings to which Vlasov had spoken, and was never repeated. The central point of the conference was a speech by General Malyshkin[53] in which he explained the position taken by the Russian Liberation Movement. The conference also adopted a resolution[54] supporting Vlasov and the political concepts which he expressed in his Open Letter.

Malyshkin opened his speech by declaring that the point had now been reached when certain conclusions could be drawn about the first stage of the Liberation Movement and that it was now essential to make clear its aims. This was necessary not only to ensure the further growth of the Liberation Movement, but so that all the members should have a firm ideological base (*tverdye ideologicheskie osnovy*) and a clear understanding of the goals.

Malyshkin then proceeded to comment on the nature of support given to the Liberation Movement. He said that not only did it find a great response within the occupied territories but also among both commanders and other ranks in the Red Army, some of whom deserted to the Russian Liberation Army even at times when the Red Army was advancing. Malyshkin went on to say that the popularity of the Movement amongst Russians had resulted in widespread publicity in the European press. It is not clear whether this statement was a product of wishful thinking or a deliberate attempt to deceive the conference, but it certainly does not seem to have been a reflection of the true state of affairs. Malyshkin added that Soviet propaganda had even asserted that Vlasov had not been captured by the Germans but was taking a rest after escaping from German encirclement. Malyshkin ascribes the success and popularity of the Russian Liberation Movement to the fact that the ideas expressed in the Open Letter were an accurate reflection of the feelings of the Soviet people. This, stated Malyshkin, was because Bolshevism was really felt to be the main enemy of the Russian nation, and only after its destruction would the Russian nation be able to create a new life for itself.

It is interesting to note Malyshkin's evaluation of the Revolution. In his view, the majority of the nation supported the events of 1917 and the Revolution could be called a 'truly National Revolution'. He made no attempt to differentiate between the Revolutions of February and October 1917, presumably because he was anxious not to emphasise any disagreements which existed on this question. The people supported the Bolsheviks because the Bolshevik party at that time was the only faction which understood the desire of the people to strive for a better future. Their aims were expressed as: 'a speedy end to the war, peace without annexations or reparations, the abolition of social and property distinctions, political power to the workers and peasants, land to the peasants'; all these Bolshevik slogans appealed to the aspirations of the people. Consequently, the nation supported their programme and it was not the people's fault that the Bolsheviks utilised this for their own interests rather than for the good of the nation. Malyshkin considered that the people had never come to terms with the slavery imposed on them by the Bolsheviks. It was resistance to slavery that had developed into armed insurrection, for instance during collectivisation, but resistance had never been successful because of the greater resources available to Stalin, namely, a well-organised army and NKVD. It was completely untrue that the Russian people had submitted to and accepted the policies of the Bolsheviks, and the constant presence of opposition to the regime could be proved by the chain of concentration camps across the country.

This section was very persuasive as an explanation of events and in making the members of the conference feel that their position was not an idiosyncratic or isolated one, that their aspirations and views were shared by the majority of their compatriots. Malyshkin's approach to this question would undoubtedly have served to convince them as to the correctness of their course of action and would also have helped to create an *esprit de corps*. The aim of Bolshevism, Malyshkin continued, was not to further the interests of the Russian nation, but to seize power throughout the whole world. Soviet involvement in the war was an example of the way in which Stalin was willing to sacrifice the Russian people to the interests of Anglo-American capitalists. Bolshevism had also failed to carry out its promises to the workers and to the peasants. The former had virtually become slaves, while the latter had been deprived of their right to own land to make use of the product of their labours. Similarly, Bolshevism had not honoured the promises made to the intelligentsia, but had demanded that their work be circumscribed by the demands of a vulgar materialist philosophy. The vast number of individuals who had suffered as a real result of the rule of terror dictated that the primary policy of the Russian Liberation Movement was the overthrow of every aspect of this rule.

Having summed up the reasons for the Movement's inexorable intent to bring down the Stalinist regime, Malyshkin tried to outline those principles which, he felt, must be instrumental in the creation of a new social and political system in Russia. Although the time had not yet come when a detailed programme of action could be made public, nevertheless Malyshkin insisted that the governing principles of the new system had to be enunciated. He began by addressing himself to the national question. Malyshkin stated that despite Bolshevik attempts to make it appear as if all the aspirations of the national minorities had been met, this was patently not the case. The Russian Liberation Movement accepted that every nationality had the right to decide its own future and that this could include the choice to secede and to claim complete independence. Malyshkin's position on this point is an interesting development of the views of the Liberation Movement, one which contrasts sharply with the strongly nationalistic tone of both the Smolensk Declaration and the Open Letter. The only caveat included by Malyshkin was that self-determination and total independence could only be achieved after Stalin had been defeated and destroyed.

The next question to be dealt with was that of the peasantry and the form of land ownership; the peasantry were to have the right to own their land and to work it as they saw fit. However, the question of land ownership must be combined with the best possible use of modern agricultural technology. This would involve forms of co-operation which would not impinge and inhibit personal initiative but would, rather, allow this initiative to be developed to optimum effect. The redistribution of land into private ownership would be organised by the state.

This was followed by a discussion on the position of industrial workers. The claim of the Soviet state was that socialism had been created and that social classes and class conflict were destroyed; that private ownership of the means of production no longer existed and an end had been put to the exploitation of the workers by other social groups. Malyshkin, however, questioned the truth of the Bolshevik assertion that as a result of the alleged changes in the structure of society the position of workers had improved significantly. Malyshkin stated that it was obvious that the lot of the working population had not improved. Its members were frequently unable to earn even the bare minimum and were greatly exploited by the authorities. The Russian Liberation Movement wished to do away with all forms of exploitation and to ensure conditions of work which would form the basis of material well-being, and allow for systematic improvements in the welfare of the worker. The state had to protect the workers' interests. The Russian Liberation Movement considered that the industrial enterprises which had been built up by the people during the period of Bolshevik rule should belong to the people, but this did not mean that individual initiative should be excluded from industry. Industry destroyed during the war would be rebuilt by the state since it would be an impossible task for the individual. The question of state or private ownership in industry would have to be determined in the light of the real interests of the people.

The rather vague and idealistic approach of the members of the Russian Liberation Movement towards the question of economic organisation shows clearly the problems with which the Movement had to contend. The question was complex, and their leaders lacked theoretical expertise in politics and political economy, as well as experience of administrative practice, to deal with the implications of this subject. The rejection of the Stalinist attitude which totally subordinated the interests of the individual to the demands of state and ideology, and at the same time the acceptance of many of the attributes of contemporary Soviet society, are easily identifiable as the two main influences on the programme of the Movement. There was no intention of repudiating Soviet society as a whole, since these Soviet citizens considered that the Revolution had brought about progress in their society.

Malyshkin then went on to speak of the position of the intelligentsia: they would be allowed to work freely, untrammelled by any ideology, but they should work in the interests of their people. The potential contradiction in this position does not seem to have been apparent to Malyshkin, and further illustrates the simplistic approach of the leadership of the Russian Liberation Movement with regard to political theory.

The relationship with Germany was the subject of the next section of his speech. A new Russia would spring from the alliance of the Russian and German peoples. Again, reference is made throughout to the people, not to the German state. Once the new Russian state was in being, then the Russians would also have their role in the creation of a new European system, where they would act in concert, and on an equal footing, with the other nations of Europe. Until now, the Russians had been cut off from their fellow Europeans during the period of Bolshevik rule.

After he had explained the tenets of the Russian Liberation Movement, Malyshkin declared that the order of priority was: first, to overthrow the Stalinist clique; second, to make an honourable peace with Germany, a peace which would not place Russia in bondage. Only then could Russians begin to create a new system of government within their country.

Malyshkin also proceeded to warn those who might feel some degree of sympathy for the Movement; first, the émigrés. For, although the White Forces had originated as opposition to Bolshevism during the Civil War, Malyshkin claimed – in a somewhat generalised and inaccurate statement which was in line with Soviet thinking on this question – that they could not have initiated the necessary progress for Russia, since they either lacked ideology, or stood for restoration of the *ancien régime*. Consequently, the Whites had been unable to attract the support of the population since the latter were well aware that there was no possibility of returning to the old forms. The Bolsheviks, however, had composed a programme which had seemed to answer to the wishes of the Russian people. Those, therefore, who dreamt of a return to the pre-revolutionary world were warned that they had no place in the ranks of the Russian Liberation Movement. Former Communist party members who accepted the views of the Liberation Movement would be welcomed, but those who had acted against the interests of the Russian people, and in particular the agents of NKVD, would not be forgiven for their past actions, and could not be accepted as allies.

At this point Malyshkin admitted that the Russian Liberation Army did not yet exist as a unified force. He expressed the hope that measures to achieve actual unity would be taken as soon as possible. Finally, he spoke of his confidence in the Liberation Movement and repeated the last passage of the Open Letter which was to become the battle cry of most later publications: it was the duty of all Russians to fight against the Stalinist regime. 'Russia is ours! The past of the Russian people is ours! The future of the Russian people is ours also!'

Malyshkin's speech shows the intellectual progress made since the first joint Vlasov-Boyarsky Memorandum to the German authorities. It illustrates a much greater subtlety on the part of the Movement's leaders towards their Russian audience and skill in bypassing the pitfalls within Nazi dogma. At the same time, it demonstrates that the opposition movement unambiguously condemned certain aspects of Soviet society. But the question of what structure should replace the Stalinist system was still under debate. A wholesale abrogation of the system was unthinkable, for many of the basic beliefs and attitudes which underpinned Soviet society were to be retained. Thus, capitalism and the Russian emigration were to be viewed as potential enemies; the fundamentally progressive basis of the events of 1917 were not to be questioned.

The conference expressed support for Vlasov and the programme as expressed in the Open Letter, and a resolution was adopted very similar in wording to the ideas expressed by the document. The resolution stressed that those attending the conference were products of Soviet society who were convinced that their duty demanded that they should fight the Bolsheviks; they called upon their fellow countrymen to unite against their common enemy.

Soviet propaganda

The effect of this activity on the part of those agitating for the formation of a Russian Liberation Army, the publication of the Smolensk Declaration, the Open Letter, and Vlasov's speeches in the occupied territories, seems to have persuaded the Soviet authorities that a change in Nazi policy was in the offing, and that the Russian Liberation Army was about to become a reality. Consequently, a change was made in Soviet propaganda directed against Vlasov in order to meet this expected threat.[55] Initially, in 1942, Soviet propaganda had remained silent on the subject of Vlasov's capture or had made it appear that he was being used against his will by the Nazi Propaganda Ministry.

By 1943, however, the position changed. Since the bulk of German propaganda was directed at military personnel, and the civilians of all sections of the Soviet population were least likely to learn about Vlasov from German propaganda, the question was ignored in the Soviet domestic press. The Red Army press, on the other hand, attempted to neutralise the effect of the propaganda which utilised the Vlasov theme. The Soviet counter-propaganda, in early 1943, argued that Vlasov had been forced to sign leaflets against his will, and this propaganda had been conceived in order to counter the effects of German setbacks at Stalingrad and elsewhere on the front. After mid summer 1943, Soviet propaganda began to include the standard charges that Vlasov was a spy and a traitor. Vlasov was accused of having participated in the Trotskyite conspiracy, of having conspired with the Germans during his tour of duty in China in 1938–9 and also of having been a German agent since 1941 when his army was encircled at Kiev.

Some propaganda also answered various points in the Smolensk Declaration. It attacked the vagueness of the wording and refuted Vlasov's claim that he was working in the interests of the Russian people. The slogan 'without Bolsheviks and exploiters' was countered by reports of Nazi excesses and their treatment of the population in the occupied territories. The partisan media also insisted that ROA had been formed purely as cannon fodder, and the fact that the name ROA had been coined only in 1943, and not in 1941, must have lent credence to this statement. In 1943, after the defeat at Stalingrad, the tide had begun to turn, the Red Army was beginning to advance and was driving the Wehrmacht out of occupied areas of Russia. In this situation, the Wehrmacht was in need of reserves, and so the argument that the ROA was formed solely to help German interests, must have appeared a plausible analysis.

In addition to this overt propaganda, Major Semion Nikolaevich Kapustin[56] was ordered to desert and to join ROA with orders to kill Vlasov and to set up subversive cells within the Russian Liberation Movement. Kapustin was given detailed instructions as to the kind of propaganda and the themes that he was to use in order to gain followers. He was to stress that Germany wanted to enslave, not liberate the Russian people, that ROA was a German and not a Russian enterprise, and that its conception was the result of a shortage of German manpower. These first two statements contained nothing new, but the third subject for dissemination, which stated that Soviet troops before the German invasion had no aggressive intentions against Germany but wished to forestall possible German expansion into the Dardanelles and Turkey, was a line of thought designed to appeal to nationalist aspirations within ROA.

Kapustin was told to elaborate the thesis that the Soviet authorities had already satisfied many of the demands of the people: they had, for example, reopened the churches and abolished the Comintern and the commissar system within the Red Army. The next point in Kapustin's brief states that:

the war has proved the instability of the Communist international idea of a Soviet Union of Republics. The whole burden of the war lies on the Great Russians. All other nationalities have failed. After the war not one of the former Republics of the Soviet Union will have their independence restored, they will all be abolished and will be merged in one undivided red [Soviet] Russia.

This idea, once again, was obviously intended to appeal to Great Russian nationalists within the Movement. It presumably was intended to sow dissension within the ranks of ROD which was slowly evolving to allow greater autonomy and independence to the minority nationalities. This idea may also have been included in order to sow dissension within the anti-Soviet movement generally, particularly since the non-Russian nationalities were being supported by the Ostministerium.

Furthermore, Kapustin was ordered to propagate the view that various changes would come about within the political structure of the Soviet Union. As well as the dissolution of the Union Republic system, the Communist party would be reformed and become a party of the people. Collective farms would be dissolved and Stalin would be replaced by Andrey Andreyevich Andreyev, because 'he is in no manner compromised'. Andreyev was a member of the Politburo and was a rather weak, mediocre figure, certainly not the obvious choice for a leader. However, since he had come to power before Stalin had consolidated his position, he could perhaps be considered not as one of Stalin's creations and therefore a suitable candidate for a propaganda platform of unity for the anti-Stalinists and Soviet adherents in a semi-communist conglomeration. Kapustin was then to say that Soviet prisoners-of-war would be well treated and that members of ROA who returned to the Soviet Union would be decorated and given a new uniform. There followed a call for Russian unity since once again Russia was standing alone against the whole of Europe. They could manage their own affairs without help from anyone.[57]

The whole of this propaganda is of interest because it throws into prominence those aspects of the programme and ideas of the Russian Liberation Movement which Moscow found most worrying. It was, therefore, thought necessary to present an alternative programme designed to interest disaffected individuals to dissipate the support for the platform of the Russian Liberation Movement. However, once it became clear that Vlasov was not to be given the go-ahead, and that Nazi policy towards the occupied territories was not going to change, this counter-propaganda was not developed further and was phased out by the Soviet authorities. Nevertheless, even this short propaganda campaign on the part of the Soviet authorities indicates their extreme sensitivity towards the potential of the Russian Liberation Movement to attract and win over Soviet citizens. Despite this strong Soviet response, the assumptions underlying Nazi policy resulted in the Vlasov enterprise being shelved. It was only in the autumn of 1944 that Vlasov emerged once more into the limelight.

The 'Constitution' of the Russian state

Vlasov's interview with Himmler on 16 September 1944 gave the approval for the official publication of the programme of the Russian

Liberation Movement, which finally appeared on 14 November 1944, in Prague, and became known as the Prague Manifesto. According to S. Ausky,[58] the first variant of the Manifesto showed clearly that KONR not only proclaimed its independence from the Nazi regime but made clear as well the difference between KONR and the monarchists in the emigration. Ausky states that the text consisted of fourteen points and can be considered a 'progressive-democratic' (*progressivno-demokraticheskoe*) programme. If this document corresponds to a typescript, twenty-three pages long, entitled 'The Constitution of the Russian State',[59] now in the Nikolaevsky archive in the Hoover Institution, then this 'Constitution' cannot be termed 'progressive-democratic'. Nothing is known about the authors or process of composition of this document. It is very dissimilar to other programmes of the Russian Liberation Movement and gives the impression of being composed by individuals who were certainly unrepresentative of the Movement as a whole.

The 'Constitution' is divided into fourteen subsections with 244 separate points, which deal with the new social order, the central administration and the regional administration, the legal structure, the rights of the citizens, and the electoral system. The thirteenth section refers to the heraldic arms of the state, the flag, and the capital which was to be both Moscow and Petrograd. The fourteenth section consisted of one sentence indicating how the constitution might be altered. The whole document gives a rather uneven impression. The administration is divided into a great many self-governing units with assemblies of elected representatives. The smallest proposed unit would be a village assembly and similar district councils in the towns. These assemblies would elect the head of the administrative area. The main legislative assembly would be known as a 'Sobor'[60] and this assembly would elect a ruler, who was known as the Ruler of all the Russias, '*Pravitel' Vseya Rusi*' (a title also given to Admiral Kolchak when he became military ruler in Siberia in 1918), and had almost unlimited power (as well as a specially designed uniform!), in contrast to the Zemsky Sobor which had various checks placed on its authority. The economy in this new state would be mixed. There would be state ownership as well as property which belonged to society, co-operative ownership and private property. The distinctions between these different types of ownership were not altogether clear and involved a degree of overlap. The whole project is completely lacking in any theoretical underpinnings, although the 'Constitution' bristles with detailed descriptions of aspects of the future state, and the authors seem to have been strongly influenced by a romantic 'slavophile' vision of Russia's past. The terminology is strongly reminiscent of this.

Certain anomalies are glaringly apparent – when the autonomous areas of the state are listed, the Great Russian area is not mentioned at all. The detail with which the different sections of the Cossacks are described would suggest that one of the authors may have been a Cossack with all the notions of loyalty to his people that such a background implied. On similar lines, one could deduce that there was no one of Baltic nationality among the authors. Although the 'Constitution' posits that self-determination will be granted to all nationalities, article 31/5 notes that since the Baltic states block access to the Baltic Sea, the Russian regime must solve this vital question, although they had no desire to enslave any other nation. Several articles of the Constitution dwell on the position of the Orthodox Church; other religious faiths are mentioned only in passing. Two points can be considered for their similarity to ideas expressed by the Russian Liberation Movement: one, there was considerable emphasis on the need to take the particular historical development of a nation or an area into account; two, there was an attempt to do away with the ideas of social class – citizens of this new state are referred to as labourers (*trudyashchiysya*). Members of the Russian Liberation Movement did put forward the opinion that by ignoring or doing away with their heritage, the Bolsheviks did violence to the true essence of the nation. However, with regard to the second point, the authors of the 'Constitution' are not consistent and the term 'workers' (*rabochie*) appears from time to time. It seems safe to conclude that this 'Constitution' is unlikely to have been approved by, or to reflect the majority opinion within the Russian Liberation Movement. It could perhaps be regarded more as an interesting anomaly, representing some views held by Russians (one of whom was possibly a Cossack who might have served with Kolchak and was an émigré) which were then put on paper in a rather disjointed and illogical fashion.

2 REALITY

The Prague Manifesto

Accounts of the actual process of composition of the Prague Manifesto vary. After Himmler had given permission for the publication of the programme of the Russian Liberation Movement, Zhilenkov, at the end of September or beginning of October 1944, called together Kovalchuk, editor of *Zarya* and formerly Zykov's deputy, Zaitsev, the senior lecturer at Dabendorf, and Noreikis, a member of the press department at Dabendorf, and ordered them to compose a manifesto. Zhilenkov, as the head of the propaganda section in the Russian Liberation Movement, apparently carried out many of the negotiations with the German authorities.

The two survivors of this authorial trio describe the process of composition differently. Noreikis[61] recalled that Zhilenkov called all three together and demanded that they write a manifesto instantly. Zhilenkov added that he would not let them go until they had produced a suitable text. Noreikis then wrote the draft of a declaration which Zhilenkov criticised as too journalistic. Zaitsev,[62] coming to Noreikis's defence, opined that journalism was only to be expected, considering the circumstances of composition. Then,[63] the draft was taken away and nothing more was heard of it.

Zaitsev alters various details and adds to the above account. Thus, when Zhilenkov asked for a text suitable for the official Manifesto, he added that he needed the draft for a political declaration and that Vlasov wanted it to include a historical background to the programme.[64] Zaitsev said that he could only work independently, not in a collective under pressure. It was decided that Kovalchuk should write the introduction, Zaitsev the articles of the programme, and Noreikis the conclusion. Noreikis rejects this version of a division of labour.[65] Zaitsev then asked for permission to leave as he said he could not compose a programme without a period of reflection. Accordingly, he then left in order to get a copy of the NTS programme and any other documents that he considered necessary. Apparently, he composed the fourteen-point programme that night with his future wife typing from his dictation.[66] A couple of days later, he returned his version to Zhilenkov, who was pleased with it. Zaitsev heard nothing more of his text for about a month when it was discussed in committee. He claims that the second point of the Prague Manifesto was changed slightly from his original draft.

However, since the political programme in the Prague Manifesto is so similar to the Smolensk Declaration, it seems rather unlikely that the former programme was the product of one man's work, or that there was so little further discussion and adaptation. Other accounts[67] state that a variety of individuals were asked to submit drafts of a possible manifesto, amongst them Shtifanov, another lecturer at Dabendorf, and also Captain Galkin, who worked in the newspaper office at Dabendorf. Most of these drafts were rejected, and reworked versions were discussed in eight subcommittees[68] before a final text was agreed upon and presented to KONR. All that remains of these discussions[69] is one variant which appeared in a Russian publication in Shanghai.[70] Presumably someone obtained a copy before publication, unaware that it had not been finally approved. Once the various drafts had been discussed, the final version is thought to have been edited by Zhilenkov and Koval-chuk.[71]

The Manifesto[72] is addressed to 'our fellow-countrymen, brothers and sisters' of the Committee for the Liberation of the Peoples of Russia. It began with the statement that it was imperative to decide the fate of their country, their nations and themselves. This intro-duction listed the forces fighting the war: the imperialists of Britain and the United States, those determined to achieve international hegemony led by 'Stalin and his clique', and the freedom-loving nations. This was followed by an enumeration of the offences committed by the Stalinist regime both against the other nations of the world, and in particular against the peoples of the Soviet Union, who had been tricked, ill-treated and deprived of their rights in every possible manner. As a result, representatives of the peoples of Russia had created a committee whose aim was to organise the struggle against Bolshevism. The aims of this committee were: first, to overthrow the tyranny of Stalin and to return to the people the rights which they had fought for in 1917, second, to make an honourable peace with Germany, and third, to create a new free political system which could be for the benefit of the people, where there would be no places for Bolsheviks and exploiters. The principles governing such a state were then listed in a fourteen point programme. Finally, the Committee listed the military formations on whose support they could depend. The concluding paragraphs reaffirmed the need for unity and immediate action and urged their compatriots to join in the campaign.

The Prague Manifesto demonstrated that the leadership of the Russian Liberation Movement had, with the passage of time, acquired a much clearer appreciation of the realities confronting them. The title itself, 'The Manifesto of the Committee for the Liberation of the Peoples of Russia', as compared to the original 'Russian Committee', illustrates the shift that had taken place. Thus, the leaders of the Russian Liberation Movement had come to realise that greater recognition of the rights and desires of the national minorities of the USSR was essential for the creation of a united anti-Stalinist force.

The question of self-determination and independence, which had been listed eighth in the programme of the Smolensk Declaration, became the first point in the Prague Manifesto. Records[73] show that many Soviet prisoners-of-war, when first captured, were surprised by, and did not understand, the German insistence of differentiation between the various nationalities of the Soviet Union. Although Russians were familiar with ideas of cultural autonomy, they were less able to come to terms with the proposal to dismember the USSR, which had so much support in Nazi circles.

However, since the policies put forward by Rosenberg and the Ost-ministerium meant that military formations and committees of representatives of the national minorities were to be encouraged, it soon became evident that the Russian Liberation Movement should try to unite all these organisations under the umbrella of one anti-Stalinist force. To do so, the leadership of the Russian Liberation Movement had to persuade the representatives of the national minorities of their sincerity, that the question of national autonomy would be decided according to the wishes of the various nationalities immediately after Stalin's overthrow. Nevertheless, many of the members of the various ethnic minorities expressed great scepticism as to the veracity of the sentiments which voiced support for national movements by the Russian Liberation Movement. Despite seemingly candid and honest statements by Vlasov and the other leaders, members of the national minorities felt that these were a mere cover for the real designs of Russian 'Imperialists'. Furthermore, the leadership of various national groups objected to the idea that they should be subordinated to Great Russians under the command of Vlasov.[74]

In some cases, members of these groups were not adverse to Vlasov as a leader of one group amongst many, but they did not wish him to be the overall commander.[75] It would seem that this scepticism to the motives of KONR and the Great Russians was not justified. Undoubtedly, the nationalist sentiments expressed by the Great Russians were popular. Soviet propaganda[76] considered that the chauvinistic element was one of the essential components of the Russian Liberation Movement. A candidate member of KONR, Muzychenko,[77] considered that over and above any element of

narrow nationalism, Russians within the Third Reich supported
Vlasov and KONR because it was a Russian and not a German
organisation. Here they met with their compatriots on an equal
footing, no longer 'subhumans' officered by Germans. This feeling,
that the Russian Liberation Movement was a refuge in an alien
environment, would not have been produced purely by nationalist
and patriotic sentiment but was rather a product of the circumstances in which the Russians found themselves. They felt beleaguered and had to retain some sense of their own identity and
integrity. This would have led to greater emphasis on nationalism,
and already existing ideas of this kind were further reinforced by this
feeling of isolation. However, this attitude towards the Russian
Liberation Movement does not in itself provide evidence of the
existence of Great Russian chauvinism.

Pozdnyakov[78] strikes a rather apologetic note when he explains
that there was no other course of action open to Vlasov except that of
trying to create a united anti-Stalinist organisation and promising
the national minorities the right to complete independence if they so
wished. The tone of these remarks suggests that not everyone agreed
with this policy towards the minority nations of the USSR; nonetheless, there is no documentary evidence to support Kroeger's remark[79]
that the Russian Liberation Movement favoured the policy of 'Russia
one and indivisible', the old slogan of the White Armies. The
leaders of the Movement realised that without unity among the
anti-Stalinists, nothing could be effected; their firmly stated object
was that the peoples of Russia must be allowed to decide their own
future. Consequently, everyone would be allowed to exercise the
right of self-determination.

In the paragraph describing the warring parties in the conflict, the
imperialists are said to be led by the plutocrats of England and the
United States. If the term plutocrat is considered as 'one of the very
rich' and not merely a term of abuse for all capitalists, then this
phrase can be seen as a modification of previous statements of the
Russian Liberation Movement where capitalism as a system was
held up to scorn. A similar modification of greater sophistication and
subtlety can be seen in the slogan 'A New Russia without Bolsheviks
and exploiters'. The term 'exploiters' can be seen as embracing a
whole range of evils in the Stalinist, Nazi and non-totalitarian worlds.
Capitalism is not, then, presented in the same black and white
manner of earlier pronouncements.

This criticism of the Allies was included in the Manifesto on the order of Himmler. Apparently, Himmler had demanded that the Prague Manifesto should include criticism of both the Allies and the Jews.[80] Vlasov is said to have refused, saying that both attitudes were repugnant to him. Finally, a compromise was reached; nothing anti-semitic would appear in the Manifesto but criticism of the Allies would be included.[81]

Whether criticism of the British and Americans was merely just a compromise sentence used to exclude the Jewish question and to placate Himmler, or whether it was a reflection of genuine anti-Allied sentiment has also been a matter for some discussion. Nikolaevsky asserts that Vlasov acquired anti-British attitudes during his tour of duty in China and that it later became very difficult to persuade him to adopt any other point of view.[82] At the same time, Vlasov's and Boyarsky's initial letter to the German authorities seems to indicate that the opposition to Stalin would have considered allying themselves with the British and Americans if this opportunity had been open to them.[83] Added to this, the supporters of the opposition movement seem to have had almost unlimited and unjustified faith that the Allies would not only understand the aims of the Liberation Movement, and the reasons which had prompted its formation, but that after the war with the Third Reich, they would embark on a campaign against the totalitarian order within the USSR.[84] Towards the end of the war, proof of the Allies' friendly stance towards the Liberation Movement was seen in the fact that Allied aeroplanes had not bombed KONR formations although it had lain in their power to do so.[85]

After the more general preamble about the nature of the conflict, the introduction to the Prague Manifesto criticised Stalinist policy in greater detail. Once again, the Manifesto expressed the view that the national and cultural heritage, which the Stalinist regime had done its best to destroy, must be defended. Claims as to the aggressive nature of the Soviet Union could be illustrated by the fact that the Soviet Union had not confined itself, during the war, to the defence of its borders, but had invaded Rumania, Bulgaria, Serbia, Croatia and Hungary. The aim of this Stalinist aggression was to strengthen Stalinist hegemony.

The Manifesto considered the cause of Bolshevik tyranny, and the events of 1917 were discussed, albeit in a very schematic manner. Here, as in the Open Letter, the Russian Liberation Movement provided an answer to the question which had been raised by all Russians involved in an analysis of their society; how should the Revolution be understood? The answer in the Manifesto was equivocal, in that it refers to 'the Revolution of 1917' without specifying whether this means February or October. This blurring of the issue was intentional in order to create a common platform between those who believed that February had ushered in a new era, the course of which had been diverted by the Bolshevik seizure of power, and those for whom October had responded to the real wishes of the population, and who considered that February 1917 had not signalled any real alteration in the nation's life. According to Galkin, a member of the press department at Dabendorf, the dividing line very frequently ran between the civilian members of the Russian Liberation Movement who regarded February as the true revolution, and the military members who were inclined to see the justification for the October Revolution. The majority of the émigrés accepted February 1917 and not October, although some, like the NTS, tried to come to terms with the realities of the Bolshevik seizure of power and realised that history did not permit the clock to be turned back.

In the Prague Manifesto, tsarist rule was described as outdated and unable to fulfil the desire of the people for a just and free social order. However, the Manifesto stated that the parties and politicians (i.e. the Provisional Government) were not able or willing to take the necessary steps and carry out the reforms the people required. Consequently, 'the people spontaneously followed those who promised them immediate peace, land, liberty and bread'. The Manifesto explained that it was not the fault of the people either that they had been deceived or that the rights for which they had struggled had been denied them by the very party which they had brought to power. Then followed an outline of the effect of Bolshevik rule on the people. The people had been deprived of the right to organise society as they wished and the right to enjoy a number of freedoms ranging from free speech to the freedom to take one's place in society according to one's abilities. Peasants had been denied the right to work the land as they chose, workers to choose their own work and the intelligentsia the right to be creative in the way they wished. All such rights and qualities had been supplanted by terror, party privilege and arbitrary conduct. The Bolsheviks were accused of bringing the country into a state of continuous poverty and slavery and of involving the population in needless suffering. The Bolsheviks justified their policies with lies about democracy and the need to build a socialist society. As a result of such sufferings, the peoples of Russia had come to realise that it was imperative to get rid of the Stalinist system. So, KONR had been formed in order to organise the campaign, and the fourteen point programme outlined the principles for the organisation of the new state.

Equality and self-determination for all the nationalities of Russia were affirmed in the first article. The second article defined the nature of the social system as national-labour (*natsional'no-trudovoy*). This definition, which is absent from the 'Shanghai' version[86] of the Manifesto, is probably primarily due to the influence of the NTS (see discussion pp. 185–93) who, like the members of the Russian Liberation Movement, felt that any new social system in Russia would have to combine the elements of both national culture and heritage and that the international aspects stressed by communism would prove to be of much less importance. Also, they believed that everyone who worked would do so on equal terms, that it would be effort rather than any other characteristic, e.g. class, party membership or ownership of capital, which determined an individual's place in society. However, an additional explanation which further clarified the nature of the national-labour system and which had been added to this second article by Zaitsev, was not included in the final programme.[87] The text of this additional clarification no longer exists. It would also be true to say that although the phrase 'national-labour' was one which was used by the NTS, it also seemed to convey ideas which were of moment to members of the Russian Liberation Movement who were not members of the NTS. Although the NTS and the Russian Liberation Movement did not share a common policy, their political philosophy frequently appears to have developed in parallel and this is a case in point. They both viewed the idea of nationhood as crucial, and opposed Stalinist policy with its emphasis on international communism. At the same time, despite their dislike for Stalinism, they accepted what they considered were the achievements of communism in improving the status of the work force.

The third article stressed the need for good relations on the international level and the fourth article exhorted the government to take measures to strengthen the family and the position of women. These two articles may reflect émigré influence, and especially that of the NTS, which saw the family as the basis of society and the place where correct moral principles could be inculcated.

The last ten articles did not differ greatly from those of the Smolensk Declaration. Forced labour and the collective farm system would be abolished, workers, peasants and intellectuals would be allowed the freedom to choose how they wished to work, and how to use their abilities and energy. Private property and trade would be reinstated. However, the state would still have a considerable role to play in the organisation of society, and all citizens would be guaranteed free education, medical aid, leisure time and pensions. The government would also be responsible for paying indemnities to the war wounded and their families, for rebuilding war damaged industrial enterprises as well as damaged housing. Freedom from exploitation would be guaranteed, freedom of speech, conscience and assembly would be allowed, all would be equal in the eyes of the law.

The fourteen articles end with a paragraph which reaffirmed the urgent need to destroy Bolshevism, and the Committee expressed its conviction that the efforts of the peoples of Russia 'would be supported by all the freedom-loving peoples of the world'. This rather high-flown phrase reflects the Movement's optimistic view of the Allies, who, it was hoped, would understand and support KONR's point of view.

Then the Manifesto listed the forces at KONR's disposal. Since this mentioned, *inter alia*, the Ukrainian Liberation Army (*Ukrains'ke Vyzvol'ne Viysko*) whose nominal commander, General Shandruk, viewed Vlasov and his avowed aims with the utmost suspicion,[88] as well as the Cossack troops, whose leader, General Krasnov, had not the slightest intention of surrendering his command,[89] this list must be considered as propaganda or a product of wishful thinking. The Manifesto also stated that KONR's leaders intended to call on the support of the growing anti-Bolshevik forces in the Soviet rear. Those forces were probably imaginary, and in the case of the Ukrainian Insurrectionary Army (*Ukrains'ka Povstans'ka Armiya*), even if Vlasov had some kind of nebulous plan to ally his forces with the UPA, the Ukrainians involved considered him as merely another example of a Russian imperialist.[90]

The conclusion of the Manifesto repeated a number of points made throughout the utterances of the Liberation Movement. The need for unity in the struggle was of the utmost importance. Peace would be made with Germany, and German help would be accepted provided this did not impinge on the independence and honour of the peoples of Russia. Finally, the Manifesto called for the help and support of all

Russians, both inside and outside the borders of the Soviet Union, to fight for real peace and freedom.

On 18 November 1944, the Manifesto was made public at a ceremony at the Europa-Haus, Berlin; a number of speeches were made supporting the programme.[91] The only slight difference was that in Vlasov's speech, he seemed to give more weight to the legitimacy of the February Revolution at the expense of October, whereas in the Prague Manifesto this question appeared less clear-cut. The overall effect of these speeches was that a brave front was put on a hopeless situation. The utterances on the successful advance of the Red Army, which now conclusively demonstrated the true predatory nature of Bolshevism to a people even less inclined to support the Soviet regime than at earlier stages of the war, had no ring of conviction to them. For, although the Manifesto reflected the criticism of Soviet citizens towards the Stalinist regime, few of them could have believed that there was still a serious chance of putting their ideas into practice at this late date.

Anti-semitism

The absence of all reference to the Jewish question is one of the striking features of the Manifesto. The attitude of Vlasov and KONR towards the Jews has been the subject of great controversy. The alleged anti-semitic attitudes of the Russian Liberation Movement was the subject of much criticism from Russian émigrés after the war.[92] This criticism was based, almost exclusively, on the evidence provided in the columns of the Russian newspaper in Paris, *Parizhskiy vestnik*, and in particular, on the evidence of the text of Malyshkin's speech[93] which was published in the newspaper after his visit in June 1943. This speech contained three references to Jews. At the beginning of the speech there is a statement that the Russian people were tricked by a group of adventurers, who were 'a group of Yids (*Zhidy*) and Bolsheviks who had managed in the course of twenty-five years to keep it [the people] in obedience ...' Further on, there is reference to the 'judaeo-Communist yoke' and half-way through the speech Malyshkin apparently said that the aim of the Liberation Movement was 'the creation of a New Russia without Bolsheviks, Yids and capitalists'. Opponents of the Russian Liberation Movement considered that the general tenor of *Parizhskiy vestnik*, which was known to support Vlasov, and of this speech in particular, proves that the

Russian Liberation Movement was basically anti-semitic.[94] Others have replied in their defence, that the phrase: '. . . a new Russia without Bolsheviks and capitalists . . .' was one of the slogans of the Movement, and that the editor of the newspaper had merely inserted the word 'Yids' into the text, and doctored the other two quotations in the same way.[95] Certain considerations would seem to support this assertion. If Malyshkin had really been anti-semitic, then it would be logical to assume that this sentiment would be evident throughout the speech, yet there is no such consistency. Both the opening lines and the conclusion of the Paris speech state that the Movement aims to overthrow Stalin and Bolshevism; there are no anti-semitic remarks where, logically, one would expect to find them. There is no reference to Jews in the speech where Malyshkin mentions international forces, which would normally be the cue for such statements. Furthermore, one would expect an anti-semitic note to be struck in all official pronouncements of the Russian Liberation Movement and not solely in one speech. None of the previously mentioned documents and declarations which are central to the development of the Movement contain references to the Jewish question. Nor did Malyshkin make anti-semitic remarks in other public appearances. In a speech that he made to a congress organised by the German Institute of International Politics,[96] Malyshkin made no mention of anti-semitism, although the ambience would have been very favourable to such a statement.

Parizhskiy vestnik was edited by Yurii Sergeevich Zherebkov, the son of a Cossack general, who was close to Krasnov. Zherebkov had embarked upon a career on the stage before being appointed, somewhat to his surprise and greatly to his embarrassment, to oversee the Russian émigré colony in Paris. Zherebkov asserted that 'he was a Russian patriot first and foremost, and he did not consider that the Jewish question was of great importance when discussing the predicament and future of Russia. Consequently, as a result he *frequently* employed anti-semitic remarks as it facilitated getting an article passed by the Nazi censor.' In the case of Malyshkin's speech, he declared that: 'the anti-semitic remarks had been uttered and had remained in the text' and that he, Zherebkov, 'had deleted some anti-Cossack remarks because he felt that revealing the cracks in Russian unity did nothing to further the Vlasov cause'.[97] Since the stenographic report of Malyshkin's speech has disappeared, it is no longer possible to verify the matter in one way or another.

Of the other newspapers sympathetic to Vlasov, *Volya naroda*, the official KONR newspaper published between November 1944 and

March 1945, contains no anti-semitic remarks. The editors were Russian and despite various difficulties with the Nazi authorities, managed to maintain their position and to avoid parroting Nazi slogans. *Zarya* was a Russian language newspaper written for civilians and *Dobrovolets* was published for Russian-speaking troops. Both these newspapers were under German control and anti-semitic remarks appear in both publications. It is said by his colleagues that when Zykov became editor of *Zarya*, he tried to minimise German control and to make the paper of greater interest and relevance to its readers.[98] He is said to have instigated the policy of taking articles from the *Völkischer Beobachter* and prefacing them with the sentence: 'As the *Völkischer Beobachter* says ...' whenever the censors demanded that Nazi ideology, and in particular anti-semitic articles, should appear in the Russian language publications.[99] Since it has proved impossible to locate a complete run of either *Dobrovolets* or *Zarya*, it has not been possible to check the accuracy of this explanation. However, if it is true, it would seem to be in line both with the general attitude of the Movement's leaders and with the approach followed by Zykov, in which he attempted to find forms of words and expressions whch would satisfy German demands and yet allow the Russians to present the views of the Russian Liberation Movement.

Zhilenkov gave an interview to the *Völkischer Beobachter*[100] in which a number of anti-semitic remarks were made. However, given the content and the profile of this newspaper, this would hardly be unexpected. Vlasov was highly critical of Zhilenkov's interview.[101] Vlasov's own reply to German concern about the Jewish question was that it was an internal Russian problem and would be dealt with after they had accomplished the primary aim of overthrowing the existing regime.[102] That Vlasov was able to withstand Nazi pressure, as well as possible anti-semitic sentiment exhibited by some Russian émigrés and Soviet nationals (see later discussion of the NTS), is greatly to his credit. Dr Taubert, the official of the Propaganda Ministry who was an expert on Soviet propaganda, complained that: 'It is important that [within the Russian Liberation Movement] a struggle against Jewry does not occur and in general that the Jewish question is not recognised as such.'[103]

Bloknot Propagandista

Bloknot Propagandista,[104] the last publication of the Movement of major ideological significance, appeared in January 1945 and was written by Captain Galkin and Shtifanov, both of whom worked at Dabendorf. This publication was intended to help those trained at Dabendorf to explain the programme of the Russian Liberation Movement. It was planned as the first part of a series, in which it was intended to discuss all the aspects and questions arising out of the Prague Manifesto. It seems, however, that only one issue appeared. Known as the 'Basic Underlying Ideas' (*Ideynye Osnovy*) of the Liberation Movement of the Peoples of Russia, the subject was discussed in two parts: first, the basic tenets of the ideology, divided into nine sections, and second, a critique of communism, divided into six sections. The publication is an interesting commentary on the Prague Manifesto and a reflection of some of the problems faced by the exponents of the anti-Stalinist point of view.

The introduction stated that it was essential to be positive when propounding these theories. It was not sufficient to know what one opposed, one also had to recognise the alternative. It was explained that the White Armies had lost the Civil War because they were unable to agree on a positive attitude. They could only say that they were 'against the Bolsheviks' and this was an insufficient platform to produce more support. The Bolsheviks, however, put forward an attractive positive approach: the victory of Bolshevism worldwide, and their certainty of inevitable success attracted people to their cause. The Manifesto indicated the principles on which the new system would be based. Under the pseudonym 'Pershin', Shtifanov explained that the Manifesto did not describe all the minutiae of the new state system but had considered the actual state of affairs, and as a result of this had settled on the possibility of putting the programme into action (*printsip vypolnimosti*). The unchanging idea behind this was to improve the welfare (*blagodenstvie*) of the nation, both to better the lot of the individual and also to strengthen the position of the state. Since the programme was designed to please the majority of the population (*narodnykh mass*), it had to be constructed with their cooperation.

The introduction, signed by 'Pershin', listed the subjects which the authors hoped would be discussed in the issues of *Bloknot Propagandista*. However, Shtifanov continued, statements in the booklet should not be taken as incontrovertible assertions, but rather as topics for discussion. This remark suggests that a more democratic system was envisaged. 'Pershin' proceeded to contrast favourably the ideas advanced by the Russian Liberation Movement, with the ideals of communism which are designated as 'idealistic delirium' (*sugubo idealisticheskim bredom*) which failed to take into account the realities of life. The Manifesto emanated from the people, and its ideas had nothing in common with Bolshevism. Indeed, it was the support of the populace, 'Pershin' stressed, which achieved the overthrow of the pre-revolutionary government. The introduction ended with an exhortation to those whose job it was to propagate the ideas of the Movement, not to procrastinate in discussing them with the Russian people.

The first half of this publication recapitulated and elaborated the basic principles underlying the programme of the Russian Liberation Movement, the second dealt with 'the Communist Utopia'. The rallying cry of the Movement was 'For the well-being of the people and the state, Nationalism and Unity!' (*Za Narodnoe Blagodenstvie, Natsionalizm, Edinenie!*) These objectives were to replace the goals of Bolshevism, and create the basis for a new state and a new social system.

The first section of *Bloknot* defined the USSR as an ideocratic state in which political power belonged to the Communist party whose members had agreed to achieve certain predetermined aims. In an interesting aside, Galkin explained that since the death of Lenin, the party had undergone substantial changes. As a result, the party had become merely a vehicle for the ideas of the leader, Stalin, rather than a platform for any specific ideology. This development had resulted in much greater repression and the analysis would appear to lay the blame for the situation in the Soviet Union squarely on Stalin's shoulders, not on the nature of the system.

Section two defined the main features of Bolshevism, which were seen as closely connected and leading one from another. The first, communism was the ideal which had inspired the Bolsheviks[105] and shaped events in 1917. Since, according to Marxist-Leninist theory, communism could not be created until the proletariat was victorious world-wide, the second basic feature, internationalism, emerged. The principle of internationalism meant that revolution must be encouraged all over the world. Revolution could be brought about through the medium of class warfare, the third integral aspect. Following this summary outline of Bolshevik ideology, Galkin declared that the tenets of the Russian Liberation Movement would supplant those of Bolshevism.

Communism was subjected to an examination in the light of practical experience in section three. Galkin declared that the socialist economic order[106] had not created a better society. Capitalism was criticised, in this section, for its attendant miseries of unemployment and imperialist wars, but communism neglected the importance of individual initiative by subordinating everything to the collective control of the Bolshevik state. Further, this type of cooperative under communism had merely been a camouflaged form of state ownership of the means of production.

Galkin considered that the building of communism had really meant that the government had forcibly seized and expropriated the property of various social groups and concentrated the means of production in its own hands. Communism had turned the population into slaves at the mercy of one single capitalist, the Bolshevik state. Under capitalism, it was explained, workers displeased with their employer, could leave and seek work elsewhere. Under communism, however, if the state was displeased with a worker, he was doomed to death by starvation since there was no other employer. Capitalist exploitation of the workers had been replaced by the immeasurably harsher exploitation of the state, since everything was produced by the state and all depended on the state for work. The Bolsheviks, working on these lines, had been unable to manage the economy and instead of the anticipated abundance of material wealth, the population had been beggared. The government apparatus used to organise the life of the country had turned out to be excessively top-heavy and expensive. Galkin concluded that the exclusion of individual initiative from the economic life of the country had in fact been a crime. It was also held that communism did not confine itself just to the reorganisation of the industrial base. Galkin asserted that communism also endeavoured to inculcate attitudes into the people in the light of the reorganisation of the economy and communist society. This attempt caused the greatest conflict between the population and communism.

Galkin contended that the ideas of communism were anti-national and alien to the attitudes of contemporary man. The people found themselves engaged in both active and passive resistance to this tyrannical power, which then reacted by using dictatorship, terror and persecution to crush any opposition. In these conditions people became not only economic but psychological slaves. The phrase: 'in the society of slaves the ideal of society (*obshchestvenny ideal*) dies too' was used by Galkin to explain the attitude of both soldiers and civilians, who, during the first phase of the war, refused to defend the

USSR and surrendered to the enemy. After this, Galkin continued, Bolshevik propaganda had to be altered to express patriotic ideas. A soldier imbued with a feeling of national honour would, in the author's opinion, sound a death knell for communism. The first priority, therefore, was to do away with the conflict between the aspirations of the people and those of communism, and the way to do this was to create a new social system. Thus the National Labour system (*Natsional'no-Trudovoy Stroy*) was put forward as the alternative. In this system, the welfare of the nation, unity in the state, and nationalism took pride of place.

Section four of the first section of the *Bloknot Propagandista* proceeded to elaborate the idea of well-being of the population (*narodnoe blagodenstvie*). This welfare was to replace both capitalism and communism, which were extreme solutions to economic questions. A solution between these two extremes would have to be found – it was defined by Galkin as the principle of the optimum solution (*printsip optimalizma*) – to settle the question of how the state should be run, and along which social and economic lines, for this to be in the best interests of the people as a whole. This would mean that the economy would be a mixed one, with large concerns such as military industry, heavy industry, transport and communications nationalised. Other enterprises, particularly consumer goods, would be left to private concern. Agriculture would be developed almost entirely under private ownership. All the land would be given to the peasantry. The division between private and state ownership would have to be decided in the light of the best interests of the nation. An idealistic explanation was added to the effect that it was hoped that by taking into account the wishes of the population and the best interests of the country, the government would then refrain from adhering blindly to the ideology of any party with predetermined aims and views.

Galkin explained that the principle of well-being within the state could be understood, in a primitive and vulgar fashion, to mean that the state was only concerned in supplying the population with sufficient food. He considered, however, that the principle of well-being involved more than this. Well-being was not limited to fulfilling the material and psychological needs of the present generation but also had to take into account the welfare of future generations. Nevertheless, the needs of the present could not be sacrificed to the prospects of future prosperity, as the Soviet government had always required. In concluding this part of the discussion, Galkin considered that to struggle for the future only made sense when the immediate situation also gained something from it.

Social justice was one of the goals of the National-Labour system. The phrase, 'from each according to his abilities and to each according to his needs' was defined by the author of *Bloknot* as merely a clever demagogic trick, which was unrealistic, could not be put into practice and also aimed to fool the masses. Therefore, in Galkin's opinion, the principle of welfare within the state demanded both unremitting amelioration of the material position of the nation and improvement of its cultural level. With the growth in the economy, the standard of health would be enhanced, as would the psychological attitude of the individual. This would result in the growth of nationhood and the 'spiritual' authority of the state.

This section can be seen as a direct reaction against the ideocratic Soviet state which put the demands of ideology above those of practical considerations and the augmentation of policies which would benefit the country. This idea, 'well-being within the state', was a call for pragmatism, which appeared to be lacking in the Soviet administration.

Section five discussed the principle of internationalism. It began with an exposition of the Marxist-Leninist position: that communism could only be achieved after the victory of Bolshevism in the entire world. Once all national divisions and differences had disappeared, after a period of time which would allow for further economic development, communism would be established. Thus, Bolsheviks had always attacked nationalism and attempts by nations to live according to their cultural traditions as products of bourgeois mentality and ideology. Lenin allowed for some qualification of this theory, i.e. that although the national question was bourgeois, it was 'essentially peasant'.[107] Stalin averred that in all nationalist movements the prime force is the bourgeoisie,[108] and that bourgeois nationalist forces were a product of capitalism. The author of *Bloknot Propagandista* argued that Bolshevik theory was incorrect, and that Stalin's amendments were obviously untrue, since it could not be said when the Russians defeated the Poles and forced them to retreat from Moscow in 1612,[109] that this was a rising of Moscow merchants rather than a national response to the aggressor. Galkin commented that in light of their theory, Bolsheviks regarded all national movements as possessing a political character which had to be utilised in the interests of achieving world revolution. The author warned that Stalin's exploitation of national sentiment during the war ought not to be viewed as evidence of a change within Bolshevism, which was not able to reject the doctrine of internationalism lying at the core of its ideology. Bolshevism was not interested in the fate of any given nation but in the position of the proletariat world-wide. Following this analysis of the theoretical basis of internationalism and its place in the communist ideology, the author called on the practical experience of his reader. During the war, millions of Soviet citizens had come into contact with citizens of other countries, and with very few exceptions it was evident no one was concerned with the world proletariat whereas everyone was interested in the fate of their own country. The world-wide solidarity of proletarian interests was shown up as merely a product of communist rhetoric.

Galkin proceeded to explain Bolshevik policy. Whereas it had originally been expected that revolution in Russia would be followed by revolution elsewhere, this had not occurred. The Bolsheviks realised that revolution could frequently be avoided by wise government and consequently Bolsheviks tried to bring about revolution by artificial means. Therefore, peasant, national, colonial, religious and other disputes or movements were manipulated to this end. The Comintern apparatus was maintained for this reason, financed by the people of the Soviet Union. All the needs of the people were subordinated to the fermentation of upheaval and revolution. The author concluded that this policy bred a hatred of the Soviet Union by other nations, and brought the Soviet people untold suffering. The last part of section five repeated the message which had been spelt out in each article of the *Bloknot Propagandista*: to reach the goal of international revolution, Bolshevik policies would violate the wishes and aspirations of the Soviet people and cause them needless harm. Consequently, it was necessary to overthrow this Bolshevik regime, and to replace the bankrupt ideal of internationalism with that of nationalism which reflected the true wishes and interests of the people.

Section six dealt with the question of nationalism. The Bolshevik view that nationalism was a bourgeois phenomenon was held to be wrong, and love for one's own people and country could be experienced by all social groups. Furthermore, the author was of the opinion that national feeling existed before capitalism came into being, and would outlive it. Galkin was in no doubt that the nation was acknowledged to be of the highest value to society and it was only by taking account of national forms that the full potential of a people could be realised. He defined the nation as an organic unity of individuals creating their own culture, linked together by it and by their economic, state and psychological interests, their shared history and by a common attitude towards the future. The energies of a people should be directed to resolving the internal problems of their country, rather than creating conditions favourable to world revolution. The National-Labour System of the New Russia should therefore strive to establish good relations with the other nations of the world.

The last few paragraphs summarised the section. The claim was made that the kind of nationalism advocated in the *Bloknot* was neither internationalism nor national chauvinism, but lay somewhere between the two. National consciousness, it was asserted, had grown beyond narrow feudal boundaries or class distinctions and had evolved into an awareness of national brotherhood. Ideas of international unity had shown themselves to be based on false premises. Consequently, Galkin summed up the argument by reiterating that for the Liberation Movement the nation was considered to be the highest social form. International cooperation was not inappropriate but it had to be based on mutual respect, friendship and a common interest in progress.

The substance and tenor of these remarks and ideas can be seen as a direct reaction to communist ideology and policies. The writer of *Bloknot Propagandista* believed that the interests of the population of the Soviet Union had been neglected in the name of communism and in particular the Soviet attempts to achieve world revolution. It is of interest that the term 'feudal' is used, as is the term 'class', not in a precise historical context but in a vulgarized interpretation of Marxism. It appears that having rejected the communist view of development, and their notion of nationalism as a product of bourgeois society, Captain Galkin felt the need to replace these terms with another frame of reference, namely the idea of nationalism and particularly its historical evolution. His analysis did not correspond very accurately to actual historical events, and the idea of the nation seems to have an almost symbolic significance. Despite such strictures, given the attitudes of his audience, Galkin was probably correct to seek a philosophy with which to replace the tenets of communism, to try and provide an alternative method of viewing the world. On a more immediate level, his appeal to nationalist, or patriotic sentiment, undoubtedly met with approval amongst members of the Russian Liberation Movement.

Having criticised the concept of internationalism, section seven proceeded to enucleate class warfare. Two parallel forces, it was explained, existed in any human society: the force of unity and that of separation. An awareness of common aims and interests gave rise to a feeling of cohesion and unity, and encouraged progress in any given society. The pursuance of selfish interests and conflict brought about disunity. Some defined this division as a class struggle. The position of the idea of class conflict within Soviet ideology was given a brief outline and it was further explained that Stalin's own contribution to this question was to say that class warfare does not fall into abeyance once all classes have disappeared within the socialist state. Class warfare, according to Stalin, continued because elements of 'capitalist thinking' remained in the minds of individuals.[110] Galkin believed that class warfare had always been encouraged since it weakened the warring groups and allowed the Bolsheviks to seize power. However, since the Bolsheviks, once in power, were unable to create an order which satisfied the needs of the people, they decreed that class warfare was to be continued and that the class enemy must be eradicated. Yet in Galkin's opinion, the definition of class enemy changed over the years, as Soviet experience clearly demonstrated. At first, class enemies were the representatives of the privileged elements in society: the landowners, entrepreneurs, clergy, officers of the armed forces and a large part of the intelligentsia. Later, while NEP held sway, class enemies were those involved in anti-Bolshevik activity, members of the counter-revolutionary White movement, nationalists, the socialist-revolutionaries, as well as NEP men, the clergy, and towards the end, the richer peasantry. The class enemies in the period of collectivisation were defined first as the wealthy peasantry, and then the peasantry as a whole. During the *Ezhovshchina* – the purges of 1936–9 when Yezhov was head of the NKVD – the definition of class enemy widened considerably, and the term 'enemy of the people' (*vrag naroda*) appeared. This category often included party workers, and members of the intelligentsia who originated from the proletariat. Finally, anyone who voiced criticism of the state became 'an enemy of the people'. In conclusion, Captain Galkin considered that their concept of class warfare had led the Bolsheviks to define the entire population as class enemies. Having thus alienated the nation's citizens, the Bolsheviks had sown the seeds which would bring about their own downfall. In the future, the concept of class warfare had to be replaced by that of social unity. The principle of unity was dealt with in section eight. In order to prevent class conflict originating amongst various social groups with differing aims, a national state (*narodnoe gosudarstvo*) would have to be built, which would bring about social justice. This national state would have no vested class interests and, therefore, class conflicts would not occur.

The state would decide maximum profit levels and the minimum wage, and thereby eliminate greed and arbitrariness on the part of the entrepreneurs, and would also ensure that the minimum demands of the workers were met. The author explained that it was not possible to create a classless society if one class destroyed all the other groups, but only by singleness of purpose and cohesion of all social divisions. 'Unite and strengthen' rather than 'Divide and rule' should be the principle underpinning state policy. Unity would be achieved when the social, spiritual and material needs of the population were met under the following seven conditions: social justice; the national-labour solidarity of interests; the existence of nationhood; liberty, justice and the rule of law; the liberation of labour (i.e. not directed and over-regulated labour); the education of society in the light of acceptance of general ethical norms; and finally, when a correct balance was reached between the demands of the individual and the community. This last criterion could be fulfilled not by resolving this question to the detriment of any one group, but by subordinating the wishes of all the parties concerned to the highest national interest and the aim of achieving social progress. Although the individual interest was in general subordinate to that of the community, individual desires should not be ignored and the rights of the individual should be respected. Society should not deprive anyone of freedom, but at the same time nobody should infringe the liberty of others by their actions. To achieve such harmony and unity in society, people had to be instructed in the requisite ideas such as common solidarity of interest. These concepts would then replace feelings of hatred, suspicion and lack of respect for the individual which were encouraged by the Bolsheviks. Captain Galkin felt that for these reasons the Ministry of Education would be of prime importance within the future Russian state. Citizens of a New Russia had to be given every opportunity to develop their personalities fully, as well as their mental and physical capabilities.

Section nine summed up the preceding pages. It stated that the ideas and goals of the Liberation Movement had surfaced because of the sufferings of the population under Soviet rule. At the same time, these ideas had roots in the Russian past. The Liberation Movement was opposed both to communism and to capitalism, and sought to complete the national revolution; this, it was stressed, would not involve any kind of restoration of the *ancien régime*. After the initial and unavoidable turbulent period following the change of order, the new National-Labour system hoped to develop along evolutionary rather than revolutionary lines, with the motto: 'For the well-being of the people and the state, Nationalism and Unity' (*Za Narodnoe Blagodenstvie, Natsionalizm, Edinenie*).

The second part of *Bloknot Propagandista* was entitled: 'The Communist Utopia; a summary' (*Ob utopii Kommunizma – konspekt*). Captain Galkin introduced his criticism by explaining that even among members of the Liberation Movement who rejected Stalin and all his policies, there still existed the conviction that communism remained the desirable goal of working people. Stalinism was seen as a distortion of the true nature of socialism, and a betrayal of Marxism-Leninism. It was Galkin's aim to show that all these ideas were untenable, and that it was not the case that Stalin had emasculated socialism, but that the whole of communist ideology was based on false premises. Since Galkin had very limited space at his disposal for this task, he defined communism as a social ideal with certain characteristics. These he listed under six main headings: first, that all the means of production, transport, communications, land, and housing were expropriated and private ownership was ceded to society as a whole; second, that the state became unnecessary and withered away; third, that division of the material wealth of this society was decided on the principle: 'From each according to his abilities, to each according to his needs'; fourth, that the antithesis between the town and the country was done away with; and fifth, that the antithesis between mental and physical work also was abrogated. The sixth characteristic of the communist state was that war and the causes of war would disappear. Galkin then proceeded to examine each of these propositions in turn.

He argued that public ownership, as Soviet reality had demonstrated, could be put into practice. If the government was in full control it could do whatever it liked. Under the totalitarian Soviet regime, people had died because of artificially created famine as in 1933; whole nations, for example the Kalmyks, had been deported to

Siberia, critical attitudes in millions of individuals had been suppressed, and so on. If the state could do all this there would not seem to be any reason why private ownership could not be suppressed. However, in order for industry to work, even if it was nationalised, society as a whole could not be involved in the administrative process, and organisations concerned solely with this came into being.[111] Such organisations, up to the present, had been called the state. This brought Galkin to a discussion of the second feature of communism, the prerequisite that the state should wither away.

Galkin considered that the Marxist definition of the state was wrong. The state was not merely 'the oppression of one class by another'. The function of the state could not be reduced, even under the most totalitarian and dictatorial regime, merely to the uncontrolled exercise of oppression and terror. Galkin said that in any system, the state had to carry out certain administrative functions which could not be termed simply as oppression. Furthermore, Galkin was of the opinion that a state, which consisted either of one nation or a group of nations, had two basic areas of policy to consider; that of the internal problems and administration, and that of foreign policy. Even if Bolshevism took over the whole world, and abolished all barriers between different states, and thereby did away with the need for foreign policy, the problem of internal administration would still exist, and then Galkin considered that an organisation similar to the state would be needed. Therefore, this second feature of the communist state was most unlikely ever to be put into practice and was not a realistic programme.

The idea 'from each according to his capabilities, to each according to his needs' was defined as the central feature of communist society. However, before this ideal society was reached, the horror of wars and revolution would have to be endured, and the aftermath of all this upheaval could be vividly illustrated by what had occurred in the Soviet Union. However, Galkin conceded that perhaps it was possible to imagine a communist utopia. He qualified this with the remark that the inhabitants of any perfect society were required to have angelic souls, and he considered that the character of the ordinary individual was far from angelic. He added that it was most unlikely, even after the effect of the teachings of communism, that people would be so self-sacrificing that their own estimates of their capabilities and needs would correspond to the dictates of society. Galkin considered that since Christianity, over a period of two thousand years, had been unable to eradicate selfishness from human nature, it was less than likely that communism would do so, and achieve a just distribution of material goods. As a result, the central aspect of communist ideology, too, was rejected as being unrealistic.

Section four dealt with communist ideas on the ending of the antithesis between town and country. Galkin considered this to be complete nonsense, as it was impossible to achieve. For purely practical reasons, the type of work, social and cultural institutions, and methods of transport were all quite different in towns than in villages. Further, the growth of industrialisation, and the consequent expansion of the towns showed that society was developing in the opposite direction from the concept where everyone lived in cottages surrounded by gardens.

The fifth feature of communism, that of the liquidation of the antithesis between intellectual and manual labour was, according to Galkin, unworkable. Furthermore, it had evoked a variety of responses, showing that the concept had been misunderstood. Some considered that it meant that all work would be carried out by machines. Others supposed that everyone would be trained as engineers, and would alternate periods on the factory floor as an ordinary member of the work force with periods as chief engineer. Some had thought that work would alter, with one year spent in agriculture, the next in industry and so on. Stalin clarified the issue by declaring that, in fact, the cultural level and technical skills of the entire working class should be raised to those of the managerial classes,[112] a solution which, Galkin observed, altered the nature of the question without providing an answer to something which, in essence, was impossible.

Section six explored the communist position on war and the contention that it would disappear once world-wide communism had been established. Galkin agreed that if the Bolsheviks seized world power then external conflicts would not occur. He pointed out that this had not yet happened; indeed, the application of communist ideas in the Soviet Union had led to great opposition in the country, which in turn had resulted in the use of terror against the population. From his examination of five aspects of communism, Galkin concluded that the population of the world would continue to resist the imposition of such an oppressive and unrealistic ideology and it could never be put into practice. Thus, conflict would remain, even come the dawning of a communist society.

In a footnote, Galkin addressed himself, very briefly, to those communist ideas which he had not scrutinised: the question of relations between men and women, the position of the family, the disappearance of nations, and the need for a common language. Once again, Galkin indicated that none of the policies put forward were realistic. In the case of the family, the Soviet regime had abandoned its early policy of 'free love' and was now attempting to strengthen the position of the family as a unit. The policies to remove nationalist consciousness and establish a common language, would only involve force and oppression and would impoverish the quality of life.

In conclusion, Galkin stated that since five of the characteristic features of communist society were impossible to put into practice, this was ample proof that the theory and the ideal were also mistaken. In fact, one could say that it was not only a mistaken theory but a criminal idea (*prestupnost'*) since, attracted by this mirage, various political opportunists had pushed nations on to the path of self-destruction. Of the leaders of the Bolsheviks, Lenin had died, Stalin had come out on top, but the rest, of whom Galkin named Bukharin, Trotsky and Zinoviev, had perished in bitter internecine struggle over the methods by which communism should be achieved and over the question as to what form communist society should take. In practice, much suffering had been endured by the Russian people, and a great deal of conflict appeared to lie ahead, and for all these reasons communism was not the right model on which the development of society should be based.

The last seven pages consisted of instructions on how best to explain the content of this publication to an audience, and also gave a glossary of various terms used. This section was perhaps the most obvious illustration of the problems with which the Russian Liberation Movement had to contend. Not only was the audience unused to thinking along the lines required by the Liberation Movement, but those supposed to be inculcating this new *Weltanschauung* had almost as little experience.

This section on methods of presentation started by suggesting that although the brief analysis of communism followed the section on the principal ideas of the Liberation Movement, it would be clearer for an audience if the speaker were to begin by criticising communism and only then illustrating how the ideas of the Russian Liberation Movement would replace the faulty Bolshevik ideology. The instructor was advised, when he was short of time, to concentrate on the practical consequences of given policies, rather than on more abstract discussion. Galkin insisted that it must also be made clear that there was no one philosophic system at the root of the ideas of the Russian Liberation Movement. Marxism claimed to be an all-embracing scientific world view, and therefore, those educated under the influence of Marxist ideas usually wished to know the philosophic basis of any other ideology. However, members of the Russian Liberation Movement should realise that it was unnecessary to have a single comprehensive philosophical system as the basis of an ideology. None of the ideologies of liberalism, capitalism, fascism and national-socialism were based on a particular philosophical system. In fact, the application of Marxism-Leninism had demonstrated that linking an ideology with a particular well-defined philosophy tended to prevent further development and caused that ideology to be increasingly inappropriate for the life of society. Moreover, philosophy needed freedom in order to evolve. However, Galkin continued with the remark that it was undeniable that every ideology contained some features which are products of a given philosophy. The main and most important difference between Marxism and the ideas of the Russian Liberation Movement was that the former emphasised the decisive role of economic factors, whereas the latter considered the human personality the most important feature in any system. Finally, the benefits of a pluralistic vision were stressed, rather than attempts to fit everything into one particular ideological straitjacket.

Because so few copies have survived, historians have completely overlooked the importance of *Bloknot Propagandista*.[113] However, this publication is fundamental to our understanding of the Russian Liberation Movement in a number of ways. First, it provides a very clear illustration of the problems faced by the ideologists of the Liberation Movement. The avowed purpose of this publication was to provide a teaching aid for those instructing their compatriots in the ideas of the Movement, by explaining the implications of basic policies referred to in the Prague Manifesto. The persistent emphasis on the faults inherent in the communist system shows, as Galkin himself admitted, that the adherents of the Liberation Movement had by no means rejected communism *per se*, still less their Soviet inheritance. Consequently, a large proportion of *Bloknot* was devoted to a rather unsophisticated critique of communism, establishing on the basis of practical experience that the ideology of communism was based on incorrect assumptions, and could not be put into practice without subjecting the mass of the population to oppression and suffering. This section also demonstrates the low level of education of those for whom this publication was intended. Undoubtedly, even at the highest levels, the Movement suffered from the fact that there were very few who were used to philosophical discussion or abstract thinking.

The leadership consisted either of professional military men, or of civilians whose higher education had been in scientific fields or who had undergone technical training. There was almost no one, with the possible exception of Zykov, who had received higher education in the humanities. This undoubtedly influenced the way in which the ideology was developed, since the ideologists had little knowledge of history or political science, and tried to develop a political programme on the basis of their own experience. At all levels the position was further complicated by the effects of Soviet education and propaganda. In Stalinist Russia people had learnt that it was best not to indulge in philosophical speculation, which to the listener might imply criticism of the regime. This meant that the readers for whom *Bloknot* was intended possessed almost no experience of dealing with political concepts or with abstract speculation. The point is made clearly by the glossary at the end of *Bloknot Propagandista* which even included such words as 'idea' and 'dictatorship'. The intellectual level of the general reader and recipient of the instruction offered by *Bloknot Propagandista* meant that it had to be written in very concrete, simple terms, nothing could be abstract or purely theoretical. Furthermore, given the complexion of the ideologists, this kind of factual approach would be natural to them. Both reader and publicist had experienced the negative side of Soviet reality and could analyse it without great difficulty.

The authors of the Prague Manifesto had attempted to create a positive goal and common platform around which the opposition to Stalin could unite. The authors of *Bloknot Propagandista* expressed the opinion, more clearly than in the Prague Manifesto, that it was necessary to replace the faulty ideal of communism with a positive programme, and so from their criticism of Marxism, evolved their motto: 'For the well-being of the People and the State, Nationalism, Unity!' This section might well be considered weaker than that of the criticism of communism, as it often appeared to be based, for example, on an idealised view of the nation or on the existence of motivation, inherent in the citizens, to subordinate their private interests to those of the mass of their compatriots. But, given the conditions in which *Bloknot* was written, where time was running out, where the need to create a consensus was still of paramount import- ance and where external political pressures were very complex, it is not surprising that the future of Russia was delineated in vague terms. Questions of legislative forms or processes were too involved to be examined in detail in such a publication, and the authors implied that this would be tackled at some later date. Indeed, since the authors lacked experience in political science and constitutional law, it is difficult to see how such questions could be discussed in any really constructive manner. Certainly, the authors of *Bloknot* har- boured suspicions of Western forms of government, and the social and economic order of capitalism and democracy. Shtifanov advo- cated orally, if not in print, that the future Russian government should be 'a democracy without parties'. In his view, the concept of a political party carried a very negative connotation. Similarly, the national question is not elaborated or significantly advanced: in *Bloknot Propagandista* nationalism and patriotism are espoused as positive characteristics, but the question of the future of the national minorities in the Soviet Union is avoided.

 Bloknot Propagandista is not merely a commentary on the Prague Manifesto, clarifying certain principles and subordinating many contentious issues to the need for unity. It is also an ideological document in its own right, showing certain shifts in positions from those adopted by the Prague Manifesto. The authors of *Bloknot Propagandista* rejected communism *in toto*. The repudiation of Marxist theory was stated more firmly in *Bloknot* than in any other document of the Russian Liberation Movement. In earlier ideological pro- nouncements, the implication was that Bolshevism, as practised under Stalin, was to be rejected, that the ideals of the Revolution had been betrayed. But the leaders of the Movement did not, in these statements, lay the blame for these distortions on the basic nature of Marxism itself. Galkin did so. He opined that the features of the Stalinist regime – the rule of terror, lack of freedom, poor economic performance – all of which had produced so much opposition among the population, were inevitable, given the fundamental assumptions of Marxism. However, having drawn this conclusion and having made categorical statements to this effect, Galkin did not appear to accept all the implications of such a position. In the light of this,

Galkin's attitude to the Revolution could be considered ambiguous. He did not reject the Revolution, and stated that the aim of the Russian Liberation Movement was to complete the struggle of 1917, but in the name of the people, not of Marxist principles. It was not evident from the wording whether Galkin favoured the February or the October Revolution, but it could be assumed, given the tenor of this publication, that on the whole, he considered February the real revolution.[114] References to Lenin are also equivocal; although he was mentioned twice in *Bloknot Propagandista*, his name did not appear in the other documents of the Russian Liberation Movement. It was not clear how Galkin considered Lenin's role *vis-à-vis* the Revolution and how the implementation of communism should be interpreted. It would appear, from the way in which he was mentioned, that the official doctrine of Lenin, as the father of the Soviet state, still held. In fact, none of the pronouncements of the Russian Liberation Movement expressly rejected Lenin. The contradictions between an acceptance of this view and a rejection of communism were not explored by Galkin.

Bloknot Propagandista must be seen as expressing one of many points of view which existed in the Liberation Movement. Although, doubtless, the text had to be passed for publication by the leadership, it cannot be assumed that everything in *Bloknot* would have been accepted without reservation or qualification by either the leaders, or by the adherents of the Movement.[115] *Bloknot Propagandista* must be understood as part of a continual debate[116] among members of the Liberation Movement on the problems facing them in their opposition to the Stalinist regime.

Bloknot Propagandista, nevertheless, showed a considerable development in the thinking of the leaders – Galkin and Shtifanov clearly belonged to the intellectual elite – of the Russian Liberation Movement since their earlier pronouncements. The implications of the stand taken by the Movement were far more clearly seen, as was the need to come to terms with some of the major problems of Soviet development – questions which, even today, concern Soviet intellectuals, the problem of the primacy of Lenin over Stalin, their relation to Marxist doctrine in general, as well as its application to the Soviet Union. The answers provided were incomplete and lacked sophistication, yet the contents of *Bloknot Propagandista* revealed a new realisation that a discussion of these subjects must be embarked upon. *Bloknot Propagandista* was a tentative approach and exemplified a way of thinking of both the authors and their colleagues. It is for this reason that this hitherto neglected source is of such importance for our understanding of the philosophy underlying the actions of the Russian Liberation Movement.

Biblioteka Propagandista

George Fischer called the school at Dabendorf 'one of those unique islands of relative privacy within the totalitarian sea of Hitler's Germany'.[117] Dabendorf was vital for the evolution of the programme and outlook of the Russian Liberation Movement. The participants of the Movement unequivocally acknowledge the important influence that discussion at Dabendorf had on their outlook and way of thinking.[118]

Unfortunately, little of this is reflected in the series of publications known as *Biblioteka Propagandista*.[119] These publications were supposed to be a summary of the teaching done in the courses at Dabendorf. The programme of study was inherited from the Wehrmacht Propaganda courses run at the prisoner-of-war camps at Wustrau and Wulheide,[120] and later at Lückenwalde,[121] and as such had a pro-German bias.[122] The aim of these courses was to produce Russian prisoners-of-war trained as anti-communist propagandists. The syllabus was subdivided as follows:

Section I. Germany
(1) Historical survey of the development of Germany (to Versailles)
(2) History of the National-Socialist Movement
(3) The foundations of National-Socialism
(4) The Jewish question
(5) The state and social structure of Germany
(6) The labour question in Germany
(7) German agriculture
(8) Social relief in Germany
(9) The German family and the education of youth

Section II. Russia and Bolshevism
(10–14) Brief familiarisation with the history of the Russian people and the development of Russian statehood
(15) Ideological oppression in the USSR
(16) Soviet agricultural policy
(17) The labour question and stakhanovism

(18) The Soviet intelligentsia and culture
(19) The family, youth upbringing and education in the USSR
(20) The struggle of the authorities against the population
(21) Soviet economic policy
(22) The USSR's foreign policy
(23) The Jews and Russia
(24) Russia under Bolshevik rule
(25) England, Russia's traditional enemy
(26) The Russian and the German peoples
(27) The USSR and Germany

Section III. The Russian Liberation Movement
(28) The foundation of the Russian Liberation Movement

Subjects one to four, devoted to German and National-Socialist history, were dealt with in lectures; five to nine, German society, were dealt with in a less structured manner and included contributions from participants of the courses. Subjects ten to fourteen, history of the Russian people and the development of the state, and fifteen, ideological oppression in the USSR, were again lectures, whereas sixteen to twenty-three, which dealt with social and economic questions, were taught in seminars. The last five subjects, Russia under the Bolsheviks; England, Russia's traditional enemy; the Russian and German peoples; the USSR and Germany; and the Russian Liberation Movement, all demanded a more theoretical approach, and instruction took the form of lectures.[123]

The chief instructors at Dabendorf, Zaitsev and Shtifanov, both assert that despite the seemingly German orientation of the programme, as the course progressed less time was spent on the German aspects of the syllabus, and more attention was given to questions that interested or perplexed the Russians.[124] In fact, Zaitsev might well have been arrested for anti-German remarks, if Strik-Strikfeldt had not intervened on his behalf.[125]

The complete set of all the pamphlets does not appear to exist, although a summary of the outline remains. Certain of these summaries, in particular those on the Jewish question, show clear evidence of Nazi influence, although as George Fischer remarks: '... it is, on the whole, noticeably restrained in its parroting of Nazi dogma. Seen from a Nazi point of view, even the vulgar anti-semitism of the Dabendorf pamphlet is remarkably moderate and unorthodox.'[126]

The main conclusion to be drawn from reading *Biblioteka Propagandista* is that under the Nazi and Stalinist regimes, those sections dealing with, for example, the family, reflect both Nazi views as expressed in their propaganda, and Soviet experience of the effect of totalitarian rule.

Dabendorf published another booklet, which again demonstrated that the level of political and philosophical sophistication amongst members of the Russian Liberation Movement was low. This booklet, entitled 'ROA's soldier, his ethics, appearance and behaviour',[127] consisted more of instruction on personal conduct and good manners, than on any philosophical discussion of ethics or morality.[128] Not all publications were quite so naive. A booklet designed to provide guidance for those who were trying to spread the ideas of the Russian Liberation Movement[129] demonstrated that most of these individuals were very inexperienced in this area, but at the same time presupposed a relatively high level of political and cultural awareness. Crude propaganda was to be discouraged and instructors were advised to use as wide a variety of methods as possible to make their point clear.

One of the most important influences at Dabendorf was that of the NTS. Trukhin,[130] Vlasov's chief of staff, and chief training officer at Dabendorf in succession to Blagoveshchensky, had become a member of the NTS, as were a number of the teaching staff, including both Zaitsev and Shtifanov. The NTS (see discussion on pp. 183–93), as an émigré organisation, had been able to examine various problems and now, when émigrés met Soviet citizens, was able to provide a framework which acted as a catalyst for discussion. The phrase *natsionalno'-trudovoy* (national-labour), which was used to describe the future social and political system in Russia, was of NTS origin, although it also included features of Soviet society, based on nationhood and free labour, without oppression, and without continuous domination of the demands of ideology, party, birth, or any other form of social distinction or stratification. Many Soviet members of the Liberation Movement, who were not members of the NTS, considered these points important.[131] However, the evidence of interviews with leading members of the teaching staff, demonstrates quite clearly that Dabendorf's role in the evolution of the Russian Liberation Movement was crucial, even if this was not reflected in *Biblioteka Propagandista*.

An unknown, but percipient observer, writing in Russian whose comments have been completely overlooked by historians, explained in December 1944[132] that the history of the Russian Liberation

Movement could be divided into three stages. The first could be defined as the 'psychological' stage when thousands of Red Army soldiers saw the advancing German armies as liberators and surrendered to them, often eventually becoming volunteers in the German forces. This 'elemental' mass action began to take on a direction, in the second stage, with the publication of Vlasov's Open Letter, the Smolensk Declaration and the creation of Dabendorf. However, the Germans regarded all of this purely as being of value for propaganda purposes. The third stage was initiated on 14 November 1944.

During the second stage the spontaneous outburst of anti-Stalinist sentiment began to acquire a more definite form, even if the pressure of Nazi propaganda frequently imposed limits on the expression of Russian aspirations. In the last stages of the Russian Liberation Movement, the programme shows that the leaders and ideologists were attempting to come to grips with a number of problems. Subtlety of expression demonstrates that there was an increasing awareness of the complexities of their situation. The unknown observer, cited above, considered that in the third stage of the Russian Liberation Movement a wish to compromise with the realities of the Soviet regime is discernible; Shtifanov, on the other hand, considered that in the final stages the Russian Liberation Movement shifted perceptibly to the right, i.e. more to an acceptance of the February Revolution of 1917, as opposed to October, since it was necessary to compromise with the old émigrés. Both commentators are, in a sense, correct. The need to create a unified force was the overriding consideration in the composition of the Prague Manifesto. The influence of the Zykov line is less evident at this point, but at the same time, the ideologists of the Movement would not and could not reject Soviet reality, and the general outlook of their adherents. Another influence on the last stage of the Movement was that of the NTS who provided a great stimulus to their Soviet compatriots and, unlike many other émigré organisations, considered that Soviet reality must be taken into account. The confusion that existed in the NTS programme,[133] between what form society actually took and what should exist in a just society, between the materialistic and idealistic views, can be discerned also in the outlook of the ideologists of the Liberation Movement, although this could also stem more from a lack of experience in dealing with political philosophical abstractions than from the direct influence of the NTS.

The unknown commentator considered that the idea of 'the

Russian nation' was another major influence on the programme in the third stage of the Movement. He stated that opinion was divided into four main directions on this question: first, there were those who espoused the point of view of *edinaya i nedelimaya* ('Russia one and indivisible') in which case any division or loss of territory was regarded as a national slight. Second, there were those who considered that a Russian federation should be established along the lines of the United States. Third, there were extreme Russian nationalists espousing the slogan 'Russia for the Russians' and fourth, there were those who favoured the Soviet organisation, and wanted a union of republics. For the observer, this last group and the federalists were most influential, and certainly there is no obvious evidence, on the strength of the statements of the Movement, or in the Prague Manifesto, that the Russian chauvinists had any very large following. Whether this commentator is accurate in his analysis of the composition of groups concerned with the national question is difficult to determine, since there is no written evidence of such divisions or arguments along these lines. However, he is undoubtedly correct in that the national issue in general was important in the development of the Movement.

Members of the Russian Liberation Movement have cited an impressive array of predecessors of their cause. This includes Radishchev, Chaadaev, the Decembrists, the Westernisers, in particular Belinsky, Herzen, Dobrolyubov and Chernyshevsky, as well as the revolutionary organisations of the nineteenth century.[134] There is, however, very little which links the ideas of any of the above with the programme of the Russian Liberation Movement. The link exists only in the fact that the leadership of the Russian Liberation Movement believed that they followed in the spirit of those whom they saw as fighters for national freedom, and as such could be considered their descendants. At Dabendorf the idea was put forward that the Russian Liberation Movement was also the descendant of a whole series of national risings, starting with that led by Minin and Pozharsky against the invading Polish forces in 1612. Amongst these risings, some members of the Russian Liberation Movement would have included the White Armies of the Civil War, but Vlasov did not agree with this analysis.[135] These attempts to define their place in Russian history as a whole stem from the conviction of the leadership that their ideas were truly of the people (*narodnye*) and therefore a product of Russian attitudes, rather than of German policy.

In addition to the increased awareness of the need to compromise, and greater subtlety of expression, the third stage of the Liberation Movement also shows that the leaders were beginning to explore the implications of their position and policies. In so doing, it became clear that two questions which had worried Russian intellectuals since 1917 had to receive some kind of answer: was communism at fault fundamentally? Or was it the distortion of ideology which had occurred in Soviet practice that had been responsible for Stalinism? Given the circumstances in which the Russian Liberation Movement developed, and the limitations imposed upon it, the answers were inevitably very tentative, and somewhat naive. Nevertheless, the Russian Liberation Movement provided a platform for the discussion of these ideas in a manner which had not been possible in Stalin's Russia, and thereby enabled Soviet citizens to consider these subjects and to contribute to the debate which asked the questions, 'What was Russia?' and 'How should the country develop?'

NOTES

1   See p. 41.
2   Vlasov and Boyarsky's letter. Vinnitsa 3 August 1942. German translation: Armee Oberkommando 16.1c.Do.12.9.1942. Captured German records US National Archives Reichsführer SS TI 175 66 EAP 161-b-12/195 258 2721. Translation back into Russian from the German text in Pozdnyakov, V. V., *A. A. Vlasov*, pp. 36–41.
3   See pp. 107–13 on M. A. Zykov, who is said to have influenced the texts of the Smolensk Declaration and Vlasov's Open Letter.
4   Interview: A. N. Zaitsev. Krasnov-Levitin, A., *Likhie gody 1925–1941*, Paris (1967), p. 327.
5   'An den Generalstab des deutschen Heeres. Eingabe des Kgf. früheren Kdeurs, des I. selbst. Schtz.-Korps der Roten Armee Oberst Michail Michailowitsch Schapowalow'. US National Archive Reichsführer SS TI 175 66 EAP 161-b-12/195 258 2721.
6   Countless memoirs provide testimony of the fact that Soviet information about the Nazis was not believed; see, for example: Krasnov-Levitin, A., *Ruk Tvoikh zhar 1941–1956*, Tel Aviv (1969), p. 22. In any case members of the Red Army were frightened to discuss the German question. Ternovsky, Yu., 'V plenu' in Pozdnyakov, V. V., *Rozhdenie ROA*, p. 8.
7   *KPSS o vooruzhennykh silakh Sovetskogo Soyuza*, pp. 298, 305–6, 318–19.
8   Dudin, L., 'Velikii mirazh', *Materialy k istorii Osvoboditel'nogo Dvizheniya Narodov Rossii 1941–45*, London (Ontario) (1970), vol. 2; p. 15.
9   Bogatyrchuk, F. P., *Moy zhiznenny put' k Vlasovu i Prazhskomu Manifestu*, p. 123.
10 See, for example: Levitin-Krasnov, A., *Ruk Tvoikh zhar*, p. 46, and Fevr, N., *Solntse voskhodit na Zapade*, Buenos Aires (1950), p. 249.
11 YIVO German document 480/RAB/IX.42. See p. 44.

12 Strik-Strikfeldt, W., *Against Stalin and Hitler*, p. 79.

13 It is not altogether clear what decided the wording of this sentence. The demands of Nazi propaganda clearly meant that the blame for the hostilities must be laid at the door of the Soviet Union. At the same time there were many who remembered Stalin's opportunistic diplomatic manoeuvres just before the signing of the Molotov-Ribbentrop Non-Aggression treaty in 1939, which had in the long run made it more difficult for Stalin to prepare for war without antagonising Hitler. Letter of G. A. Homyakov to the author 7 April 1983.

14 Werth, A., *Russia at War 1941–1945*, London (1964), p. 211.

15 Original from the Cossack Library, New York, printed in *Bor'ba*, 75/76 (November 1979), pp. 17–20. Buchbender, O., *Das tönende Erz*, pp. 226–7. See Appendix, pp. 206–9.

16 See p. 45.

17 This is reminiscent of Stalin's speech on 3 July 1941 when he addressed his countrymen as 'Comrades, brothers and sisters, fighting men of our Army and Navy, I am speaking to you, my friends.'

18 See discussion of the Prague Manifesto, pp. 126–7.

19 Nikolaevsky, B. I., 'Porazhenchestvo 1941–5 godov i general Vlasov', *Novy zhurnal*, 19 (1948), pp. 220–1.

20 Buchbender, O., *Das tönende Erz*, pp. 62–3, 100.

21 US National Archives NOKW 3569.

22 Dallin, A., *German Rule in Russia*, p. 567, n. 2.

23 '"Pochemu ya stal na put' bor'by s bolshevizmom." Otkrytoe pis'mo generala Vlasova', *Zarya* (3 March 1943) and in *Dobrovolets* (7 March 1943). See p. 51 and Appendix pp. 210–15.

24 For accounts of him see: Kitaev, M., *Communist Party Officials*, New York (1954), and *Materialy k istorii Osvoboditel'nogo Dvizheniya Narodov Rossii*, 1941–45, SBONR, London, Ontario (1970); Pozdnyakov, V. V., 'Meletii Aleksandrovich Zykov', *Novy zhurnal*, 103, (June 1971), pp. 153–68; Nikolaevsky archive, 201.1.2.

25 Interview: D. Galkin.

26 Kazantsev, A. S., *Tret'ya sila*, p. 174.

27 Dallin, A., *German Rule in Russia*, p. 530.

28 Steenberg, S., *Vlasov*, p. 44.

29 Kitaev, M., *Kak eto nachalos'*, New York (1970), pp. 10–11.

30 Strik-Strikfeldt, W., *Against Stalin and Hitler*, p. 105.

31 Typescript: 'K vospominaniyam o Zykove' Ot Pozdnyakova; Nikolaevsky archive, 201.1.2.

32 Nikolaevsky archive, Menlo Park.

33 Letter to author from A. Artemov, 30 April 1980. Theory put forward by A. N. Neimirok.

34 Interviews: K. G. Kromiadi, P. I. Kruzhin.

35 'Zagadka maiora Zykova', *Chasovoy*, no. 315 (January 1952).

36 Kitaev, M., *Materialy k istorii Osvoboditel'nogo Dvizheniya; Communist Party Officials; Kak eto nachalos'*. Op cit.

37 Kitaev, M., *Communist Party Officials*, p. 158.

38 See, for instance: Kromiadi, K. G., *Za zemlyu, za volyu ...*', pp. 157–8.

39 Kazantsev, A. S., *Tret'ya sila*, pp. 177–8.
40 Interview: N. G. Shtifanov.
41 Kitaev, M., *Communist Party Officials*, p. 153.
42 Kitaev, M., *Kak eto nachalos'*, pp. 12–13.
43 Kitaev, M., *Kak eto nachalos'*, pp. 18–19.
44 Veche was the town meeting or assembly. In Novgorod at the end of the eleventh century, the entire administration had become elective. It remained the dominant political body in the state until 1478 when Novgorod was annexed by Muscovy.
45 Stepan Timofeevich Razin, Cossack Ataman, who in 1670 led a rebel army up the Volga. The commanding officers of the garrisons, boyars and wealthy merchants were massacred. The rank and file were invited to join the rebel army and the municipal governments were reorganised along Cossack lines, with a general assembly of citizens which elected municipal officers. Peasants and local tribes joined the movement against their local landlords. In the autumn of 1670 the Moscow government put a regular army in the field which defeated Razin's army. Razin fled to the Don, but in 1671 was handed over to the Muscovite authorities and publicly executed.
46 Bogdan Khmelnitsky was a member of the Ukrainian gentry and Hetman of the Ukraine who in 1648 led the Zaporozhie Cossacks against the Poles and was instrumental in the incorporation of the Ukraine with the Russian state in 1654.
47 Emelian Pugachev, a Don Cossack who claimed to be Peter III, announced the abolition of serfdom and liberation of peasants belonging to serf owners and led a peasant revolt. He was executed in 1775.
48 Ivan I (1325–41) was prepared to co-operate with the Mongols, yet also increased his own territory and ransomed Russian prisoners from the Mongols.
49 Interviews: D. Galkin, N. A. Noreikis, N. G. Shtifanov.
50 'General Vlasov v 16'oy Armii' in Pozdnyakov, V. V., *Vlasov*, p. 95.
51 Demsky, A., 'A. A. Vlasov v batal'ione Volga'; Pozdnyakov, V. V., *A. A. Vlasov*, p. 82; Hromenko, G. D., 'Diary' in Pozdnyakov, V. V., *A. A. Vlasov*, p. 102; '"General Vlasov v Rige"', Vospominaniya morskogo ofitsera Aprel' 1943', *Russkoe vozrozhdenie*, vol. 10, New York (1980), p. 105.
52 Fischer, G., *Soviet Opposition to Stalin*, p. 61.
53 'Doklad general-mayora V. F. Malyshkina na I-oy antibol'shevistskoy konferentsii voennoplennykh komandirov i boytsov Krasnoy Armii, stavshikh v ryady Russkogo Osvoboditel'nogo Dvizheniya', Pozdnyakov, V. V., *Rozhdenie ROA*, pp. 139–51; *Zarya* (18 April 1943).
54 Pozdnyakov, V. V., *Rozhdenie ROA*, pp. 152–5.
55 Dallin, A., and Mavrogordato, R. S., 'The Soviet Reaction to Vlasov', *World Politics*, 8 (April 1956), pp. 307–22; Armstrong, J. A., *Soviet Partisans in World War II*, pp. 243–6; Hoffmann, J., *Die Geschichte der Wlassow-Armee*, pp. 331–57.
56 'Aufzeichnung: Betr. Vernehmung des Spions Kapustin der unter anderen mit dem Auftrag herüberkam, terroristiche Gruppen zum Zwecke der Ermordung von Wlassow zu bilden'. Captured German files. FCO 997/305 056-058, 997/305 067-071. Armstrong, J., *Soviet Partisans in*

World War II, pp. 246–8.

57 Kapustin is not mentioned in any of the Russian literature on the Liberation Movement. After his interrogations in July 1943, Kapustin's name does not reappear in the German files. It can only be supposed that after his interrogation he was shot as a Soviet spy.

58 Ausky, S. A., *Predatel'stvo i izmena*, p. 26.

59 'Konstitutsiya Rossiiskoy Derzhavy (proekt KONR)', B. I. Nikolaevsky Collection No. 201, Box I. 1.4. Hoover Institution.

60 Sobor, or council, is often thought of in connection with 'zemskii sobor' dating from the Muscovite period. A sobor could be either an electoral or a consultative body.

61 Interview: N. A. Noreikis.

62 Interview: A. N. Zaitsev.

63 Interview: N. A. Noreikis.

64 Interview: A. N. Zaitsev.

65 Interview: N. A. Noreikis.

66 Interview: A. N. Zaitsev.

67 Interviews: D. Galkin, S. B. Fröhlich, N. G. Shtifanov.

68 Interviews: S. B. Fröhlich, N. G. Shtifanov.

69 See pp. 7–8 and 61–2.

70 'Russkoe Osvoboditel'noe Dvizhenie. Komitet Narodov Rossii'. On the back cover: Deutsche Informations Stelle, 7, Chang An Lui. (Gt. Western Road), Shanghai. 1944. From the mistakes in the spelling it seems reasonable to assume that the document was translated from Russian into German and then back into Russian. N. Ivanov. Private archive.

71 Interviews: D. Galkin, N. A. Noreikis, N. G. Shtifanov, A. N. Zaitsev.

72 Text in *Volya Naroda* (15 November 1944) and see Appendix pp. 216–23.

73 Interviews: N. A. Noreikis, R. N. Redlich, A. N. Zaitsev and Anon.

74 BA. NS 31.34 Besprechung mit dem Vertreter der Aserbeidjaner. BA. NS 31.28 Zusammenfassung der nichtrussischen Gruppen. IZ. Thorwald ZS 399. Armstrong, J. A., *Ukrainian Nationalism*, London (1963), p. 182. Shandruk, A., *Arms of Valor*, New York (1959), pp. 203–4.

75 BA. NS 31.30 National-Turkestanisches Einheitskomitee.

76 See section on Soviet propaganda, and the instructions given to Kapustin, pp. 120–2.

77 Interview: Y. A. Muzychenko.

78 Pozdnyakov, V. V., *A. A. Vlasov*, p. 185.

79 Kroeger. Letter 24 March 1979 to the author asserts that the policy of KONR was the continuation of the idea 'edinaya i nedelimaya'. An unidentified commentator also considers that there was a group within KONR who favoured this approach, but that they were not very influential. BA. NS 31.28 Kurze Information über die wichtigsten Prinzipien der Ideologie des Komitees zur Befreiung der Völker Russlands.

80 For antisemitism see pp. 133–5.

81 Pismenny, Y., 'Ob odnom voprose svyazannom s Manifestom', *Vlasovets*, no. 3, Munich (1950) pp. 7–8. There is no documentary evidence on this point, and given the circumstances of composition, it would be foolish to expect there to be such evidence.

82 Nikolaevsky, B. I., 'Porazhenchestvo 1941–1945 godov i gen. A. A. Vlasov', *Novy zhurnal*, 18 (1948), p. 225.

83 See above, p. 91.

84 Interviews: A. Kiselev, M. V. Schatoff, A. N. Zaitsev, US National Archives SHAEF, 12th Army Group, 24 April 1945.

85 Interview: Anon.

86 See p. 161, n. 70.

87 Interview: A. N. Zaitsev.

88 Shandruk, A., *Arms of Valor*, pp. 203–5.

89 'Pis'mo generala Krasnova', *Kazach'ya zemlya*, 12 (16 March 1945); 'Otvet gen. A. A. Vlasova' and 'Otvet Kazach'ego Upravleniya pri KONR', *Put' na rodinu*, 2 (3 April 1945); reprinted *Bor'ba*, 29/30 (1950). See p. 64.

90 Tys-Krokhmaliuk, Y., *U.P.A. Warfare in the Ukraine*, New York (1972), p. 46.

91 For a transcript of the proceedings, see Pozdnyakov, V. V., *A. A. Vlasov*, pp. 142–65.

92 See: Aronson, G. Ya., 'Po povodu statey B. I. Nikolaevskogo o vlasovskom dvizhenii', *Novy zhurnal*, 20 (1949), p. 274; Aronson, G. Ya., *Pravda o vlasovtsakh, problemy novoy emigratsii*; Dvinov, B., *Vlasovskoe dvizhenie v svete dokumentov*; and the correspondence in *Sotsialisticheskiy vestnik* following article by Abramovich, R., 'O chem my sporim' (1948).

93 'Rech' Gen. Malyshkina', *Parizhskiy vestnik*, no. 59 (31 July 1943).

94 See, for example: Aronson, G. Ya., 'Po povodu statey B. I. Nikolaevskogo o vlasovskom dvizhenii', *Novy zhurnal*, 20 (1949), p. 274.

95 Nikolaevsky, B. I., 'Otvet G. Ya., Aronsonu', *Novy zhurnal*, 20 (1949), pp. 281–92.

96 US National Archives, 'Doklad general-maiora V. F. Malyshkina na konferentsii, sozvannoy Germanskim Institutom Mezhdunarodnoy Politiki' and *Volya naroda* (24 January 1945).

97 Interview: Y. S. Zherebkov.

98 Kazantsev, A. S., *Tret'ya sila*, p. 179. Kitaev, M., *Kak eto nachalos'*, p. 7.

99 Strik-Strikfeldt, W., *Against Stalin and Hitler*, p. 114.

100 Zhilenkov, G. N., 'Das ist die UdSSR', *Völkischer Beobachter*, Berlin (20 January 1945).

101 Pozdnyakov, V. V., *A. A. Vlasov*, p. 203.

102 Interview: N. G. Shtifanov.

103 YIVO 6.PA. 14 Dr Taubert, 'Querschnitt durch die Tätigkeit des Arbeitsgebietes'.

104 *Bloknot Propagandista Osvoboditel'nogo Dvizheniya Narodov Rossii*. No. 5–6, January 1945. Izdatel'stvo glavnogo upravleniya propagandy Komiteta Osvobozhdeniya Narodov Rossii. According to the introduction, *Bloknot Propagandista* was going to discuss the following subjects: (1) The ideological basis of the Movement; (2) The social basis of the new national-labour system; (3) The basis of the new state; (4) The economy (labour, property, industry, agriculture, trade, etc.); (5) Social policies; (questions of material, physical and moral strengthening of the people) (6) The psychological (*dukhovny*) life of the nation (culture, education, religion, etc.); (7) The outlook for the political and military struggle

against Bolshevism; (8) The outlook for the formation of the national-labour system. However, with the exception of Nos. 5–6, which dealt with the ideological basis of the Movement, no other parts of *Bloknot Propagandista* were published. Written by Galkin, with an introduction by Pershin.

105 The terms Bolshevism and communism are used almost interchangeably in *Bloknot Propagandista*. However, communism is more frequently used when referring to the theory, whereas Bolshevism is used to describe a Soviet reality, and in that case Bolshevism has a pejorative connotation.

106 As Galkin explains in *Bloknot Propagandista*, p. 13, Soviet society had been declared to be socialist in 1935, at the Seventh Congress of the Comintern. Manuil'sky, D. Z., *Itogi sotsialisticheskogo stroitel'stva v SSSR*, Leningrad (1933), p. 4.

107 Bystryanskiy, V. and Myshin, M. (eds.), *Leninizm, khrestomatiya*, Leningrad (1933), p. 485; letter from Galkin to author, 2 April 1984.

108 Stalin, I. V., 'Marxism i natsional'ny vopros', [1913], *Sochineniya*, 2, Moscow (1946–55), p. 305.

109 Kozma Minin's and Prince D. M. Pozharsky's defence of Moscow in 1612 became a symbol of patriotic heroism during the Second World War both for Stalin and for the Russian Liberation Movement.

110 Stalin, I. V., 'Otchetny doklad XVII s'ezdu partii o rabote TsK VKP(b)', [26 January 1934], *Sochineniya*, 13, p. 348.

111 Galkin's view is extremely simplified. See, for instance: Kolakowski, L., *Main Currents of Marxism*, London (1981), vol. 1, p. 360.

112 Stalin, I. V., 'Rech' na pervom vsesoyuznom soveshchanii stakhanovtsev', [17 November 1936], *Sochineniya*, 14, pp. 83–4.

113 *Bloknot Propagandista* is not mentioned in any English language study of the Russian Liberation Movement. Fischer in *Opposition to Stalin* devotes a great deal of attention to the ideas of the movement, but does not seem to know of *Bloknot*. I was able to obtain a copy after correspondence and an interview with the author of *Bloknot*, Captain Galkin.

114 Galkin was considered to be among the more 'left-wing' of the staff at Dabendorf. Interview: N. G. Shtifanov. He was a friend of Bushmanov, who was discovered to be a communist agitator and who was eventually shot by the German authorities. Nemirov, A., 'Sud'ba polkovnika Bushmanova'. Pozdnyakov, V. V., *Rozhdenie ROA*, p. 97.

115 The so-called 'left-wing' point of view left little in the way of written evidence of its position. Since the chief exponent of this attitude was Zykov, who was supposed to be a Marxist, it is likely that, had he still been alive, he and his supporters would have taken issue with Galkin over *Bloknot Propagandista*. Kitaev, M., 'Russkoe Osvoboditel'noe Dvizhenie', *Materialy k istorii Osvoboditel'nogo Dvizheniya Narodov Rossii 1941–1945*, pp. 53, 65.

116 Galkin considered that the ideology of the Russian Liberation Movement existed not so much in the written statements of the Movement but in the constant discussions of the members. Captain Galkin, D., 'Predislovie. Ideologicheskaya doktrina osvoboditel'nogo dvizheniya', *Bor'ba*, no. 6/7 (June/July 1949), III.

117 Fischer, G., *Soviet Opposition to Stalin*, p. 69.
118 Shtifanov, N., 'Dabendorf', *Novoe Russkoe Slovo* (8 February 1974); Interviews: D. Galkin, A. N. Zaitsev; Pshenichny, G., 'Dabendorf' in Pozdnyakov, V. V., *A. A. Vlasov*, p. 64.
119 *Biblioteka Propagandista*, izdanie kursov propagandistov Russkoy Osvoboditel'noy Armii (1944).
120 Pshenichny, G., 'Kursy propagandistov v Wulheide' and 'Dabendorf' in Pozdnyakov, V. V., *Rozhdenie ROA*, pp. 22–7, 44, 59.
121 Ternovsky, Y., and Bezdetny, T., 'Lager' nadezhd i razdumiy' in Pozdnyakov, V. V., *Rozhdenie ROA*, pp. 28–30. Pozdnyakov, V. V., 'Podgotovitel'nye kursy ROA' in *Rozhdenie ROA*, pp. 31–8.
122 Strik-Strikfeldt, W., *Against Stalin and Hitler*, pp. 95–102.
123 Pozdnyakov, V. V., 'Kursy propagandistov ROA v Dabendorfe' in *Rozhdenie ROA*, pp. 103–9.
124 Interviews: A. N. Zaitsev, N. G. Shtifanov.
125 Interview: A. N. Zaitsev. Strik-Strikfeldt, W., *Against Stalin and Hitler*, pp. 117, 199.
126 Fischer, G., *Soviet Opposition to Stalin*, p. 68.
127 *Voin ROA* (*etika, oblik, povedenie*), izdatel'stvo shkoly propagandistov Russkoy Osvoboditel'noy Armii (1944) in Pozdnyakov, V. V., *Rozhdenie ROA*, pp. 205–38.
128 The booklet was written by Zaitsev's future wife. She explained that she had entitled the booklet 'Ethics' instead of 'Etiquette' since the idea of etiquette would have been rejected out of hand by its readers as being synonymous with snobbery, and unnecessary. Andreyev, N., Memoirs, pp. 940–1.
129 Spiridonov, Polkovnik, A. I., *Formy i metody ustnoy propagandy*. Izdatel'stvo glavnogo upravleniya propagandy Komiteta Osvobozhdeniya Narodov Rossii (1945).
130 Strik-Strikfeldt, W., *Against Stalin and Hitler*, p. 115. Kitaev, M., 'Russkoe Osvoboditel'noe Dvizhenie', *Materialy k istorii Osvoboditel'nogo Dvizheniya Narodov Rossii 1941–1945*, p. 40.
131 Captain Galkin, D., 'Predislovie. Ideologicheskaya doktrina osvoboditel'nogo dvizheniya', *Bor'ba*, no. 6/7 (June/July 1949), III.
132 BA. NS 31 28 Kurze Information über die wichtigsten Prinzipien der Ideologie des Komitees zur Befreiung der Völker Russlands.
133 *Skhema Natsional'no-Trudovogo Stroya* (1944).
134 Kitaev, M., *Kak eto nachalos'*, pp. 18–19; *Materialy k istorii Osvoboditel'nogo Dvizheniya Narodov Rossii 1941–1945*, p. 35. Interview: N. G. Shtifanov.
135 Interview: N. G. Shtifanov.

3

The Russian Idea

After the initial expression of dissatisfaction with the Stalinist regime, coupled with their desire to turn this discontent to good account, the leadership of the Russian Liberation Movement was confronted with the problem of creating a programme with a positive content. It was not sufficient to state that the Russian Liberation Movement aimed to abrogate Stalinist policies; Vlasov and his colleagues had to try and provide a forward-looking plan of action for their adherents. As the leadership worked on this task, they began to realise some of the political and ideological implications of their position. Since the Movement was critical of Stalinism, the question of the genesis of the Stalinist system – the two Revolutions of February and October 1917 – had to be discussed.

An evaluation of these Revolutions has proved to be at the core of debates not only in the Russian Liberation Movement but for all groups and movements opposed to the Soviet regime, both within the Soviet Union and supported by Russians outside the country. Such opposition is faced with the question as to whether the February Revolution of 1917 should be seen as the signal for democratic progress, and whether the achievements of February were subsequently subverted by the Bolshevik *coup d'état* in October. If Bolshevism had been imposed from above by an unrepresentative group of revolutionaries who made use of coercion to put their ideas into practice, then Stalinism could be seen as a product of Bolshevik ideology. Or would it be true to say that the February Revolution had not made any significant difference to the country's political structure and that the October Revolution had been the manifestation of the will of the people? According to the latter interpretation, Stalinism has to be understood as a corruption of the ideals of October rather than as a product of these aspirations. Any assessment has to take into account the fact that the peasantry had been given the land, which they regarded as theirs for many generations, as a result of the October Revolution, whereas the revolutionaries of February had postponed decisions of this question. Any appraisal of the Revolution means that the position of Lenin, his views and actions, also must be assessed. The answers to these questions determine the parameters and path of the programme of any Russian movement of opposition.

Such a schematic analysis obviously ignores nuances of historical interpretation and generates disagreement. In order to avoid the inevitable divisions which the answers to these questions would produce, the leadership of the Russian Liberation Movement tried to minimise the differences of emphasis. The Prague Manifesto referred to 'the Revolution of 1917' without specifying whether this meant February or October and without elaborating on any of the issues raised about the nature of the two revolutions. According to Galkin, who did not provide an explanation for this division of opinion, by and large the military leadership of the Russian Liberation Movement felt that October 1917 had been the signal for real progress and that the Bolshevik seizure of power had been in response to the wishes of the people. There was considerable pressure from many of the civilians in the Movement, as well as from émigré supporters, to modify this point of view and accept the February Revolution as the signal for democratic progress, thereby designating October as a *coup d'état* by the Bolsheviks. The leaders of the Russian Liberation Movement, while anxious to preserve an alliance between those of differing opinions, were not prepared to repudiate their view of October and thus denigrate Lenin. Despite the lengthy and detailed criticism in *Bloknot Propagandista*, not only of Stalinism but also of communism, the question of the relation of Stalinist policies to the Revolutions of 1917 was not raised. Similarly, the role of Lenin and his connection with communism was not discussed since the diverse answers to these questions would not only have destroyed the broad consensus of opinion, which the leadership of the Russian Liberation Movement strenuously sought to create and maintain, but by implication would have raised the issue of the legitimacy of the Soviet regime itself, a concept which was very hard to accept for those who were products of the system.

The acceptance of the October Revolution as initiating a genuine democracy in Russia, links the Russian Liberation Movement with the best known of all the risings against the Soviet regime, the Kronstadt rising of 1921.[1] While it is clear from occasional references, found chiefly in memoirs,[2] that other risings and revolts have occurred in the USSR, the authorities have not made information about such incidents available and the paucity and inaccessibility of the material makes it very difficult to assess the nature of these uprisings. Notable exceptions to this rule were revolts which occurred in the wake of the Civil War: the Antonov peasant rising in Tambov province and the revolt led by Makhno in the Ukraine, where sufficient material exists for research to be pursued. Although an account of a conspiracy amongst the Far Eastern Command[3] has been greeted probably incorrectly, with scepticism, by Western scholars,[4] no reliable criterion has been adduced to prove or disprove its author's contentions.

After the Second World War, survivors of the Russian Liberation Movement considered that their efforts to criticise the regime in the Soviet Union in many aspects bore a striking resemblance to the views expressed by the Kronstadt sailors and with hindsight saw the Kronstadt revolt as a direct precursor of the wartime opposition.[5] The wartime documents do not provide much written evidence to show that the supporters of the Russian Liberation Movement thought a great deal about the Kronstadt rebellion, although the war hardly provided the opportunity for historical research; yet interesting similarities between the two movements exist which support this post-war appreciation[6] of the relationship between these two attempts to put forward an alternative programme for the government of the USSR.

In the Kronstadt programme political demands took pride of place even though the economic hardships of War Communism produced the conditions which fuelled the revolt. These demands reflected the insurgents' experience of 1917. Democracy was to be produced by having free elections to the Soviets. This would end the hegemony of the Communist party and give workers and peasants the political rights which they had obtained after the October Revolution of 1917. The Kronstadters did not consider that the February Revolution had effected any real change in the power structure. They abhorred the tsarist regime and scorned the bourgeoisie and the Constituent

Assembly. When change was achieved in October 1917, the Bolshevik party claimed that it alone represented the wishes of the
workers and of the peasantry. The insurgents on board the battleship
Petropavlovsk passed a resolution which they hoped would correct this
appropriation by the Bolsheviks of power entrusted to them. The
Resolution[7] specified certain administrative changes: secret ballots,
increased freedom of the press, abolition of the political departments
in order to allow the other socialist parties the opportunity of
expressing their views. For the Kronstadters, democracy was a
privilege which was to include only the left wing groups: socialists,
Marxists and anarchists; there was no provision for the expression of
centrist or right-wing views.

The insurgents were concerned with the issues of 1917: power and
democracy. Lenin had sacrificed democracy to considerations of
power, and the Kronstadters wished to rectify this. Although the
Kronstadters saw democracy, as expressed by the system of local
Soviets, which they had lived through in 1917, as the best way to
express their views, they were not merely harking back to an earlier
situation but felt that the revolutionary spirit could and must be
utilised to make further progress. In a key article, 'What we are
fighting for' (*Za chto my boremsya*) one of the editors, A. Lamanov,[8] put
their views very clearly: 'Here in Kronstadt we have laid the first
stone of the *third revolution* [my emphasis–C.A.] which will free the
working masses from their remaining fetters and open new wide
paths for socialist development (*sotsialisticheskoe tvorchestvo*).'[9] This
elaboration of the *Petropavlovsk* Resolution indicates an awareness
that the processes started in 1917 remained incomplete and that a
return to the earlier forms of Soviet democracy would not suffice.
Lamanov must have realised that although the vision of the people's
democracy of 1917 was a powerful rallying cry, it was not enough to
look back to the achievements of a bygone era, a way forward had to
be found and further evolution of the programme was necessary.

Many of these attitudes and ideas are echoed in the programme of
the Russian Liberation Movement. Western democracy was viewed
with caution by members of the Movement, and political parties were
thought to be power-hungry and more interested in their own
well-being than that of the country as a whole. The Kronstadters and
the supporters of the Russian Liberation Movement shared a
common outlook on the achievements of the Soviet state. For
example, they were not prepared to repudiate the state *in toto*, as did

those on the White side in the Civil War, but wanted instead to work for peaceful reform which would lead to a modification of the hegemony of the Communist party. Where the Kronstadters hoped to achieve this by calling for new elections to the Soviets, supporters of the Russian Liberation Movement hoped that national elections would provide a true representation of the views of the population.

Both the Kronstadters and the supporters of the Russian Liberation Movement saw 1917 as the inauguration of a process which could only be brought to fruition by a new 'third' revolution. The Kronstadters had been influenced by ideas current in 1917 when so many theories were in the melting pot, and this gave them a clearer idea of what might be expected by such a 'third revolution'. Supporters of the Russian Liberation Movement had to elaborate their idea in the hostile environment of the Third Reich yet lacked the revolutionary experience of the Kronstadters to develop this concept. However, in his Open Letter, Vlasov called for 'the completion of the national revolution' and it is clear that many Vlasovites considered that the Bolsheviks had subsequently used the power entrusted to them by the people in October to further their own ends. The 'national revolution' was to complete the process begun in February 1917 and was to give back to the people their right to decide their own future.

2 FROM FOREIGN SHORES

Although superficially it might appear that the experience of the Russian émigré communities after 1917 had little bearing on the lives of their Soviet compatriots, such a judgement would ignore the exchange of ideas and influences between the Soviet Union and the Russian emigration. The history of the Russian emigration, particularly the first emigration, which left after 1917 and the Civil War, is part of Russian cultural history.[10] Literature and art cross-fertilised with one another. Equally ideas originating within the emigration must also be considered part of the development of social and political thought within the Soviet Union. The emigration remained passionately interested in developments within the Soviet Union and constantly discussed and evaluated events there. The émigrés were able to discuss ideas when their Soviet compatriots did not have the freedom to do so. These ideas filtered back through official and underground channels. Communication was particularly easy and open in the 1920s, but even when links were more difficult to maintain, viewpoints were exchanged and still continue to be so. Some groups, such as the Change of Signposts Group (*Smena vekh*),[11] had an immediate impact on Soviet society; other movements and concepts took much longer to filter back, but nevertheless the émigré world remained an important powerhouse of ideas.

Since the Russian communities abroad after 1917 had left their country because of the Revolution and the Civil War, it was axiomatic for them that in order to give voice to their opposition to the Soviet regime, an assessment of the Revolution was ineluctable. The period 1920–39 saw a variety of émigré responses to this need for an evaluation of the Revolution and subsequent Soviet policy.

It might be argued that the post-1917 emigration had little in common with the Russian Liberation Movement since the émigrés had not experienced the realities of Soviet society, whereas the Movement was a product of that environment. However, one of the Russian émigré organisations, *Natsional'no-Trudovoy Soyuz*, NTS, (the National Labour Alliance)[12] had a very significant influence on the Liberation Movement. Members of the NTS made contact with their 'Vlasovite' compatriots and discussed the theories of the NTS in the light of the experience of these Soviet citizens. Areas of agreement between the two groups became apparent. The NTS performed a valuable service not simply by providing an outline programme, but rather by suggesting ideas and expressing opinions which stimulated members of the Movement to elaborate political alternatives for the Soviet Union. It is indisputable that the ideology and programme of the Russian Liberation Movement was developed *in part* as a result of the reaction of its members to ideas which they found current among the émigrés. The NTS, in its turn, was undeniably a product of émigré political development. Within ten years of the beginning of exile, the younger émigrés decided that their elders were conducting the struggle against Bolshevism incompetently, and that their views of the new Russian state were becoming increasingly out of date. In the throes of their reaction against the policies and ideas of their elders, these younger people grouped together and a new political party, the NTS, evolved. The members of the NTS belonged predominantly to the younger generation of émigrés who had received their education abroad.

What then were the ideas against which the members of the NTS reacted and which new developments were they seeking? The diversification among the main émigré political groupings had certainly not succeeded in developing a coherent line of action *vis-à-vis* the Soviet Union.

Exact figures for those who left Russia following the Revolution and the Civil War do not exist, though most estimates range between one and two million people.[13] A large proportion of those who had left were well-educated[14] and most believed that their exile would be of a short duration.[15] Their belief in the inevitability of a speedy return home was not simply the product of purely human reaction that it was inconceivable that they would never see their homes again, or that the difficulties of émigré existence could only be surmounted with the aid of such a belief. Neither was it merely the result of their inability to suppose that they could have so mismanaged events that power 'had been left lying on the streets' and that the riff-raff of society had been able to seize it and drive the former ruling classes from the country. Developments in Soviet politics reinforced the émigré view that the regime was bound to collapse or to evolve so substantially that everyone would be able to return home. In 1921 Lenin had been forced to introduce the New Economic Policy as a result of the failure of War Communism. His modification of policy seemed to provide clear proof that the Bolsheviks had at last realised that their ideological position as originally conceived was not tenable. Thus the émigrés concluded that further evolution of the regime was inevitable.[16] In addition to this apparent economic liberalism, relative ease of communication with Russia now became possible and Soviet citizens were permitted to travel abroad. Some intellectuals left the USSR,[17] while others returned home.[18] Many refugees, particularly rank and file members of the armed forces, including a large number of Cossacks, also returned.[19] The works of some Russian writers were being published both outside and inside the Soviet Union in the early 1920s.[20] However, with Stalin's rise to power this freedom was sharply curtailed. As a result, the émigré world found itself cut off from and ignorant of events within Stalinist Russia. In the 1930s Stalin was understood to be propagating nationalist policies which were on the whole acceptable to many Russians abroad.[21] When it became clear that war between the Third Reich and the Soviet Union was likely, patriotism took precedence over the previous political judgements of many members of the emigration.[22] For although they considered the government of the Soviet Union to be their ideological foe, the inhabitants were nevertheless their compatriots, and they did not wish to see their country defeated and dismembered.[23] Only after the war, during the period 1945–7,[24] did it finally become evident to the émigrés that the Soviet regime had not changed, that fundamental reforms would not take place in the near future, and that the desired return home was not feasible.

The old emigration had been concentrated in Europe. Berlin, the centre in the early 1920s, soon gave way to Paris as the cultural, social and political hub of the emigration. German visas had been easy to obtain and the cost of living was low, but with the onset of severe inflation in 1923, this was no longer the case.[25] Furthermore, with the treaty of Rapallo, in 1922, came the improvement of relations between Germany and the Soviet Union, and Germany became a less welcoming place for anti-Soviet political exiles. In addition to Paris and Berlin, large communities could be found in Prague and Belgrade as well as in Poland, the Baltic States and Bulgaria. Further émigré communities existed in the Far East. Because they believed that their stay abroad would be of a temporary nature, the Russian émigrés did not see any real necessity to assimilate into their host societies. Despite difficulties arising from financial need and their status as 'stateless persons', most émigré activities centred on Russia and were justified in terms of the country's future. In the early 1920s the military continued to speak of a new campaign directed at the Bolsheviks,[26] so military formations and organisations were preserved for this purpose. Children were educated in Russian, along traditional lines of Russian education.[27] Many young men studied law, since any new post-Bolshevik regime would require administrators; a knowledge of law would equip them for that profession.[28] The same held even more true for émigré politics. Russia remained the focus of all discussions and it was a common assumption that the Bolsheviks were unlikely to retain power for long.

Russian émigré politics represented a vast spectrum of opinion. On the right wing, there were those who believed in autocratic monarchism, and those like Markov II[29] who was, in addition, extremely anti-semitic. There were representatives of the constitutional period of the Russian monarchy and of the Civil War. On the left, the views of Socialist Revolutionaries (SRs), Mensheviks, anarchists, and with the arrival of Trotsky abroad, the Bolsheviks, found a place.

The pre-revolutionary parties tended to relive their experience of tsarist government and of 1917, and continued the arguments which had originated in that period. Of these, the Constitutional Democrats or the Kadet party survived the shortest time in emigration. By 1920, splits among its members were evident. Some felt that General Baron Wrangel, still fighting in the Crimea, and the policy of military intervention, had to be supported. Others, led by Milyukov, considered that the party had to rethink its position and its policies. Milyukov advocated a tactical coalition with the socialists in order to work for an 'all-Russian' political coalition. Milyukov's ideas were derided both by the socialists and by those Kadets still supporting Wrangel.[30] The division among the leadership was symbolised by the appointment of V. D. Nabokov as editor of the Kadet newspaper *Rul'* in Berlin, supported by I. V. Gessen[31] and P. I. Novgorodtsev.[32] Milyukov became editor of the Paris daily newspaper *Poslednie novosti* from 1921–40. In July 1921, Milyukov announced the formation of the Democratic Group of the Party of National Freedom (*Demokraticheskaya Grouppa Partii Narodnoy Svobody*),[33] and the split appeared to be complete. In March 1922, after Nabokov's assassination,[34] the Kadet party was bereft of leadership and later that year was officially dissolved,[35] although *Rul'* continued to appear until 1931 and *Poslednie novosti* until 1940. The Kadet point of view could be said to have been expressed by the group around Milyukov even if the party no longer existed officially.

The divisions in the socialist bloc of the emigration appear to have been rather ill-defined and members of the SRs participated in a large number of publications. V. M. Zenzinov, V. I. Lebedev and O. S. Minor, as well as A. F. Kerensky, edited a daily paper in Prague, *Volya Rossii*. This closed in 1921 but was resurrected in 1922 as a weekly newspaper by V. I. Lebedev, and the other SRs, M. L. Slonim and V. V. Sukhomlin. Later, it became a fortnightly newspaper and in 1924 a monthly publication, a metamorphosis which was typical of many émigré publications. Those who supported Kerensky worked on the Berlin daily newspaper *Golos Rossii* which was replaced by *Dni*. Shortly afterwards *Dni* was moved to Paris. In Paris *Sovremennye zapiski* became a quarterly, and was edited by the right wing SRs, V. V. Rudnev, M. V. Vishnyak and A. I. Gukovsky.[36]

The Mensheviks were most successful in preserving their organisation in the emigration while also retaining one within the Soviet Union, although this came increasingly under attack. A further centre of the party grouped around the editorial board of

Sotsialisticheskiy vestnik. There were party organisations in Berlin, Geneva, Liège, Paris, Bern and New York. However, no new members joined the party, with the exception of the offspring of the existing members! The Mensheviks lacked a medium from which to recruit new and trustworthy members. Despite party discipline, rifts occurred in 1927 with the left being led by F. I. Dan, and the centre by R. A. Abramovich, D. Yu. Dallin and B. I. Nikolaevsky. The split occurred over the question as to whether the Soviet regime was evolving. The rightists considered their original position, taken in 1917 – that Lenin's seizure of power would not evolve into true democratic socialism and therefore should not be supported – as correct, and consequently defended it.[37]

Although the old pre-revolutionary groups continued to exist, they became, to a large extent, politically redundant. Events had overtaken them and shown their programmes to be irrelevant. They no longer had an environment within which to function and from which they could attract support. Furthermore, their loyalties to past traditions and points of view made it difficult for them to adapt to radically changed circumstances.

The need to come to terms with the fact of the Revolution and Bolshevik seizure of power, as well as the need for the émigrés to rationalise their own situation and to find a role for themselves produced a number of new departures and new approaches. One of these was the *Smena vekh* (Change of Signposts) Movement, named after a publication which appeared in Prague in 1921 under the same title.[38] This collection of essays was written by six members of the émigré community. The best known of them, N. V. Ustryalov, had been a Kadet and a supporter of Admiral Kolchak. All of them had links with the right wing of the White Movement during the Civil War. Ustryalov had first published his essay in Harbin in 1920.[39] The authors of these essays did not agree on all details but their overall attitude was similar. They wished the émigrés to come to terms with the fact of Bolshevik power and to acknowledge that their resistance to the Bolshevik regime had been mistaken. The contributors to this volume urged their fellow émigrés to come to terms with the fact that 'a Third Revolution would not occur'[40] and that opposition to the Soviet regime would only plunge the country into further bloodshed. S. S. Chakhotin considered that the émigrés had two potential roles to play. First, they could and should educate the populace in every possible way and support all the steps taken by the new state in this direction. Second, they had to take the most active part possible in the economic regeneration of the country.[41] This was seen not as support for Bolshevism but its transcendence (*preodolenie*), as most of the contributors to *Smena vekh* considered that the regime was showing signs of evolution which would continue. The émigré intellectuals were asked to acknowledge the national character of the Revolution and to abandon their prejudice that Bolshevism had no support within the country.[42] A few months after the publication of the *Smena Vekh* essays, a weekly journal under the same title was published in Paris. The last issue, no. 20, appeared on 25 March 1922 and was replaced by the daily paper *Nakanune* (*On the Eve*) which was published in Berlin and survived until 1924. A number of leading émigré writers[43] became interested in this ideology of National-Bolshevism, as Ustryalov's ideas came to be called, but the ideas of the *Smena vekh* group were alien to the mass of the emigration who saw these views as a betrayal of the aspirations of both the émigrés and of Russia. *Smenovekhovstvo*, however, seems to have had a considerable following within the Soviet Union, and it has been argued that the ideas of National-Bolshevism lay at the root of many of Stalin's policies.[44]

The Eurasian Movement was another attempt to come to terms with the Revolution and to delineate a role for those intellectuals who found themselves in emigration. This Movement emerged in 1921 with the publication of a volume of essays, *Iskhod k Vostoku* (*Exodus to the East*),[45] and was followed by a further seven volumes, the last appearing in 1931. The *Eurasian Chronicle* appeared in twelve volumes between 1925 and 1937, in addition to other literary endeavours and programmes of the Movement.[46]

The Eurasian Movement found a following mainly among Russian émigré intellectuals and students. The Eurasians also claimed that they had support within the Soviet Union, and the 1927 programme of the Movement was supposed to have emanated from Moscow.[47] Contributors to the Eurasian Movement were predominantly scholars, and their attempts to provide a definition of Eurasia, its position geographically and culturally, and the qualities that it entailed, resulted in contributions to many fields of study, regardless of their links with Eurasia. N. S. Trubetskoy and R. O. Jakobson were philologists, G. V. Vernadsky was a historian; all took part in the Eurasian symposia and all became leading scholars in their respective disciplines.[48]

The unsigned introduction to *Iskhod k Vostoku*, probably written by P. N. Savitsky,[49] a geographer and one of the originators and longest-standing contributors to the Movement, explained that the Eurasians saw the Revolution as a cataclysmic event, which heralded a new age. The West was on the decline and the East would succeed as the centre of world culture.[50] The nature of this new culture was elaborated and developed in all later Eurasian publications. The Revolution was considered by the Eurasians to have a positive side. It was viewed as the logical culmination of Peter the Great's reforms and his attempt to turn Russia towards the West.[51] In so doing, Peter had created a rift between the rulers and the ruled. The Revolution, however, had unleashed forces which could be utilised to free Russia from Western influence, much of which was alien to her real nature. At the same time, the Eurasians were opposed to communism, and sought a new ideology, based on Christianity, to replace it.[52] One of the main faults of communism was that it took on many aspects of religion, although it had a purely materialist outlook. The religious dimensions of this new ideology would, in the opinion of the Eurasians, create an undivided 'symphonic' personality, both of the individual and of the state.[53] Thus, alienation of the individual and divisions within the state could be healed. The Eurasians saw life as the incarnation of an idea, and they conceived the state to be an ideocracy, that is, the reign of an idea, and led by a party which represented that idea. The model government was defined as demotic, broadly supported by the people, and acting in the interests of the people, but not democratic.[54] One author ascribes this opposition to democracy as a product of a general tendency to react against the petit-bourgeois (*meshchanskiy*) West and strongly emphasised the Eurasian conviction that Russia had a special path.[55]

This view of the uniqueness of Russian development as well as the religious basis of Eurasianism had obvious links with Slavophilism of the nineteenth century and with Danilevsky. The Eurasians criticised Catholicism and Protestantism as heretical and schismatic forms of Christianity, which did not allow for the development of the total personality. Orthodoxy, as the highest and purest form of Christianity, did so.[56]

The Eurasians recognised some of their debt to the Slavophiles but also expressed the view that they were not populists and did not link their ideas of individualism with that of a collective economic system as Herzen had done.[57] N. V. Riasanovsky considers that despite a

similarity in certain attitudes between the Eurasians and the Slavophiles, the Eurasian idea is a distinct break with previous Russian
intellectual traditions.[58] This can be explained first and foremost by
the traumatic effect of the Revolution on the Russian intelligentsia,
who, as a result, had to find a new way of assessing both their own
situation and what happened to their country.

In 1928, one of the founding members of Eurasianism, and a
contributor to *Iskhod k Vostoku*, G. V. Florovsky, broke with the
Movement and explained his reasons in an article, 'Evraziiskiy
Soblazn'.[59] He considered that although the Movement asked the
right questions about Russia's problems, it was not providing the
correct answers. His critique alleged that, although the Eurasians
considered that they would replace communism with an ideology
based on religion, they seemed to have mistaken the nature of faith,
and consequently had begun to adulate what they perceived as the
positive side of communism: this had led to support for what they saw
as acts of strength, which in Florovsky's view were merely barbarism
destroying the real nature of Russia. Although Florovsky's criticism
is based on a religious concept, which is at odds with that of the
Eurasians, he had pinpointed the cause of the increasing tension to be
found within the Movement. The attitude towards the Soviet Union
caused dissension within the ranks of the Eurasians[60] and was the
reason that other members of the Movement, notably S. G. Push-
karev, felt that they could no longer support Eurasianism.

Krest'yanskaya Rossiya (Peasant Russia) was a political organisation
of a rather different type. It originated in Moscow in 1920,[61] when a
number of individuals left the SR party. Details of the organisation
were smuggled abroad by one of its members. *Krest'yanskaya Rossiya*
began its official émigré existence with the publication of S. S.
Maslov's book in 1921, *Rossiya posle 4-kh let revolutsii* (*Russia After Four
Years of Revolution*), and in May 1922 the first official meeting of
members of *Krest'yanskaya Rossiya* took place in Prague. In October
the first nine issues of *Krest'yanskaya Rossiya* appeared, edited by A. A.
Argunov, A. L. Bem[62] and S. S. Maslov. After the formation of the
Prague group, further party organisations were created in Yugoslavia, Poland and, in 1927, in the Far East. In 1924, a hectographed
news-sheet was produced in Prague, which in 1925 appeared as a
printed newspaper, *Vestnik Krest'yanskoy Rossii*. In 1933 the name was
changed to *Znamya Rossii*, and publication continued until March
1939.

In 1925, at its first conference, *Krest'yanskaya Rossiya* officially designated itself a political party, took on the name of *Trudovaya Krest'yanskaya Partiya* (TKP) (Peasant Labour Party) and approved its detailed programme. It was agreed that the party should operate within the Soviet Union and that their links with people within Russia made it imperative that both the form and aims of the organisation should be very clear.

The programme[63] explains that while the party accepted the socialist analysis that society was divided into classes, it did not accept that the only possible relationship between classes had to be one of conflict. Members of *Krest'yanskaya Rossiya* considered that common interests did exist between different classes. From this it followed that, although they were the party of the peasantry as a whole – and it was further clarified that no one section of the peasantry was to be afforded preferential treatment – this did not mean that they would pursue their interests at the expense of all other classes in society. All forms of labour (*trud*), both manual and intellectual as the title of the party suggested, were valued, and it was hoped that the intelligentsia in particular would lend their support. *Krest'yanskaya Rossiya* took issue with the Russian Marxists who considered that the peasantry did not have interests in common with the proletariat and were really a part of the 'petty-bourgeoisie'.[64]

The programme of *Krest'yanskaya Rossiya* expounds the position of the peasantry as a separate class which had three separate roles. The peasantry included the farmer (*zemledelets*), the owner (*khozyain*) and the labourer (*rabotnik*). The growth of political consciousness among the peasantry as a separate identifiable class had created a sense of unity and purpose. *Krest'yanskaya Rossiya* considered that this process, the attempt by the peasantry to obtain a political voice and to participate in the political process, was particularly evident in Russia. However, this striving by the peasantry to become a political force did not mean that the interests of the country as a whole would be ignored. *Krest'yanskaya Rossiya* had produced an ideology, as the programme made clear, which was not a copy of socialist or liberal thinking, but which followed those ideas and had links with them. *Krest'yanskaya Rossiya* was an evolution of the existing situation rather than a replacement.

The basis of the ideology of *Krest'yanskaya Rossiya* was a concern for the welfare of the individual (*obshcheznachimoe blago chelovecheskoy lichnosti*). In order to carry this out, it was necessary to accept the importance of labour in all spheres of life and to democratise all the main areas of human life and culture. The section of the programme devoted to the ideology[65] of the party discussed nine subjects: the social ideal of the party, labour, the democratisation of culture, the basic method of democratisation, the basis of socio-economic policy, the socio-economic position of the peasantry, the peasantry and Russia, the intelligentsia and the peasantry, Russia's position in the world. *Krest'yanskaya Rossiya* would strive for freedom and this had to take the interests of labour into account. The interests of all labourers demanded that democratic processes should function in all areas of human endeavour. Democracy had to be achieved via education, which was acknowledged to be a slow process. With regard to the economic system, the party was not opposed to private property as such but was against exploitation and parasitical forms of private ownership of capital. *Krest'yanskaya Rossiya* favoured a mixed economy and considered that co-operative practices were most likely to be in the interests of the whole of society. Since the peasantry had interests both as landowner and as labourer, it was considered that they would find both the socialist conception of a nationalised economy and the unlimited power of capital equally alien. Thus, it was thought that the peasants would work for the best interests of all labouring groups and for equality of opportunity. Since the peasantry was the most important class in Russian society, its interests had to be taken into account, otherwise a conflict would occur. The intelligentsia were called upon to participate with the peasantry to work for the good of the country. The programme then detailed the type of society it hoped to achieve.[66] The unity of the country was to be preserved, Russia was conceived as a federation with responsible government elected by free and secret ballots. The judiciary was to be autonomous and easily accessible. All nationalities would be equal. The economy was to be developed, paying particular attention to agriculture and rural industries. Education was to be encouraged but was to be free of political interference. The programme also maintained that *Krest'yanskaya Rossiya* would allow freedom of religion, support for family life, introduce social benefits for less fortunate members of society and would improve health care. In international politics Russia would strive for world peace.

This very detailed programme, which was designed to supplant Bolshevik policy, seems to have had a certain amount of success. The TKP had made it clear that they would never co-operate with the Bolsheviks.[67] The Moscow group of *Trudovaya Krest'yanskaya Partiya* was proscribed by the authorities in 1925.[68] The émigré section of the party continued to send in illegal literature[69] via contacts in the frontier areas of the Soviet Union. These links were largely destroyed during collectivisation when most of the peasants in the frontier areas were resettled. Solzhenitsyn states that Stalin had considered having a show trial of members of TKP, but had then reconsidered this idea.[70] Solzhenitsyn suggests that this may have been because Stalin sensed that such a trial would merely have brought attention to the discrepancy between Soviet policy and the desires of the peasantry.[71] Even though this trial never took place, the Soviet authorities appear to have taken the activities of the émigré section of the TKP quite seriously. Once the Red Army controlled Prague in 1945, a specially detailed NKVD officer, who was an expert on TKP and its leaders, was sent to Prague to arrest the officers of the party and bring them back to the Soviet Union.[72] A. L. Bem committed suicide by jumping out of a window, while being interrogated by SMERSH.[73]

Emigré attempts to come to terms with the Revolution and with events inside the Soviet Union and to find a solution to their country's problems continued throughout the 1930s. An added element enters the picture: the disagreement between generations known as 'Fathers and Sons'.[74] The younger generation of émigrés, most of whom had left Russia at an early age and had received most of their education abroad, reacted not only against the pre-revolutionary politicians as their fathers had done, but also against the views of their elders, the older generation of émigrés.

Novy grad[75] was a journal which produced fourteen issues between 1931 and 1939. Many of its contributors, for example, I. I. Fonda-minsky-Bunakov, F. A. Stepun and G. P. Fedotov, had been involved in *Sovremmenye zapiski*,[76] one of the leading journals of the emigration. N. A. Berdyaev was also closely associated with *Novy grad*. The contributors to this journal, although part of the so-called older generation, displayed many of the characteristics of the younger 'émigré sons'. They were becoming increasingly dis-enchanted with democracy, which was seen to be weak and was also linked to the capitalist system. They were further disappointed by the failure of the anti-Bolshevik struggle. The contributors to this journal perceived that the world was in crisis,[77] and that a war was in the offing, with which the democracies would be unable to cope. The solution proposed by the *Novogradtsy* was a form of 'Christian Socialism', although they did not use this term. They considered that freedom was the most important feature of their programme. 'We defend the eternal truth of the personality and its freedom, above all the freedom of the spirit from fascism.'[78] This could only be done by means of Christianity which affirmed 'the equality of the whole and its parts, of the individual and of the world, the church and human souls'.[79] The *Novogradtsy* rejected the bourgeois and socialist solutions to the world crisis and believed that a 'New Man' (*novy chelovek*) was arising in the Soviet Union. V. V. Rudnev criticised this whole movement in an article in *Sovremennye zapiski*, considering that the position taken up by *Novy grad* was far too vague.[80]

Novy grad, however, in its rejection of the bourgeois, capitalist world and its anticipation of the emergence of some new force from the Soviet Union, was typical of many émigré movements. Similar sentiments, although without the Christian basis, were expressed in the journal *Utverzhdenie*,[81] whose aim was to try and unite the post-revolutionary political trends (*porevolutsionnye techeniya*); but again, this journal was criticised for putting forward very vague and unoriginal ideas.

Perhaps one of the most bizarre post-revolutionary movements was the *Mladorossy*[82] (Young Russians), which was led by Alexander L'vovich Kazem-Bek (1902–77). The *Mladorossy* professed to be monarchists and supported the candidature of the Grand Duke Kirill Vladimirovich, who had been the first member of the Imperial Family to accept the Provisional Government in 1917, and had marched his men, with red cockades in their hats, through the streets of Petrograd.[83]

In 1923, at a rally of student organisations, *Soyuz Molodoy Rossii* (the Union of Young Russia) was established and Kazem-Bek was elected leader. The name was later changed to *Soyuz Mladorossov*, and in 1926 they made their headquarters in Paris. The organisation produced *Mladoross – opoveshchenie Parizhskogo ochaga Mladorossov* (*Young Russia – the Declaration of the Parisian Section of the Young Russians*), which appeared in 1928 and 1929. From 1930, the newspaper, no longer produced on a duplicator but printed, appeared as a monthly until 1932. *Mladorosskaya Iskra* (*The Young Russian Spark*) was published from 1931 to 1940, to start with as a fortnightly newspaper – and then at less frequent intervals. Additional publications appeared: *K molodoy Rossii* in 1928, and *Rossiya, Mladorossy i emigratsiya* in 1935.

The *Mladorossy* considered that Russia required a government which would lead the country to greater national awareness and achievement, and that such a government could only be monarchical. Therefore, when the communist government had been overthrown, the national revolution could be fulfilled in the person of a tsar. The *Mladorossy* believed that a monarchical form of government would best be able to comprehend Russia's historical legacy and would lead the country forward to greatness. At the same time, the *Mladorossy* were resolutely opposed to restoration of the old regime. The new monarch would take into account the revolutionary ethos of Soviet Russia, would initiate radical policies[84] and would allow for the free election of the Soviets. From these ideas the *Mladorossy* coined their slogan *Tsar i Sovety* (The Tsar and the Soviets!).

The romantic revolutionary rhetoric and the simplified ideology, often presented in the form of slogans and placards, was the target of much criticism from the liberal and socialist émigré press.[85] The right-wing émigrés were less critical and welcomed the youth and enthusiasm of the *Mladorossy*.[86] This organisation seems to have met with considerable success among the younger generation of émigré Russians, and had particularly strong followings in Belgium and France. The *Mladorossy* provided an opportunity for the younger generation of émigrés to express not only their discontent with the policies of the older generation, but also their disillusionment with democracy which was not willing or able to mount an effective campaign against Bolshevism. Neither were the democracies able to cope with the problems of their own societies nor to protect their democratic systems from their opponents. The *Mladorossy* were impressed by the seeming strengths of Italian fascism and adopted various external attributes, saluting Kazem-Bek with outstretched right hand and chanting '*Glava! Glava! Glava!*' (Leader!). The *Mladorossy* also saw Stalin's policies of the 1930s as a revival of nationalism[87] within the Soviet Union and as such signalled the end of communism within Russia.

It was rumoured within the emigration that Kazem-Bek had links with the security services of the Soviet Union. After the war Kazem-Bek left France for America and in 1956 returned to the Soviet Union. He began to contribute to *Zhurnal Moskovskoy Patriarkhii* (*Journal of the Moscow Patriarchate*) and assisted the Metropolitan Nikodim who was head of the International Department of the Patriarchate. A church activist was warned to be careful since Kazem-Bek was a very dangerous man.[88]

3 SPLICING OLD AND NEW

Against this background of attempts by the Russian emigration to understand the antecedents and the effects of the Revolution, to produce some kind of system of ideas which would explain their situation and to find a role for themselves, the NTS[89] came into being.

No detailed and reliable account of the history of the NTS organisation exists.[90] It has proved difficult to establish the details of the development of the pre-war organisation since many of the publications have proved extremely difficult, if not impossible, to find. Undoubtedly, much of this material must have disappeared during the war, when members of the NTS were imprisoned by the Gestapo. Further, after the Second World War there were disagreements over the future of the organisation and there was a split in the leadership. Later, the NTS attracted members who were ignorant of the NTS pre-war activities and who might well have disagreed with some of the early policies. Thus, evidence of the organisation's past became lost or purposely obscured.

The younger generation of émigré 'sons' who eventually joined the NTS suffered a similar feeling of disaffection to that of the *Mladorossy*. In the 1920s various groups of Russian youth intimated their dissatisfaction with the activities of their elders and expressed concern for the future of Russia. In 1928, suggestions were made by *Natsional'ny Soyuz Russkoy Molodezhi* (the National Union of Russian Youth) in Bulgaria and *Soyuz Russkoy Natsional'noy Molodezhi* (the Union of Russian National Youth) in Yugoslavia that all these groups should unite. In 1929 these two groups united and renamed themselves *Natsional'ny Soyuz Russkoy Molodezhi za Rubezhom* (the National Union of Russian Youth Abroad) and this was followed by the creation of similar groups in other centres of the emigration. The official birth of the NTS took place at a conference of these groups in Belgrade from 1 to 5 July 1930, which included representatives from the younger generations of Russians from Yugoslavia, France, Bulgaria, Czechoslovakia and the Netherlands.[91]

The organisation was renamed *Natsional'ny Soyuz Russkoy Molodezhi* (the National Union of Russian Youth), a constitution was adopted and the conference elected a council. The Duke of Lichtenberg was elected president and an executive committee of two members and a chairman, V. M. Baidalakov, were also elected. In May 1931, P. B.

Struve agreed that part of the newspaper *Rossiya i Slavyanstvo*,[92] of which he was editor, would devote a section to the organisation, which would give an opportunity for the NTS leadership to publicise their views.

In December 1931, a new conference was convened where the name was altered to *Natsional'ny Soyuz Novogo Pokoleniya* (NSNP)[93] (the National Alliance of the New Generation). In 1936 this was changed to *Natsional'no-Trudovoy Soyuz Novogo Pokoleniya* (the National-Labour Alliance of the New Generation).

The constitution was amended and further sections added to the programme. In 1932, the organisation began to publish a newspaper in Sofia, *Za Rossiyu*, which in 1935 changed its name to *Za novoyu Rossiyu*. From 1935 onwards the NTS published literature explaining the aims of the organisation and its ideas. In 1936, K. D. Vergun became the head of the ideological sector of the NTS and he organised small groups of members to discuss, clarify and develop the programme.[94] The NTS seem to have attracted members who were inspired by the conviction that they had a responsibility towards the Soviet Union and that it was their duty to fight the communist regime and establish a better future. It was this belief in a mission rather than the content of the NTS programme which induced many of the younger generation of émigrés to support the NTS.

At the conference in 1930, the ideological statement (*polozhenie*) of the organisation was published.[95] It stated that Russia was to be visualised not only as a territorial unit and state but as a complex organism of national and cultural ideas and values, which the state had a duty to develop and encourage.

The Russian state should be based on national interests, immutable law, private ownership and the possibility for personal creativity, all within a religious framework and in the best interests of the state. The renascence of Russia could only be achieved by taking her past into consideration. Five essential features of the new order were elaborated. There would be strong central government which would be above class interest. Personal liberty would be established, all would be equal before the law, and privileges of class or estate would not exist. Foreign policy would be conducted with the national interests in mind. The various nationalities making up the Russian state would be given the opportunity for cultural independence. The agricultural problem would be solved by allowing private ownership of land.

Many of the elements of this initial resolution can be found in the later programmes of the Movement, published in 1931,[96] 1935, 1938, 1940 and 1944.[97] The publications of the Movement were designed to explain the underlying principles and produce a programme of action. Educational and explanatory publications provided courses of study which could be followed by members of the NTS.[98] The NTS refused to enter into the émigré debate about the form of a future Russian government – the debate centred on the virtues of a monarchical form of government versus republicanism.[99] The NTS considered this debate irrelevant and did not propose to elaborate on this question or give precise details of how the struggle against the Soviet regime would be conducted.[100] There is no reliable information on the NTS pre-war underground activity in the Soviet Union. Certain individuals do appear to have been sent there but it is very difficult to discover trustworthy evidence about such missions.[101]

The NTS wished to create a new *Weltanschauung* and to put forward a new philosophy which they termed *Natsional'no-Trudovoy Solidarizm* (national-labour solidarity). This philosophy was designed to replace Marxism, and solidarity was based on three main components which the NTS termed idealism, nationalism and activism.[102]

Idealism meant that in addition to material attributes, both the individual and society had a spiritual (*dukhovnoe*) dimension which took precedence over material aspects. Thus, in the opinion of the NTS, ideas played a far more important role in history than material considerations. A materialist explanation of history was, consequently, incomplete and one-sided. Since ideas were deemed to be one of the driving forces in the process of the development of society, the NTS considered that strong personalities such as Napoleon[103] or Peter the Great[104] played a significant role in historical events. Chance was also held to influence historical developments. The NTS considered that these factors demonstrated the flaws inherent in materialist historical interpretation.

The NTS defined the nation as people united by a common culture, common state and economic interests, sharing a common past and common aims for the future.[105] Since the nation was an organic unity of ideas and culture, the NTS considered that only within a national framework was true creativity possible. Therefore, nationalism was not merely a question of national pride or chauvinism, it was considered as 'a natural fulfilment of the human desire for positive creativity, directed to the highest ideals of social justic‿ ‿‿ the name of the good of the nation, and thereby serving the nation'.[106]

The NTS called their third basic premise 'activism'. This was a result of their conviction that their ideas were correct. The members of the organisation were duty bound to create a situation where their whole philosophy of 'national-labour solidarity' could be put into practice.[107] This meant that members of the NTS not only had to familiarise themselves with the concepts of this *Weltanschauung*, but also to educate themselves in all the relevant areas of philosophy, economics and history to be able to proselytise those ideas of solidarity within the Soviet Union itself. This section was intended to oppose the Marxist concept that 'being determined consciousness'. This section was purposely drafted to read as a call to action. Russian émigré youth had a responsibility towards their country and were bound to carry out a variety of actions in order to try and fulfil this duty. It was in light of these assumptions that answers to all the main social and political questions, as defined by the NTS, were outlined. This was not supposed to be a definite programme (a concrete plan of action was provided in another publication), but merely an indication of the priorities of the NTS. However, the authors of the programme and the ideology were not entirely sure how to differentiate one from the other and some duplication occurred.[108]

The NTS concept of the new state was based on their idea of national-labour solidarity.[109] Solidarity would ensure that the relations between the state and the individual were harmonious, since only then could the process of true co-operation be achieved. The national-labour order meant that the NTS rejected what they considered to be the basis of liberal democracy: the political party. Instead, the government would be responsible to working organisations (*trudovye grouppy*), representatives of such groups would form the government of the country, and these representatives would be responsible to the groups which had elected them. The NTS recognised the importance of the relationship between freedom and equality. It was considered that the freedom of the individual would be maintained by law, but the NTS at the same time rejected the idea of unlimited freedom, termed by them as 'the liberal and capitalist' concept, where the liberty of one individual might impinge on that of others. Concerning private ownership, the NTS considered that this was necessary but rejected the role of private ownership of capital in industry. All industries of national importance would have to be in the hands of the government. National-labour solidarity would be achieved by co-operation between all those who worked, not by conflict of interest. In agriculture, the operation of the principle of solidarity would be achieved by encouraging co-operative practices in the use of machinery. At the same time, land would be given into private ownership. It was envisaged that these measures would solve Russian agricultural problems. It was imperative that workers (*rabochie*) should be made to feel like valued citizens with equal rights. Far-reaching labour legislation would be enacted in order to protect them from exploitation, to assure them a high standard of living and good educational and cultural opportunities. Authority (*vlast'*) should be stable, above class and party influence and would therefore act in the national interest. The administration would be decentralised and organised on a regional basis. It is not clear how the NTS envisaged the relationship between the 'stable' and strong centralised power and the local administration. The NTS rejected ideas of federalism or any form of secession of minorities. The NTS laid great stress on education as they considered that this would be the main way by which the idea of national-labour solidarity could be taught and disseminated. Education would be carried out in schools, by the army, and within the family, which the NTS saw as the basic unit of society.

The NTS reiterated several times that the army should be developed as a national fighting force and devote its energies to national aims.[110] The NTS also laid great stress on religion. Much of Russian culture was rooted in Orthodoxy. All religions would be given freedom of worship and of conscience but the Orthodox Church would play the central role in the religious life of the Russian people. The church would be independent of the state.[111]

There has been considerable discussion over the relationship of the NTS to fascism.[112] The NTS were undoubtedly impressed by some of the features of fascism, notably its opposition to communism and its rejection of Marxist ideology. Members of the NTS were very disillusioned by democracy. Their experience of the 1920s taught them that democracy seemed weak, unable to protect the economic or political desires of their people. Still less had democratic rule been favourable to émigré society. As foreigners, they were the first to be affected during political or economic difficulties, when they lost their jobs in favour of the nationals of the country. Fascism, in its early years, seemed to be a powerful force for the restoration of a feeling of pride in one's country and seemed to deal successfully with many of the problems to be found in European society in the 1920s.

The NTS were particularly influenced by Portuguese fascism.[113] According to Laqueur, Portuguese fascism under Salazar could not be included in a narrow definition of fascism, it was a party created from above rather than one which obtained its mandate from below and conquered power for its leaders and supporters.[114] Rather than being a genuine fascist party it was really an authoritarian system. Salazar's regime has been described as a 'conservative corporatist regime that shunned every kind of radicalism'.[115] The corporative aspect of the Portuguese state was 'supposed to denote a state which represents, and thus serves, the people who contribute to the life of the state through their family, professional, vocational and municipal groups'.[116] This idea seems to have much in common with the national-labour system put forward by the NTS. The Portuguese system also emphasised the need for unbreakable tradition within society. The importance of nationalism and the concept of nationhood as opposed to cosmopolitanism and internationalist doctrines were features held in common in both the Portuguese system and the NTS programme.

Opponents of the NTS imply that it had a certain empathy for German National Socialism. The NTS were given the nickname of '*nats mal'chiki*' or 'national boys'. The prefix '*nats*' was often considered to be derived from Nazi rather than from the 'National' of the organisation's name. However, it seems that the NTS had few illusions about the nature of the Nazi regime. In 1936, M. A. Georgievsky, the secretary of the NTS based in Belgrade, travelled to Berlin to see whether there was any possibility of joint action with the Nazi authorities, since the Nazis professed themselves anticommunists. Georgievksy's experiences persuaded him that it would be quite impossible to initiate any form of co-operation. The Nazis were too inflexible, too much in the grip of their racist theories for pro-Russian but anti-communist ideas to make any significant impact.[117] The 1938 programme explained that the Nazis presented a real threat to the Soviet Union and that war would provide an opportunity for the Russian people to bring about a revolution of national liberation. The programme reminded its readers that change within the Soviet Union could only be brought about by the people, but still the members of the NTS were asked to hold themselves in readiness.[118] This entire passage makes it clear that the

NTS wished to identify the evils of the Soviet regime and to acknowledge the imminent possibility of war in which the overthrow of the government would be possible. National Socialism is discussed only in its capacity as a potentially serious rival and threat to communism.

Many similarities between fascist ideology and the programme of the NTS exist. Both were critical of liberal democracy and capitalism, both opposed communism. Both favoured authoritarian rule with the aim of national and social integration through a single party or ruling group. However, one basic difference is striking. Fascism is largely anti-clerical and irreligious. The programme of the NTS was imbued with a religious morality. This underpinned their whole ideology and programme, which presupposed an acceptance of morality based on Christian principles. Moreover, the programme of the NTS expressed a concern for personal freedom, the furtherance of which was not a feature of fascist ideology.

When war broke out between the Soviet Union and the Third Reich, the NTS went underground. Officially, the Nazis closed down all émigré institutions, but the members of NTS were not willing to submit to this decree. The war gave them the opportunity to meet their Soviet compatriots and to find out what modifications needed to be made to the draft programmes of the NTS which would bring it up-to-date and make it relevant to the Soviet reader. Many young émigrés who were members of the NTS had received a technical or scientific training and education. This had often occurred because it was much easier for an émigré to find a job if he had these types of qualifications as opposed to an education in the humanities. These scientific and technical qualifications enabled young Russian émigrés to get permission – although they had to conceal their Russian origins – to travel to the occupied territories of the Soviet Union where they were employed in various capacities by the Ostministerium. While in the occupied territories these members of the NTS met their Soviet compatriots.[119] Conversations and discussions ensued which finally resulted in the 1944 Scheme (*Skhema*) or draft programme.[120] This 96-page document, approximately twice as long as previous publications, put forward a plan for a national-labour system divided into six sections: the social system, the state apparatus, economic and social policy, national culture, and the transitional period. In light of the previous publications by NTS, the Scheme is comprehensible. However, since its introductory section, dealing with basic principles underlying the ideas of the organisation, is shorter and deprived of reference to previous statements of the NTS, the Scheme seems unbalanced. In their description of the envisaged new society, the distinction between the present state of society and the ideal state as understood by the NTS, is not always clearly made, which leads to considerable confusion.[121]

In the development of the NTS programme, the Movement gradually evolved from an identification with some features of the pre-revolutionary anti-Bolshevik opposition and the White Movement to a more precise criticism of Stalin. In the 1935 programme, it is stated that the NTS is the heir of General Kornilov.[122] In the 1938 programme, this is omitted, and the programme includes a detailed analysis of Stalinist policy, particularly of the army purges.[123] The 1944 Scheme shows still further the influence of Soviet reality. The national revolution as envisaged by the NTS would complete the Revolution of 1917 and resurrect the true revolutionary atmosphere of 1917, directing it into channels which would fulfil the wishes of the people.[124] The detail of the Scheme reflects the extent of politicisation of Soviet society. This meant that Soviet citizens who joined the NTS considered that these questions had to be discussed. The effect of Soviet influence is particularly striking in the sections on freedom and law.[125] In contrast to earlier definitions, where the reader's knowledge was assumed, the concept of freedom of choice to travel or to choose where to live, freedom of speech, the press, belief, and assembly, are minutely detailed. The powers of the law and the courts are similarly described in great detail and include the clauses that no one may be detained without trial or arrested without charge, torture may not be used and individuals may not be arrested merely because they are related to someone who has committed a crime. These and similar details were not included in earlier programmes as they were deemed to be self-evident, but this was not the case with the new Soviet members of the NTS, whose experience had taught them that these subjects must be discussed.

The new Soviet members[126] of the NTS also contributed to a passage which stated that all the nationalities whose territories lay within the boundaries of the Russian (*Rossiskiy*) state were part of the nation. The only exceptions to this were foreigners and Jews.[127] A little further on, the Scheme stated that Jews were free to leave but were not allowed to take any capital with them, otherwise they could inhabit specially designated territories. This feature of the programme was completely new. There was no anti-semitism in earlier drafts and it did not appear in post-war programmes. It was later argued that this anti-semitic remark had appeared in response to Nazi pressure.[128] Since the NTS was in any case illegal, and many of its leaders and rank and file membership were jailed for part of the war, it is not clear why an underground organisation found it necessary to respond to this pressure.

One of Vlasov's first requests on his arrival in Berlin in the autumn of 1942 had been for copies of all the émigré political programmes.[129] He explained that he sought a basic framework which he could use as a starting point for his ideas. The only political organisation still operating, albeit illegally, was the NTS and Vlasov was given one of their programmes immediately, and was provided with details of many of the programmes of other organisations.[130] Vlasov returned this NTS programme with his comments and corrections in the margin. Unfortunately, this copy does not seem to have survived so that Vlasov's opinions remain unknown, but it is clear that the NTS as a whole had a great influence on the Russian Liberation Movement. Trukhin and Meandrov were both members of the NTS. The two senior lecturers at Dabendorf,[131] Zaitsev and Shtifanov, were also members. Other instructors at Dabendorf joined the organisation. Since the NTS had already worked out their own elaborate ideological scheme, they were able to provide significant contributions to the discussions, which seem to have been one of the most important aspects of life and work at Dabendorf. The members of the NTS were familiar both with émigré views and with some of the key questions to be discussed with regard to the Soviet Union. This enabled them to provide a stimulus for much debate, and a framework of ideas around which their Soviet compatriots, who had less experience of the diversity of political opinion, could build their own ideas.

The NTS programme had features which appealed to members of the Russian Liberation Movement. The nationalism of the NTS corresponded to nationalist feelings to be found among supporters of the Russian Liberation Movement. Similarly, the NTS opposed the internationalist aims of communism and endeavoured to work out a philosophy which would replace Marxism. In this last aim the NTS were more advanced than the Russian Liberation Movement. The NTS tried to develop a comprehensive ideology, whereas the ideologists in the Russian Liberation Movement, although opposed to certain specific policies, were only gradually beginning to explore the implications of this position. The NTS held the view that Marxism had to be replaced but at the same time, they were prepared to accept the changes in attitude which had occurred in the Soviet Union. The NTS did not propose restoration of the old regime, since they had become convinced that the policies of the previous generation had been flawed. The reasons for their opposition to the old regime by members of the Russian Liberation Movement were different, but this mutual realisation, that it was necessary to take the present situation into account and that it was not possible to turn the clock back, meant that further common ground existed. It would, however, be completely erroneous to maintain,[132] as occasionally members of the NTS have done, that without the NTS the programme of the Russian Liberation Movement would never have come into being. Despite the extensive influence of the NTS, the programme of the Russian Liberation Movement shows no sign of the acceptance of the NTS doctrine of solidarity. Furthermore, the publications of the Liberation Movement show virtually no trace of a concern central to the NTS outlook: the influence of Christianity, particularly in its Russian Orthodox version, and the rule of law. Although the second part of the Prague Manifesto termed the new system, which would be installed after the Soviet regime had been overthrown, a national-labour system, Zhilenkov, as chairman of the editing committee, refused to accept the NTS explanation of what the national-labour system entailed.[133] The members of the Russian Liberation Movement only accepted the national-labour definition inasmuch as this signified opposition to the international and party aspects of communist ideology. In this, although subject to different influences, members of the Russian Liberation Movement and members of the NTS agreed on what could be considered a desirable social and economic system. Members of the Russian Liberation Movement reached their conclusion as a result of experiencing the injustices of the Soviet system, whereas the NTS was influenced, to a large extent, by their opposition to what they had experienced in Europe.

It is perhaps slightly ironic that Soviet citizens who were members of the Russian Liberation Movement found points of contact with émigrés who were considered to be on the right of the political spectrum. At first glance, it might have been expected that the older population, on the left wing of émigré politics, would have been more in sympathy with those who were products of the Soviet system, people who were not, by and large, prepared to repudiate that system *in toto*. These émigrés, however, were not prepared to give even a sympathetic hearing to their Soviet compatriots opposed to Stalin. Such émigrés tended to see the conflict between the Third Reich and the Soviet Union in terms of black and white, i.e. between fascists and anti-fascists. It was the younger generation of émigrés who had joined the NTS who were prepared to adapt themselves to new circumstances and to understand the attitudes of their Soviet compatriots caught between the Third Reich and the Soviet Union. These younger émigrés realised that this definition of the conflict was incorrect since it failed to take the realities of the situation into account.

NOTES

1 The newspaper of the Kronstadt revolt, *Izvestiya Vremennogo Revolutsionnogo Komiteta Matrosov, Krasnoarmeytsev i Rabochikh gor. Kronstadta* was republished as the Appendix to *Pravda o Kronstadte* izd. Volya Rossii, Prague (1921), thus preserving a record of the uprising. The leader of the rising, Petrichenko, escaped to Finland and published his memoirs: Petrichenko, S. M., *Pravda o Kronstadtskikh sobytiyakh* (1921); 'V Kronstadtskie dni', *Revolutsionnaya Rossiya*, no. 16–18, Prague (1922), pp. 6–8; 'O prichinakh Kronstadtskogo vostaniya', *Znamya bor'by*, Berlin (1926). All abridged in *Kontinent*, 10 (1976), pp. 206–34. For further bibliographical material, see Avrich, P., *Kronstadt (1921)*, Princeton (1970) and Getzler, I., *Kronstadt 1917–1921*, Cambridge (1983).

2 See, for example, the Popov papers in the Bakhmeteff archive at Columbia University BAR 17.5.9. I. Popov lists five major revolts which he claims occurred in the 1930s, but provides no further information about them:

  1931   Rising in the N. Caucasus;
  1932   Siberian rising;
  1931–5 Karnaukov's Far Eastern revolt;
  1936   Rising of the Ivanovo-Voznesenskiy weavers;
  1936   Mutinies of the Kalonovsky tank brigade, the tank brigade near Kiev and the infantry corps in Central Asia.

3 Svetlanin, A., (Frolov, A. V./Likhachev, N.), *Dal'nevostochny zagovor*, Frankfurt am Main (1953).

4 Tucker, R. C., 'Problems of Interpretation', *Slavic Review*, 42/1 (1983), p. 80.

5 Interviews: N. G. Shtifanov, D. Konstantinov.

6 Schapiro, L. *The Communist Party of the Soviet Union*, 2nd revised edn, London (1970), p. 505.

7 For the text of the resolution see *Pravda o Kronstadte*, pp. 9–10, 46–7.

8 Getzler, I. *Kronstadt 1917–1921*, p. 225.

9 *Pravda o Kronstadte*, pp. 83–4.
10 See, for instance, Geller, M., and Nekrich, A., *Utopiya u vlasti*, vol. 1, p. 192.
11 See pp. 174–5.
12 In 1930 groups of émigré youth formed the *Natsional'ny Soyuz Russkoy Molodezhi* (the National Alliance of Russian Youth). In 1931 this was changed to *Natsional'ny Soyuz Novogo Pokoleniya* (the National Alliance of the New Generation). In 1936 this was altered to *Natsional'no-Trudovoy Soyuz Novogo Pokoleniya* (the National-Labour Alliance of the New Generation). But, from 1935 in literature destined for the Soviet Union, the Alliance referred to itself simply as the Natsional'no-Trudovoy Soyuz (the National-Labour Alliance), and in the autumn of 1941 the organisation finally assumed this name. See pp. 183–4. The Alliance will be referred to as NTS throughout.
13 The discussion on the exact number of émigrés continues. Alekhin, M. and Belaya, E., in 'Razmeshchenie emigratsii', *Bol'shaya sovetskaya entsiklopediya*, vol. 64, cols. 160–75, Moscow (1933) gives the total number as 860,000 but omits a number of countries: Estonia, Latvia, Bulgaria, Turkey, Finland, where sizeable émigré communities were to be found. In the 3rd edition of the *Bol'shaya sovetskaya entsiklopediya*, vol. 30, cols. 163–4, Moscow (1978) the émigrés were said to number two million. Shkarenkov, L. K., *Agoniya beloy emigratsii*, Moscow: (1981), p. 18, considers that the maximum number of those who left was two million. Simpson, Sir John Hope, *The Refugee Problem*, London (1939), discusses the various estimates, pp. 80–3. In 1922 Dr Nansen estimated that there were one-and-a-half million refugees in Europe while an American Red Cross estimate for 1920 gives the figure of 1,964,000 refugees. In 1926 the League of Nations statistics give 1,160,000 persons as having left Russia. Kovalevsky, P. E. *Zarubeshnaya Rossiya*, Paris (1971), p. 13. For a discussion of the question, see Andreyev, N., 'Ob osobennostyakh i osnovnykh etapakh razvitiya russkoy literatury za rubezhom' in ed. Poltoratzky, N., *Russkaya literatura v emigratsii*, Pittsburgh (1972) p. 24.
14 Huntington, W. Chapin, *The Homesick Millions*, Boston (1933), p. 2, concludes that one-sixth were university graduates and two-thirds had received secondary education.
15 Milyukov, P. N., *Emigratsiya na pereput'e*, Paris (1926), p. 5.
16 Ibid., p. 90.
17 In 1922 the Soviet government sent out over 160 of the leading members of the intelligentsia including N. A. Berdyaev. See Struve, G. P., *Russkaya literatura v izgnanii*, New York (1956), p. 18.
18 The best known of those who returned home were A. N. Tolstoy and M. Gorky. Williams, R. C., *Culture in Exile*, Ithaca (1972), p. 139.
19 Milyukov, P. N., *Emigratsiya na pereput'e*, p. 75.
20 Williams, R. C., *Culture in Exile*, p. 134. Soviet publishing firms such as Petropolis, Z. I. Grzhebin, and I. P. Ladyzhnikov working in Berlin published such émigré writers as I. Bunin and B. Zaitsev.
21 Hayes, N., 'Kazem-Bek and the Young Russians' Revolution', *Slavic Review*, 39, no. 2 (1980), pp. 255–6.

22 Struve, G. P., *Russkaya literatura v izgnanii*, p. 242.
23 *Oboroncheskoe dvizhenie*, Paris, no. 1 (May 1936). *Golos otechestva*, no. 1, Paris (March 1938).
24 Struve, G. P., *Russkaya literatura v izgnanii*, pp. 383–4.
25 Williams, R. C., *Culture in Exile*, pp. 111–12.
26 Milyukov, P. N., *Rossiya na perelome*, Paris (1927), vol. 2, pp. 233–7. Abdank-Kossovsky, V., 'Russkaya emigratsiya III.' *Vozrozhdenie*, 54 (1956), pp. 131–2.
27 Simpson, Sir John Hope, *The Refugee Problem*, p. 99. Kovalevsky, P. E., *Zarubezhnaya Rossiya*, devotes a very large proportion of his work to a discussion of Russian education.
28 Interview: D. A. Levitsky.
29 Laqueur, W. *Russia and Germany*, London (1965), p. 118.
30 Rosenberg, W. G. *Liberals in the Russian Revolution*, Princeton (1974), pp. 437–9, 447.
31 Williams, R. C. *Culture in Exile*, pp. 184–5.
32 Rosenberg, W. C. *Liberals in the Russian Revolution*, p. 449.
33 Milyukov, P. N., *Rossiya na perelome*, vol. 2, p. 243.
34 Nielsen, J. P., 'Milyukov and Stalin. P. N. Milyukov's political evolution in emigration 1918–1943', *Meddelelser*, no. 32, Oslo (1983), p. 3.
35 Williams, R. C. *Culture in Exile*, p. 182.
36 Slonim, M. 'Volya Rossii' in Poltoratzky, N. P. (ed.), *Russkaya literatura v emigratsii*, p. 291.
37 Haimson, L. H. (ed.), *The Mensheviks*, Chicago (1974), pp. 320–1.
38 *Smena vekh*. Sbornik statey, Klyuchnikova, Yu.B., Ustryalova, N. V., Lukianova, S. S., Bobrishcheva-Pushkina, A. V., Chakhotina, S. S., and Potyukhina, Yu.N., July 1921, Prague.
39 Struve, G. P., *Russkaya literatura v izgnanii*, p. 30.
40 *Smena vekh*, p. 91.
41 Ibid., p. 162.
42 Ibid., p. 181.
43 Struve, G. P. *Russkaya literatura v izgnanii*, p. 35.
44 Agursky, M., *Ideologiya natsional-bolshevizma*, Paris (1980), pp. 201–4 and review by Andreyev, N. 'The reality of National-Bolshevism', *Soviet-Jewish Affairs*, 1 (February 1982), pp. 76–80.
45 *Iskhod k Vostoku. Predchuvstviya i sversheniya. Utverzhdenie Evraziitsev*, Sofia, 1921.
46 A bibliography of the Eurasian Movement can be found in Böss, O., *Die Lehre der Eurasier. Ein Beitrag zur russischen Ideengeschichte des 20. Jahrhunderts*, and Lubensky, S., 'Evraziiskaya bibliografiya 1921–31', *Tridsatye Gody. Utverzhdenie Evraziitsev*, 7 (1931), pp. 285–317.
47 *Evraziistvo (Formulirovka)*, Moscow, 1927.
48 Riasanovsky, N. V., 'The Emergence of Eurasianism', *California Slavic Studies*, 4 (1967), p. 47.
49 Struve, G. P., *Russkaya literatura v izgnanii*, p. 41.
50 *Iskhod k Vostoku*, pp. iii, iv.
51 *Evraziistvo (Opyt systematicheskogo izlozheniya)* (1926), p. 45.
52 Ibid., p. 51.

53 Ibid., pp. 11–13.
54 Ibid., pp. 54–6.
55 Varshavsky, V. S., *Nezamechennoe pokolenie*, New York (1956), p. 35.
56 *Evraziistvo (Opyt systematicheskogo izlozheniya)*, pp. 18–20.
57 *Iskhod k Vostoku*, p. 5.
58 Riasanovksy, N. V., 'The Emergence of Eurasianism', *California Slavic Studies*, 4 (1967), p. 52.
59 Florovsky, G. V., 'Evraziiskiy soblazn', *Sovremennye zapiski*, 34, Paris (1928), pp. 312–46.
60 Riasanovsky, N. V., 'The Emergence of Eurasianism', *California Slavic Studies*, 4 (1967), p. 48.
61 For the history of this organisation, see *Krest'yanskaya Rossiya. Trudovaya Krest'yanskaya Partiya. Vvedenie. Ideologiya, Programma. Taktika. Ustav*, Prague (1928) and *Krest'yanskaya Rossiya*. Sbornik statey, I. New York (1953).
62 Bem was an expert on Dostoevsky who frequently wrote for *Krest'yanskaya Rossiya* under the name of Omeliyanov.
63 *Krest'yanskaya Rossiya. Trudovaya Krest'yanskaya Partiya. Vvedenie. Ideologiya. Programma. Taktika. Ustav*, Prague (1928), pp. 8–15.
64 Ibid., p. 13.
65 Ibid., pp. 15–39.
66 Ibid., pp. 41–62.
67 *Sbornik Krest'yanskoy Rossii*, 1, Prague (1922), p. 4.
68 *Krest'yanskaya Rossiya. Trudovaya Krest'yanskaya Partiya. Vvedenie. Ideologiya. Programma. Taktika. Ustav*, Prague (1928), p. 5.
69 Butenko, V., 'Partinaya zhizn. (Itogi 1930–31 goda)', *Vestnik Krest'yanskoy Rossii* (June–July 1931).
70 Solzhenitsyn, A. I., *Arkhipelag GULag*, vols. 1–2, pp. 61–2.
71 Ibid., p. 402.
72 Interview: Andreyev, N. E. Recollection of conversation with B. V. Sedakov, secretary of KTP, while both Andreyev and Sedakov were detained by SMERSH in 1945.
73 Andreyev, N., 'O russkoy literaturnoi Prage', *Russkiy Almanakh*, Paris (1981), p. 349.
74 Struve, G. P. *Russkaya literatura v izgnanii*, p. 222; Varshavsky, V. S. *Nezamechennoe pokolenie*, p. 9.
75 Bunakov, I. I., Stepun, F. A., Fedotov, G. P. (eds.), *Novy grad*, vols. 1–14, Paris (1931–9).
76 Vishnyak, M. V. *Sovremennye zapiski*, p. 309.
77 *Novy grad*, 1, p. 3.
78 Ibid., p. 6.
79 Ibid., p. 7.
80 Rudnev, V. V., 'Novy grad', *Sovremennye zapiski*, 50 (1932), pp. 438–55.
81 Struve, G. P. *Russkaya literatura v izgnanii*, pp. 223–6.
82 The only study of the movement is Hayes, N., 'Kazem-Bek and the Young Russians' Revolution', *Slavic Review*, 39, no. 2 (1980), pp. 225–68.
83 Katkov, G., *Russia 1917: The February Revolution*, p. 399.
84 Kazem-Bek, A. L., 'O porevolutsionnom monarkhisme', *Mladoross* (1 February 1930).

85 Hayes, N., 'Kazem-Bek and the Young Russians' Revolution', *Slavic Review*, 39, no. 2, (1980), p. 263.

86 *Chasovoy*, no. 123/4 (1934).

87 Kazem-Bek, A. L. *Rossiya, Mladorossy i emigratsiya*, Paris (1935), p. 31.

88 Levitin-Krasnov, A. E. *V poiskakh novogo grada. Vospominaniya III*, Tel Aviv (1980), pp. 40–4.

89 See p. 194, n. 12.

90 *Na sluzhbe Rossii*, Frankfurt, (1979), is very brief, 70 pages, and is produced by the organisation itself. Young, G., *The House of Secrets*, New York (1959), is a very popularised account dealing with the post-war activity of the NTS. Brunst, D. V., *Zapiski byvshego emigranta*, Moscow (1961), is allegedly written by one of the leaders of the NTS who returned to Moscow. The circumstances of his return are not clear. Varshavsky, V. S., *Nezamechennoe pokolenie* discusses the NTS in relation to other émigré trends.

91 For the early history of the organisation, see 'Kak sozdavalsya NTS', *Possev* (July 1983), pp. 49–51, and *Natsional'ny Soyuz Novogo Pokoleniya* (1935), pp. 70–80.

92 'Svoe slovo', *Rossiya i Slavyanstvo* (2 May 1931).

93 *Natsional'ny Soyuz Novogo Pokoleniya* (1935), p. 76.

94 Andreyev, N. E., Memoirs, pp. 643–4.

95 'Kak sozdavalsya NTS', *Possev* (July 1983), p. 51. *Natsional'ny Soyuz Novogo Pokoleniya* (1935).

96 I have been unable to find a copy of the programme for 1931.–C.A.

97 *Natsional'ny Soyuz Novogo Pokoleniya* (1935).
Za chto borot'sya (1938).
Programmnye polozheniya i Ustav, Belgrade (1938).
Natsional'no-Trudovoy Soyuz Novogo Pokoleniya. Za Novy Stroy (1940).
Skhema Natsional'no-Trudovogo Stroya, Slovakia (1944).

98 These were called *Kursy natsional'no-politicheskoy podgotovki* and were devoted to such questions as the history of Russia, Soviet economic development, the basis of a national outlook. Vol. 1: 'Osnova natsional'nogo mirovozzreniya' (1939). Vol. 3: 'Sotsial'naya, ekonomicheskaya i politicheskaya zhizn'' (1937). Vol. 4: 'Istoricheskiy otdel' (1938). Vol. 2 was never published.

99 Melnikov, F., 'Put' soyuza pravilniy', *Za Rossiyu*, no. 2 (April 1932). Georgievskiy, M., 'Voprosy programmy', *Za Rossiyu*, no. 16 (June 1933).

100 *Natsional'ny Soyuz Novogo Pokoleniya* (1935).

101 *Na sluzhbe narodu*, pp. 18–22.

102 *Natsional'ny Soyuz Novogo Pokoleniya* (1935), pp. 18–39. *Za chto borot'sya* (1938), pp. 4–8.

103 *Za chto borot'sya*, p. 6.

104 *Za Novy Stroy*, p. 9.

105 Vorob'ev, R. *Filosofskie osnovy natsional'no trudovogo solidarisma*, Menhenhof, Kassel (1946).

106 *Za chto borot'sya*, p. 7.

107 Ibid., pp. 8–9.

108 For instance, see *Za chto borot'sya*, pp. 17–19 on agriculture, and

Programmnye polozheniya i Ustav III, 'Zemel'naya politika', p. 8.

109 The basic framework of the conception of the state altered very little in the pre-war draft programmes, *Natsional'ny Soyuz Novogo Pokoleniya* (1935), pp. 21–39. *Za chto borot'sya*, pp. 9–27.

110 *Programmnye polozheniya i Ustav*, p. 12.

111 Ibid., p. 11.

112 Varshavsky, V. S., *Nezamechennoe pokolenie*, pp. 77–8. Stephan, J. J., *The Russian Fascists*, London (1978), pp. 29–30.

113 Neimirok, A., 'Novaya Portugaliya', *Za rodinu*, no. 60 (July 1937). Stolypin, A., 'Portugaliya', *Za rodinu*, no. 61 (July 1937). Interview: N. E. Andreyev.

114 Laqueur, W., *Fascism, a Reader's Guide*, London (1976), p. 9.

115 Payne, S., 'Fascism in Western Europe', in Laqueur, W., *Fascism, a Reader's Guide*, p. 302.

116 Kay, H., *Salazar and Modern Portugal*, London (1970), p. 51.

117 Interview: N. E. Andreyev.

118 *Za chto borot'sya*, pp. 29–36.

119 Kazantsev, A., *Tret'ya sila*, pp. 63–4, 77–8. Fevr, N., *Solntse voskhodit na Zapade*, p. 57.

120 *Skhema Natsional'no-Trudovogo Stroya*, Slovakia (1944).

121 For example, *Skhema Natsional'no-Trudovogo Stroya*, Slovakia (1944), p. 19, in the discussion of the existence of the forces of solidarity or conflict in society a statement of belief 'solidarity is the main force of social progress' is made to sound like a statement of fact.

122 *Natsional'ny Soyuz Novogo Pokoleniya* (1935).

123 *Za chto borot'sya*, pp. 29–36.

124 *Skhema Natsional'no Trudovogo Stroya*, p. 91.

125 Ibid., pp. 20–4.

126 Interview: N. G. Shtifanov.

127 *Skhema Natsional'no Trudovogo Stroya*, pp. 43–5.

128 Artemov, A., 'Skhema NTS i evreiskiy vopros', *Possev* (June 1975), pp. 40–3.

129 Interview: I. L. Novosiltsev.

130 Novosiltsev, I. L. 'Andrei Andreyevich Vlasov', *Novy zhurnal*, no. 129 (December 1977), p. 187.

131 See pp. 51 and 153–5.

132 Young, G., *The House of Secrets*, p. 14. Interview: A. N. Artemova.

133 See Chapter 2, p. 131. Galkin, D., 'Predislovie. Ideologicheskaya doktrina osvoboditel'nogo dvizheniya', *Bor'ba*, no. 6/7 (June/July 1949), p. 6.

Conclusion

The Second World War should have been the moment for which Russians opposed to the Stalinist regime had been waiting. Both émigré and Soviet citizens alike had reached the conclusion that individuals alone would be unable to alter the Stalinist system. State control of propaganda and the system of terror made it very difficult for the individual to act. Added to this, the sheer size of the country and state control of all communications militated against the success of any uprising in the USSR. All insurrections between the Bolshevik seizure of power in 1917 and the outbreak of the Second World War were successfully crushed by force. Consequently, those Russians who were opposed to the regime felt that change could only occur after some sort of external shock or conflict had weakened the Soviet government and provided the opportunity for substantial restructuring. They hoped that the war would be the catalyst for a change of this kind, and the moment for decisive action. Right from the moment of capture, Soviet citizens expressed a wish to fight the Soviet state, and already by the autumn of 1941 had created military formations[1] which they hoped would help them to achieve their aim.

However, the Nazis were intent on implementing Hitler's racial theories. They remained totally indifferent to the fate of the Russian people, who were to be subjugated and forced into the service of the Aryan race. The sovereign Soviet state was to be converted into a Russian one possessing subordinate colonial status. Since the Germans had not turned out to be the looked-for ally, all hopes of liberation and reform of the Soviet regime proved ephemeral as the country united in the face of Nazi atrocities in order to repel the aggressor.

If it was quite clear to many émigrés belonging to the defencist grouping, even before the attack by the Third Reich on the Soviet Union, that co-operation with the Nazis was impossible, their Soviet compatriots were less well informed. Although the Soviet public had been told in the 1930s that fascism, defined as the last gasp of capitalism, was an enemy of socialism, the Non-Aggression Pact signed with the Third Reich in 1939 meant that Nazi Germany was presented as a friendly power. On the outbreak of war, Soviet citizens were disinclined to believe Soviet propaganda about Nazi aims and methods, since propaganda had not previously proved to be a particularly reliable source of information. Initially, therefore, some captured Soviet military personnel entertained hopes that realistic political considerations could be brought to bear on Nazi policy makers. Vlasov, for instance, took approximately a year to realise that his assumptions as to the wisest policy towards the Soviet Union were not and could not be shared by the Nazi authorities. When Vlasov was captured, he met Germans who were critical of Nazi policy. His experience of the Soviet Union, where criticism of government policy could not be voiced without official sanction, led him to assume that this criticism was echoed at a higher level and, consequently, opportunity for change really existed. It was not immediately apparent to captured Soviet commanders that although the systems were similar, they were not analogous. State control was more pervasive in the USSR than in the Third Reich. Whereas it had been possible within the German officer corps to discuss plans to assassinate Hitler for a number of years, a similar situation could not have arisen in the Red Army. Such conspiracies would have been denounced very quickly.

A further belief, held by members of the Russian Liberation Movement, that they would be able to explain their views and actions to those world powers of whom they had such high hopes – Britain and the United States – proved totally untenable. First, there were practical difficulties encountered by members of the Russian Liberation Movement. They were dependent on their German sponsors and had only symbolic freedom of movement and communication. Furthermore, in Allied eyes, whatever the actual state of affairs, members of the Russian Liberation Movement were seen as Nazi hirelings, and it would have taken a very sophisticated publicity campaign for the Allied powers to begin to understand the complex position of the anti-Stalinist Russians. Such a publicity exercise was obviously unthinkable during the war. Furthermore, from the Casablanca conference onwards, the Allies were prepared to accept only unconditional surrender of the Third Reich with the corollary that they were unwilling and unable to contemplate any negotiations with groups within Germany. Moreover, the anti-Stalinist Russians, through their lack of knowledge of the West, failed to realise that their situation and aims needed to be explained. Just as in the early days of the German invasion of the USSR, it had been assumed by Soviet citizens that the Germans were fully informed about the situation within the USSR, so members of the Russian Liberation Movement considered it axiomatic that not only did Great Britain and the USA understand their predicament, but that after they had defeated the Nazis, the Western Allied armies would turn against the other dictatorship, the communists. That the Allies, like the Nazis before them, had been unable to understand the reasoning which inspired these Russians to fight against the Stalinist regime, is more than amply illustrated by the gruesome story of forced repatriation.[2]

Since the Nazis, and subsequently the British and Americans, failed to accept the Russian Liberation Movement's analysis of events, the anti-Stalinist Russians found no supporters in their struggle to transform their vision into reality, although this hope of foreign sympathy with their plight motivated their actions right to the bitter end. Soviet prisoners-of-war were more concerned with politics and political discussion than were, for example, their British and French counterparts, a situation which might be deemed surprising, given the terrible conditions in which they were held. This interest in politics arose from the attitudes of both Nazi and Soviet authorities which forced captured Soviet personnel into a situation where a decision of a political nature had to be taken *vis-à-vis* both regimes. Paradoxically, participants in the Russian Liberation Movement have affirmed that they experienced a greater sense of freedom as prisoners-of-war in the Third Reich, than they had as citizens of the Soviet Union. This feeling of intellectual liberty also provided the stimulus for discussions in which political problems were of primary importance. The future of the USSR rather than the intentions of the Third Reich, was the main subject of these deliberations. Despite the appalling conditions in which they were held, with survival the order of the day for the majority of Soviet prisoners-of-war, those who lived long enough and were able to get transferred to special camps, most notably Dabendorf, continued their theoretical and political discussions. The tenor of such debates altered with the progress of the war. In the earlier phase, when the leadership of the USSR was in disarray, and German victory seemed likely, change within the Soviet Union seemed to be a distinct possibility. Once the tide had begun to turn, the victories of the Red Army seemed to provide compelling justification for the existence and policies of the Soviet regime. Nevertheless, right up to the end of the war, members of the Russian Liberation Movement persisted in their attempts to debate the problem which concerned them most: the possibilities which the future held for their country.

By November 1944, when the Prague Manifesto was published, it was too late for the Russian Liberation Movement to achieve any spectacular military success. The Red Army was advancing through Eastern Europe, and the disaffected troops and Soviet civilians on whose support in the period of defeat and occupation Vlasov had counted, were no longer available. Vlasov seems to have realised this, even if some of his subordinates still hoped for a favourable conclusion. Regardless of the approaching catastrophe, Vlasov felt that the war had offered a chance for change in the USSR. Russians who cared about the future of their country had formed the Liberation Movement, and it was essential to leave a record of its aims and ideals so that the participants' intentions should not be misrepresented. The Prague Manifesto was to provide such a record. Vlasov thought that history would show, in the end, that he and his supporters had been right.

Corroborative evidence for this view can be found in the fact that the text of the Prague Manifesto has never appeared in any Soviet history of the war. The implication is that the Soviet authorities still have something to fear from the legacy and ideas of the Russian Liberation Movement and therefore take great care that very little information about it should reach the Soviet people. Instead, much effort has been expended in vilifying the Movement in the person of General Vlasov. Yet the available evidence shows that Vlasov was not the opportunist and Nazi hireling of such accounts. Throughout, Vlasov stressed his nationalism and strove to preserve the independence of the Movement as far as circumstances permitted. When offered the chance to fly to Spain at the end of the war, Vlasov declined to escape, feeling bound to stay with the men whom he had led into this impasse.

Soviet citizens in the Russian Liberation Movement had to contend with various major difficulties. The need to establish a *modus vivendi* with the Nazi authorities meant that particular care had to be taken over the phraseology of the Movement's publications. An allusive language had to be developed in which certain questions were avoided or glossed over so that other issues, vital to the development of the Liberation Movement, could find expression. This added the further requirement that the supporters should read between the lines and understand the hidden implication of the Movement's pronouncements. Given these constraints, it is all the more to the credit of the Movement that the leaders managed to circumvent Nazi demands for the inclusion of anti-semitic propaganda in the KONR newspaper, *Volya naroda*, and that Vlasov withstood pressure from the Nazi authorities to include criticism of the Jews in the Prague Manifesto.

Although rapid development of the programme was hindered by the inexperience of both leaders and supporters of the Liberation Movement in dealing with the political concepts, the key documents demonstrate, nevertheless, that they were gradually coming to terms with these problems and were addressing themselves to the ideological implications of their position. The experiences undergone by these Soviet citizens led them to try and come to terms with and develop further ideas which the post-1917 Russian emigration had already been discussing for twenty years. Nielsen has written that: 'The politics of the first emigration has a definite ... place in the history of Russian political and social thought.'[3] The truth of this statement can be illustrated by reference to the way in which, during the Second World War, Soviet citizens encountered some of the ideas current in the emigration and realised that these might help them solve the problems which they had come across in Russia. The post-1917 emigration consisted largely of the political, cultural and social elite of Imperial Russia. As such it was familiar with a wide variety of ideas and proceeded to develop them in emigration. The Russian intelligentsia of the nineteenth century had argued over the question as to how Russia and her history should be understood and which was the best path of development. Should Russia follow the example of the West or should she adhere to a course of her own? Was this evolution dictated by her economic development or by her cultural inheritance, particularly as expressed by the teaching and spirit of the Russian Orthodox Church, which was different from that of Western Christianity? These arguments continued in emigration, but now, too, the cataclysm of the Revolution had to be assessed. At the heart of divergent émigré polemics lay different appreciations of the causes and results of the Revolution of 1917. Were they a result of a deep-seated malaise within Russian society, and if so, what did the Revolutions demonstrate about the condition of that society and what changes might be expected to occur? Or should the events of 1917 be assessed in less apocalyptic terms and seen in the shorter perspective of the effects of the war both on Tsarism and the Provisional Government? Should February or October 1917 be seen as the true expression of the wishes of the Russian people, and how far had Lenin and the Bolsheviks fulfilled those wishes? The answers to these questions determined the way in which events within the Soviet Union in the 1920s and 1930s were interpreted. However, although émigré life provided opportunities frequently denied their Soviet compatriots, for the elaboration and discussion of concepts relating to political developments in the Soviet Union, the émigrés were denied the chance of action and their deliberations were confined to a theoretical plane. The war provided an opportunity to put some of these theories into effect. Despite their differing backgrounds, the problems raised by the emigration were fundamental to discussions of the Russian Liberation Movement. Thus, émigré Russians, especially those who were members of NTS, through their contacts with Soviet prisoners-of-war, particularly in special camps such as Wustrau or Dabendorf, provided an initial catalyst and focus for their Soviet compatriots and helped them both with the practical organisation of the Russian Liberation Movement as well as with the theoretical underpinnings of the programme.

In the Prague Manifesto itself, assessment of 1917 is phrased ambiguously. *Bloknot Propagandista* elaborated questions raised by the programme of the Russian Liberation Movement, but although it came close to addressing itself to the question: 'How should the Russian Revolutions be evaluated?', the author finally returned an equivocal answer. On one level, this ambiguity was the product of the need to create a united movement. It was not wise to generate divisions, especially amongst the leadership, over the theoretical issue whether February or October 1917 represented the real embodiment of the wishes of Russian society, when the Movement was already beset by so many practical difficulties. Secondly, it was not easy for people who were products of the Soviet system and accepted many aspects of that society, to reject or even to criticise the Revolution which had inaugurated the Soviet state. Thus, the ideologists of the Movement preferred to concentrate on the abuse of power within the Soviet state rather than to find fault with the genesis of that state.

The programme of the Russian Liberation Movement should not be considered, therefore, merely as a curious by-product of the conflict between the Third Reich and the Soviet Union. Had Soviet citizens been free to ask these questions about their society in the late 1930s and early 1940s they would, undoubtedly, have raised the issues which the ideologists of the Russian Liberation Movement addressed. How Soviet citizens within Soviet society would have answered them depended on their differing interpretations of events in 1917; and it seems unlikely that they would have found it easy to reach consensus of opinion on this very complex problem.

NOTES

1 See p. 36 on the Kaminsky and Osintorf Brigades.
2 See Bethell, N., *The Last Secret*, New York (1974); Tolstoy, N., *Victims of Yalta*, London (1979); Elliot, M., *Pawns of Yalta*, Illinois (1982).
3 Nielsen, J. P., 'Milyukov and Stalin. P. N. Milyukov's political evolution in emigration', *Meddelelser*, no. 32, Oslo (1983), p. 2.

Appendix A

The Smolensk Declaration

An appeal by the Russian Committee to the men and officers[1] of the Red Army, to the whole Russian nation, and to the other nations of the Soviet Union.

Friends and Brothers!

BOLSHEVISM IS THE ENEMY OF THE RUSSIAN PEOPLE. It has brought countless disasters to our country and finally has involved the Russian people in a bloody war waged in others' interests. This war has brought unheard-of sufferings to our Motherland. Millions of Russians have already paid with their lives for Stalin's criminal attempts to seize world-wide power to the profit of Anglo-American capitalists. Millions of Russians have been crippled and have lost their ability to work forever. Women, old people and children are dying of cold, starvation and because the work demanded of them is beyond their strength. Hundreds of Russian cities and thousands of villages have been destroyed, blown up and burned on Stalin's orders.

Defeats such as those experienced by the Red Army have never happened before in the history of our country. In spite of the selflessness of the troops and officers and the bravery and self-sacrifice of the Russian people, battle after battle has been lost. The fault lies with the rottenness of the whole of the Bolshevik system, and the incompetence of Stalin and his general staff.

At this very moment, when Bolshevism has shown itself to be incapable of organising the country's defences, Stalin and his clique make use of terror and lying propaganda to continue to drive people

---

[1] Commanders of the Red Army were increasingly referred to as officers after January 1943 when epaulettes were reintroduced on their uniforms.

to their deaths, for they want to remain in power, at least for a while, regardless of the cost in blood to the Russian people.

STALIN'S ALLIES – THE BRITISH AND AMERICAN CAPITALISTS – HAVE BETRAYED THE RUSSIAN PEOPLE. They aim to make use of Bolshevism in order to take over the natural riches of our country. These plutocrats not only save their own skins at the cost of millions of Russian lives, but they are the signatories to secret pacts biased in their favour.

Germany, meanwhile, is not waging war against the Russian people and their Motherland, but only against Bolshevism. Germany does not wish to encroach on the living space of the Russian people or on their national and political liberties. Adolf Hitler's National-Socialist Germany aims to organise a 'New Europe' without Bolsheviks and Capitalists, in which every nation is guaranteed an honourable place.

The place of the Russian nation lies in the family of European nations; its place within the 'New Europe' will depend on the degree of its participation in the struggle against Bolshevism, since the destruction of Stalin's blood-stained power and that of his criminal clique – IS FIRST AND FOREMOST THE TASK OF THE RUSSIAN PEOPLE.

In order to unite the Russian people and to lead them in their struggle against this hated regime, in order to co-operate with Germany in its struggle against Bolshevism and in its creation of a 'New Europe', we, the sons of our people and the patriots of our Motherland have formed the Russian Committee.

The RUSSIAN COMMITTEE has set itself the following aims:

a. *The overthrow of Stalin and his clique, the destruction of Bolshevism.*
b. *The conclusion of an honourable peace with Germany.*
c. *The creation, in friendship with Germany and the other peoples of Europe, of a 'New Russia' without Bolsheviks and Capitalists.*

The RUSSIAN COMMITTEE sees the following principles as forming the basis of the 'New Russia':

1. The abolition of forced labour and the provision of a guarantee to the worker of a genuine right to work so that he may create his own material well-being;
2. The abolition of collective farms and the systematic transfer of land into the peasants' private ownership;
3. The re-establishment of commerce, trades and crafts and the provision of the opportunity for private initiative to participate in the economic life of the country;

4. The provision of the opportunity for the intelligentsia to work freely for the well-being of their people;

5. The guarantee of social justice and the protection of all working people from exploitation;

6. The provision for working people of their genuine rights to education, to leisure and to a secure old age;

7. The complete dismantling of the regime of terror and the introduction of genuine freedom of religion, conscience, speech, assembly and the press; the guarantee of inviolability of persons and of their homes;

8. The guarantee of national liberty;

9. The release of all the political prisoners of Bolshevism and the return home of all those in prisons and labour camps who have suffered repression as a result of their struggle against Bolshevism;

10. The rebuilding of towns and villages destroyed during the war at the state's expense;

11. The rebuilding of factories destroyed during the war;

12. The abrogation of the payments specified in the one-sided agreements concluded by Stalin with Anglo-American capitalists;

13. The provision of a minimum living wage for war veterans and their families.

Since we believe wholeheartedly that a happy future for the Russian people can and must be built on the basis of these principles, we call upon all Russians who now find themselves in the occupied territories and in those territories still occupied by the Bolshevik authorities: workers, peasants, members of the intelligentsia, soldiers, officers, political workers, TO UNITE IN THE STRUGGLE ON THE MOTHERLAND'S BEHALF, AGAINST HER WORST ENEMY – BOLSHEVISM. The Russian Committee declares that Stalin and his clique are enemies of the people. The Russian Committee declares that all those who voluntarily joined the punitive organisations of Bolshevism – the special sections, the NKVD, the frontier detachments – are enemies of the people. The Russian Committee declares that all those who destroy the treasures of the Russian people are enemies of the people.

The duty of every honest son of the people is to destroy the enemies of the people, who propel our country towards new misfortunes. The Russian Committee calls upon all Russians to carry out their duty.

The Russian Committee calls upon all Red Army men and officers to cross over to the *Russian Liberation Army* which is allied to Germany. Furthermore, the life of all those crossing over to the fighters against Bolshevism is guaranteed and sacrosanct, whatever their previous actions and occupation may have been.

The Russian Committee calls upon all Russians to take part in the struggle against hated Bolshevism, to set up partisan units of liberation and to turn their weapons against the oppressors of the people, Stalin and his hirelings.

Russians! Friends and brothers!

Enough blood has been spilt! There has been enough starvation, forced labour and suffering in the Bolshevik torture-chambers! Arise and join in the struggle for freedom! Let us fight in the sacred struggle for our Motherland! Join in the fight to the finish to gain happiness for the Russian people! Long may peace with honour with Germany prevail! It will lay the basis for eternal friendship between the German and Russian nations!

Long live the Russian people, equal partners in the family of nations of a New Europe!

Chairman of the Russian Committee
LIEUTENANT-GENERAL A. A. VLASOV

Secretary of the Russian Committee
MAJOR-GENERAL V. V. MALYSHKIN

27 December 1942
Smolensk

Appendix B

Vlasov's Open Letter: 'Why I decided to fight Bolshevism'[1]

Inasmuch as I am calling on all Russian people to fight against Stalin and his clique, to build a 'New Russia' without Bolsheviks and Capitalists, I consider it my duty to explain my own actions.

The Soviet authorities have not harmed me personally in any way. I am the son of a peasant, and was born in the province of Nizhni Novgorod. I studied in conditions of great poverty and achieved higher education. I accepted the national (*narodnuyu*) revolution, and enlisted in the Red Army in order to fight for land for the peasants, for a better life for the workers, and for a brighter future for the Russian people. Since that time my life has been inextricably linked with the life of the Red Army. I served in its ranks without a break for 24 years. I rose from the ranks to command an army and to be deputy commander of a front. I have commanded a company, battalion, regiment, division and corps. I was awarded the Order of Lenin, the Order of the Red Banner, and decorated with the medal for 20 years' service in the Workers' and Peasants' Red Army. I have been a member of the Communist Party since 1930.

And now I am fighting Bolshevism and asking the people, whose son I am, to follow me.

Why? Anyone who reads my appeal will ask this question and I am bound to provide an honest answer.

During the Civil War I fought with the Red Army because I believed that the Revolution would give the Russian people land, freedom and happiness. When I became a commander in the Red Army, I lived with the men and their officers – Russian workers, peasants, and members of the intelligentsia, all of them dressed in

[1]Published in *Zarya*, 3 March 1943; in *Dobrovolets*, 7 March 1943.

grey [army issue] overcoats. I knew their thoughts, their worries and problems. I did not lose touch with my family and my village and was familiar with the ways and means of the peasantry.

And so I realised that none of those things for which the Russian people had fought during the Civil War had been achieved by Bolshevik victory. I saw what a difficult life a Russian worker led and how the peasant was forcibly driven to join the collective farms. Millions of Russian people disappeared, having been arrested and shot without trial. I saw that everything Russian was being destroyed, that time-servers were being given positions of command in the Red Army, people to whom the interests of the Russian nation were of no importance.

The commissar system was corrupting the Red Army. Lack of responsibility, shadowing and spying on each other, have made the commanders puppets in the hands of the party hacks in civilian clothing or in uniform.

From 1938 to 1939 I was in China as military adviser to Chiang Kai-shek. When I returned to the USSR, I saw that during that time the command structure of the army had been destroyed for no reason whatsoever on Stalin's orders. Thousands of the best officers, including the Marshals of the Red Army, had been arrested and shot or sent to the labour camps to disappear forever. Terror was unleashed not only on the army but on the whole nation. There was no family which was not involved in some way or other. The army was weakened, the terrified nation looked to the future with horror, awaiting the war which Stalin had made inevitable.

Foreseeing that enormous sacrifices would be the unavoidable lot of the Russian people in this coming war, I aimed to do everything in my power to strengthen the Red Army. The 99th Division, which I commanded, was acknowledged to be the best in the Red Army. I tried to stifle the feeling of indignation which the actions of Stalin and his clique had aroused in me by working and constantly caring for the military formations committed to my charge.

And then war broke out. It found me commanding the 4th Mechanised Corps. As a soldier and a son of my country, I considered that I was bound to carry out my duty honestly. My corps in Peremysl and Lvov faced up to and withstood the onslaught and was prepared to counter-attack but my proposals were rejected. Indecisive and chaotic leadership corrupted by commissar control brought a series of heavy defeats upon the Red Army.

I withdrew the troops to Kiev. There I took on the command of the 37th Army and the difficult job of commandant of the town garrison. I saw that the war was being lost for two reasons: the unwillingness of the Russian people to defend Bolshevik power and the system of coercion which had been developed; and the irresponsible actions of those in command of the army, which had resulted in the interference of commissars at all levels in the army's work.

My army fought in the defence of Kiev under difficult conditions and defended the capital of the Ukraine successfully for two months. However, the incurable weaknesses of the Red Army had their effect. The front was broken through in adjacent sections. Kiev was surrounded. On the orders of the High Command, I had to abandon the fortified area.

After breaking out from the encirclement, I was appointed Deputy Commander of the South-Western Front and then Commander of the 20th Army. The formation of the 20th Army took place under difficult circumstances when the fate of Moscow was being decided. I did everything I could to defend the country's capital. The 20th Army halted the advance on Moscow and then counter-attacked. It broke through the German lines and took Solnechnogorsk, Voloko-lamsk, Shakhovsky, Sered and other towns, and made the counter-attack along the whole length of the Moscow Front possible and reached the approaches to Gzhatsk.

During the decisive battles for Moscow, I saw how those in the rear helped those in the front line, but like every soldier, each worker and inhabitant behind the lines did so only because he considered that he was defending the Motherland. He bore countless sufferings for the Motherland, sacrificed everything. More than once, I chased away the question which kept coming to mind: surely it was not for Bolshevism, hiding under the sacred name of the Motherland, that the Russian nation was really spilling its blood? ...

I was appointed Deputy Commander of the Volkhov Front and Commander of the 2nd Shock Army. The command of this army was organised from the centre and was in the hands of the General Staff. No one knew or was interested in the real circumstances of the army. One order from the top would be contradicted by the next one. The army was condemned to certain destruction.

The men and officers received 100 or sometimes only 50 grams of hardtack a day for several weeks. They became bloated with hunger. Many could no longer move in the swamps, into which the orders of the High Command had led them. But everyone continued to fight selflessly. Russians died heroically. But for what? For what did they sacrifice their lives? For what did they have to die?

I stayed with the men and their officers until the end. A handful of us remained and we continued to carry out our duty as soldiers to the very end. I extricated myself from the encirclement into the forest and hid in the forest and swamps for about a month. But now the full force of these questions made themselves felt: was it worth spilling the blood of the Russian people any further? Was it in the interests of the Russian people to continue the war? What were the Russian people fighting for?

It was clear to me that Bolshevism had involved the Russian people in a war being fought in the interests of the Anglo-American capitalists. England had always been the enemy of the Russian people. England had always attempted to weaken and harm our Motherland. But Stalin, by acting in the interests of the Anglo-American capitalists, had seen an opportunity to realise his plans for world-wide hegemony, and in order to carry out these plans he had linked the fate of the Russian people with that of England, had involved the Russian nation in a war and had brought countless sufferings upon it. These wartime sufferings are the result of all the disasters which the nations of our country have had to bear under 25 years of Bolshevik power.

So, is it not a crime to continue to shed more blood? Is not Bolshevism in general, and more particularly Stalin, the main enemy of the Russian people? Is it not the first and sacred duty of every honest Russian to fight against Stalin and his clique?

While I was in the forest and swamps, I finally came to the conclusion that my duty consisted in calling on the Russian people to fight to overthrow Bolshevik power, to fight for peace for the Russian people, to fight for an end to an unnecessary war being fought for foreign interests which was spilling Russian blood, to fight for the creation of a New Russia, in which every Russian might be happy.

I reached the firm conclusion that the tasks facing the Russian people can be solved in alliance and co-operation with the German people. The interests of the Russian people have always combined with the interests of the German people and with the interests of all the people of Europe. The highest achievements of the Russian people have always been indissolubly linked with those periods of history when their destiny was interconnected with that of Europe and their culture, their economy and their way of life was formed in close association with the peoples of Europe. Bolshevism has built an impenetrable wall to separate the Russian people from Europe. It has attempted to isolate our Motherland from advanced European countries. In the name of utopian ideas which are alien to the Russian people, Bolshevism has prepared for war, opposing itself to the people of Europe.

In alliance with the German people, the Russian people must destroy this wall of hatred and suspicion. In alliance and co-operation with Germany they must build a new and happy Motherland – within the framework of the family of free European nations with equal rights.

Having thought this through and having made this decision, I was taken prisoner, together with a handful of loyal friends, in a last battle.

I spent more than six months as a prisoner. Behind the wire, as a prisoner-of-war, not only did I not change my mind, but my convictions were reinforced.

In all honesty and with complete conviction, in full realisation of my responsibility towards my Motherland, towards my people and to history for my actions, I call on the people to fight for the creation of a 'New Russia'.

How do I see this 'New Russia'? I will disclose this in due course.

History does not turn back. I am not calling on the people to return to the past. No! I call on them to go forward to a brighter future, to participate in the struggle to complete the national revolution, to the struggle to create a New Russia – a homeland for our great people. I call them to the path of brotherhood and unity with the peoples of Europe and in the first instance to the path of co-operation with the great German people.

My appeal has met with a deeply sympathetic response not only in the widest circles amongst prisoners-of-war, but amongst the broad masses of the Russian people in those areas still under the control of Bolshevism. This sympathetic response from Russians expressing their willingness to support wholeheartedly the Russian Liberation Army gives me the right to say that I am on the right track, that the cause for which I fight is a just cause, namely the cause of the Russian people.

In this struggle for our future, I openly and honestly advocate an alliance with Germany. This alliance, which is equally advantageous to both great nations, will bring us to victory over the dark forces of Bolshevism, and will free us from the oppression of Anglo-American capital.

During the last few months, Stalin, realising that the Russian people do not wish to fight for the international aims of Bolshevism which are alien to them, has altered policy towards the Russians superficially. He has abolished the Institute of Commissars, he has tried to reach an agreement with the venal leaders of the previously persecuted church and he is trying to restore the old tradition of the army. In order to compel the Russian people to spill their blood for alien interests, Stalin recalls the great names of Alexander Nevsky, Kutuzov, Suvorov, Minin and Pozharsky. He wants to make it appear that he is fighting for the Motherland, for our Country, for Russia. He needs this contemptible and base deception in order to remain in power. Only the blind could believe that Stalin would turn away from Bolshevik ideas. A forlorn hope! Bolshevism has forgotten nothing, has not retreated a step and will not retreat from its programme. He talks of Russia and the Russians today only so that he can achieve victory with the help of the Russian people, but tomorrow, armed with even greater strength, he will enserf the Russian people and force them to serve alien interests still further.

Neither Stalin nor Bolshevism fights for Russia. Our true Motherland can only be created in the ranks of the anti-Bolshevik Movement. The concern and duty of the Russians is the struggle against Stalin, for peace, for a New Russia! Russia is ours! The past history of the Russian people is ours! The future of the Russian people is ours!

The Russian people, many millions strong, throughout their history have always found the strength to fight for their future and their national independence. Thus the Russian people will not perish now and in these hard times they will find the strength within themselves to unite and overthrow the hated yoke, to unite and build a new state in which they will find their happiness.

LIEUTENANT-GENERAL A. A. VLASOV

Appendix C

The Prague Manifesto[1]

The Manifesto of the Committee for the Liberation of the Peoples of Russia.

Fellow-countrymen! Brothers and Sisters!

In this hour of great trial we must decide the fate of our Motherland, our peoples and ourselves.

Mankind is living through an era of the greatest upheavals. The present world war is a fight to the finish between opposing political systems.

It is being fought by the powers of imperialism, led by the plutocrats of England and the USA, whose greatness is built on the oppression and exploitation of other countries and peoples. It is being fought by the powers of internationalism led by Stalin's clique, who dream of world revolution and the destruction of the national independence of other countries and their peoples. It is being fought by freedom-loving nations, who yearn to live their own way of life, determined by their own historical and national development.

There is no greater crime than the one which Stalin commits, of destroying the countries and oppressing the peoples who strive to preserve the land of their forebears and build their happiness by their own labour. There is no greater crime than to subjugate another people and force one's own will upon it.

The forces of destruction and slavery camouflage their criminal aims with slogans such as the defence of freedom, democracy, culture and civilisation. By the defence of freedom they mean the conquest of other lands. By the defence of democracy they mean forcing their political system upon other states. By the defence of culture and civilisation they mean the destruction of monuments of culture and

[1] *Volya naroda*, no. 1 (Wednesday, 15 November 1944), p. 1.

216

civilisation which have been created over thousands of years by the work of other peoples.

What then are the peoples of Russia fighting for? Why are they condemned to countless sacrifices and suffering?

Two years ago Stalin was still able to deceive nations with words about the patriotic nature of the war of liberation. But now the Red Army has crossed the state boundaries of the USSR, forced its way into Roumania, Bulgaria, Serbia, Croatia and Hungary and is flooding these countries with blood. Now the true nature of the war being continued by the Bolsheviks is made clear. Their aim is to strengthen still further the mastery of Stalin's tyranny over the peoples of the USSR, and to establish his hegemony all over the world.

The peoples of Russia have experienced the burden of Bolshevik tyranny for more than a quarter of a century.

In the Revolution of 1917 the peoples who inhabited the Russian Empire sought to realise their aspirations for justice, for the general welfare and for national liberty. They rose up against the outmoded tsarist regime, which did not wish to and could not abolish those factors which gave rise to social injustice, or do away with the remnants of serfdom and the economic and cultural backwardness of Russia. But the parties and their leaders were unable to decide on bold reforms to follow the overthrow of the tsarist empire by the people in February 1917. By their ambiguous policy, their compromises and their unwillingness to take on responsibility for the future, they failed to prove themselves to the people. The people spontaneously followed those who promised them immediate peace, land, freedom and bread, those who put forward the most radical slogans.

The Bolshevik Party promised to create a social system in which the people would live happily. To attain this the people made incalculable sacrifices. It is not the fault of the people that the Bolshevik Party not only did not realise the demands of the people, but by gradually strengthening the coercive nature of the administrative apparatus, robbed the people of the rights which they had won, and forced them into permanent misery, into lawlessness and exploited them most unscrupulously.

The Bolsheviks deprived the peoples of Russia of their right to national independence, development and their own way of life.

The Bolsheviks deprived the people of the freedom of speech, the freedom of conviction, the free choice of a place of residence and the right to travel, the freedom to choose their work and the opportunity for everyone to take his place in society in accordance with his abilities. They have replaced these freedoms with a regime enforced by terror, party privilege and arbitrary treatment of the individual.

The Bolsheviks took back from the peasants the land for which they had fought, they deprived them of their right to work freely on their land and to use the proceeds of their work as they wished. By chaining the peasants to the collective farm system, they turned them into hired labourers of the state, deprived of any rights, endlessly exploited and oppressed.

The Bolsheviks deprived the workers of the right freely to choose their profession and place of work, to organise themselves and to fight for better working conditions and wages, and to influence the process of production. They turned the workers into the slaves of state capitalism, without any rights.

The Bolsheviks deprived the intelligentsia of their right to free creative work for the well-being of their people and by the use of violence, terror and bribery sought to make them a tool of lying propaganda.

The Bolsheviks condemned the people of our Motherland to permanent poverty, hunger and extinction and to spiritual and physical slavery, and finally they forced them into a criminal war fought for causes alien to them.

All this is being camouflaged with lies about the democratic nature of Stalin's constitution and the building of a socialist society. No other country in the world has ever had or has such a low standard of living, when its material wealth is so vast. No other country has known such interference with the personal freedom of the individual and such humiliation as has occurred and continues to occur under the Bolshevik system.

The peoples of Russia have lost their faith in Bolshevism forever. It is a system where the state is the all-devouring machine and the people have become indigent slaves deprived of their belongings and their legal rights. They see the terrible danger which hovers over them. If Bolshevism should succeed in asserting itself over the blood and the bones of the peoples of Europe, even temporarily, then the struggle of the peoples of Russia, carried on for years and at immense cost, would have been in vain. Bolshevism would take advantage of the nations' exhaustion in this war and would rob them totally of their ability to resist. Therefore, the efforts of all peoples must be directed towards the destruction of the monstrous Bolshevik machine and towards giving every man the right to live and work freely in accordance with his capacity and abilities, towards the creation of a society which protects the individual from lawlessness and does not permit anyone, including the state, to deprive him of the fruits of his labour.

IN VIEW OF THESE CONCLUSIONS, THE REPRESENTATIVES OF THE PEOPLES OF RUSSIA, IN FULL RECOGNITION OF THEIR RESPONSIBILITY TO THEIR PEOPLES, TO HISTORY AND TO THEIR DESCENDANTS, HAVE SET UP A COMMITTEE FOR THE LIBERATION OF THE PEOPLES OF RUSSIA, IN ORDER TO ORGANISE A UNITED STRUGGLE AGAINST BOLSHEVISM.

The Committee for the Liberation of the Peoples of Russia has as its aim:

a. The overthrow of the tyranny created by Stalin, the liberation of the peoples of Russia from the Bolshevik system, and the restitution to the peoples of Russia of those rights which they won in the national revolution of 1917;

b. An end to the war and the conclusion of an honourable peace with Germany;

c. The creation of a new free popular state system without Bolsheviks and exploiters.

As the basis for the formation of the new political system of the peoples of Russia the committee lays down the following main principles:

1. The equality of all peoples of Russia and their real right to national development, self-determination, and state independence;

2. The establishment of a national labour (*natsional'no-trudovoy*) system, where the interests of the state are subordinated to the task of improving the standard of living and the development of the nation;

3. The maintenance of peace, the establishment of friendly relations with all countries and the greatest possible development of international co-operation;

4. Extensive government measures to strengthen the position of the family and of marriage; genuine equality for women;

5. The abolition of forced labour and the guarantee to all workers of the genuine right to work freely as the basis of their material well-being; with sufficient wages for all forms of work to provide for a civilised standard of living;

6. The abolition of the collective farm system and the handing over, without requiring compensation, of land to the peasants as their private property, with the freedom to farm as they wish, the right to make what use they wish of their agricultural products, the abolition of forced norms and the abrogation of debts to the Soviet state;

7. The establishment of the inviolability of private property earned by work; the re-establishment of commerce, trades and crafts and the restitution to private initiative of the right and opportunity to participate in the economic life of the country;

8. The provision of the opportunity for the intelligentsia to work freely for the well-being of their people;

9. The guarantee of social justice and of protection for workers against any form of exploitation regardless of their origin and their previous employment;

10. The establishment for all without exception, of a genuine right to free education, medical care, holidays and security in old age;

11. The destruction of the regime of terror and coercion; the abolition of forced resettlement and mass deportation; the establishment of a genuine freedom of religion, conscience, speech, assembly and the press; a guarantee of the inviolability of persons, their property and their homes; the equality of all before the law, the independence and public proceedings of the courts;

12. The release of all the political prisoners of Bolshevism and the return home of all those in prisons and labour camps who have suffered repression as a result of their struggle against Bolshevism; no vengeance on or persecution of those who cease to support Stalin and Bolshevism, regardless of whether their support was a result of conviction or coercion;

13. The rebuilding of national property destroyed in the war – towns, villages, factories and industrial plant – at government expense;

14. State support for war victims and their families.

The destruction of Bolshevism is an urgent task facing all progressive forces. The Committee for the Liberation of the Peoples of Russia is convinced that the united efforts of the peoples of Russia will receive support from all the freedom-loving nations of the world.

The Liberation Movement of the Peoples of Russia is the continuation of many years of struggle against Bolshevism and for freedom, peace and justice. The successful end of this struggle is now assured because of:

a. The people's experience of struggle which is greater than was the case in 1917;

b. The existence of growing and organised armed forces – the Russian Army of Liberation, the Ukrainian Liberation forces, Cossack troops and national units;

c. The existence of anti-Bolshevik armed forces behind the Soviet lines;

d. The existence of growing opposition to the regime among the people, the government apparatus and the army of the USSR.

The Committee for the Liberation of the Peoples of Russia maintains that THE UNIFICATION OF ALL NATIONAL FORCES AND THEIR SUBORDINATION TO THE COMMON CAUSE OF THE DESTRUCTION OF BOLSHEVISM IS THE PREREQUISITE FOR VICTORY. The Committee for the Liberation of the Peoples of Russia, therefore, supports all revolutionary and opposition forces directed against Stalin and Bolshevism; while at the same time it decisively rejects all reactionary projects which would limit the rights of the people.

The Committee for the Liberation of the Peoples of Russia welcomes Germany's help under conditions which will not detract from the honour and independence of our country. At the moment this help provides the only available opportunity to organise an armed struggle against Stalin's clique.

In our fight we have taken upon ourselves the responsibility for the fate of the peoples of Russia. Millions of the best sons of our country are with us. They have taken up arms and already have proved their courage and their willingness to give their lives for the liberation of the Motherland from Bolshevism. Millions of people who have escaped from the clutches of Bolshevism and are working together in the struggle's common cause are with us. Tens of millions of brothers and sisters, suffering under the yoke of Stalin's tyranny and awaiting their hour of liberation are with us.

Officers and men of the Liberation Forces! The blood shed in a common struggle has united in the comradeship of battle soldiers of different nationalities! We have a common goal. We must work together. ONLY THE UNITY OF ALL THE ARMED ANTI-BOLSHEVIK FORCES OF THE PEOPLES OF RUSSIA WILL LEAD US TO VICTORY. Do not lay down the weapons which you have been given, fight for unity, above all fight against the enemy of the people – Bolshevism and its accomplices. Remember that the suffering peoples of Russia await you. Liberate them!

Fellow-countrymen, brothers and sisters in Europe! Only victory over Bolshevism will make possible your return home as citizens able to enjoy your full rights. There are millions of you. The success of the struggle depends on you. Remember that now you are working for a common cause, for the heroic Liberation Forces. Multiply your efforts and your achievements in your work.

Officers and soldiers of the Red Army! Stop fighting this criminal war whose purpose is to to oppress the peoples of Europe. Turn your weapons against the Bolshevik usurpers, who have enslaved the peoples of Russia and have condemned them to hunger and suffering and have deprived them of their rights.

Brothers and sisters in the Motherland! Intensify your struggle against Stalin's tyranny and against his war of conquest. Organize your forces for the decisive struggle for the rights of which you were robbed, for justice and the common good.

The Committee for the Liberation of the Peoples of Russia calls upon all of you to unite and to fight for peace and freedom!

Chairman of the Committee for the Liberation of the Peoples of Russia: Lieutenant-General A. Vlasov.

Members of the Committee:
Lieutenant-General
  F. Abramov;
F. Alekseev, public figure;
Professor S. Andreyev;
Professor G. Anufriev;
Lieutenant-General E. Balabin;
Shamba Balinov, public figure;
Professor F. Bogatyrchuk;
S. Bolkhovskoy, actor;
Colonel V. Boyarsky;
K. Gordienko, worker;
Lieutenant A. Dzhpanov;
Lieutenant-General
  G. Zhilenkov;
Major-General D. Zakutny;

Y. Zherebkov, public figure;
Colonel Bunyachenko;
Colonel M. Meandrov;
A. Zaitsev, university lecturer;
Professor A. Karpinsky;
Professor N. Kovalev;
A. Lisovsky, journalist;
Major-General V. Malyshkin;
Corporal I. Mamedov;
Professor I. Moskvitinov;
Y. Muzychenko, author;
N. Podlaznik, worker;
Professor S. Rudnev;
Sergeant G. Saakian;
E. Tenzerov, university lecturer;

Captain D. Zyablitsky;

Professor A. Tsagol;

Kh. Tsymbal, peasant woman;

Captain I. Chanukh;

Major-General F. Trukhin;

Ibragim Chulik, M.D.;

F. Shlippe, public figure;

F. Yanushevskaya.

Candidates for Committee Membership:

Lieutenant V. Dubovets; V. Egorov, worker; A. Kazantsev, journalist; P. Kumin, engineer; D. Levitsky, public figure; Y. Rodnyi, worker; P. Semenov, engineer; Professor L. Smirnov; Professor V. Stal'makov; Professor V. Tatarinov; Major I. Tel'nikov; A. Shcheglov, private soldier.

[The names of some members and candidates of the Committee for the Liberation of the Peoples of Russia are not published in view of their presence in the territory of the USSR or to ensure their personal safety.]

Prague, 14 November 1944.

Select Bibliography

UNPUBLISHED MATERIAL

Andreyev, N. E. Unpublished memoirs. Author's archive.

Anon. [Buchardt, F.?]. 'Wlassow-Aktion. Die Behandlung des russischen Problems während der Zeit des ns. Regimes in Deutschland' [1945?]. Author's archive.

Bakhmeteff Archive, Columbia University.

Bundesarchiv, Koblenz. RFSS Persönlicher Stab Files, Ostministerium Files.

Bundesarchiv-Militärarchiv, Freiburg im Breisgau: Oberkommando des Heeres/Generalstab des Heeres Files, Pozdnyakov Collection, Steenberg Collection.

Foreign and Colonial Office Archives, London: Captured German records.

Gornav, P. 'Ot tsarskoy kokardy do znachka ROA'. Unpublished memoirs. Munich 1951. Author's archive.

Hoover Institution, Stanford: Nikolaevsky Archive.

Institut für Zeitgeschichte, Munich: Thorwald Collection.

Ivanov, N. G., Private Collection.

London School of Economics and Political Science. Melgunov Archive.

Mihalap, L. I. 'Soviet citizens in a struggle against Stalin: the Vlasov Army, a personal reminiscence'. Paper given at the AAASS conference in 1980. Author's archive.

Nikolaevsky Papers. Menlo Park, California.

Novosiltsev, I. L. 'General-Leytenant Andrey Andreyevich Vlasov, Predsedatel' Komiteta Osvobozhdeniya Narodov Rossii. Slovo cheloveka, kotorogo Vlasov schital svoim drugom'. Transcript of a tape prepared for A. I. Solzhenitsyn. Author's archive.

Public Records Office, Kew, London: F.O. 371/36958; 36959; 36960; 43303; 47955; 48004; 56710. W.O.11119.

ROA Archive. Columbia University, New York.

U.S. National Archives. Captured German Records, Nuremberg War Crimes Trials, SHAEF Documents.

YIVO Institute for Jewish Research, New York. Material on the occupied territories.

UNPUBLISHED DISSERTATIONS

Andreyev, C. C. L. 'The nature and development of opposition to Stalin as expressed by Soviet citizens in German hands during the Second World War' (Cambridge University, 1984).

Azarenko, T. 'The Russian Liberation Movement During World War II. Historical Accounts and Works of Fiction' (Georgetown University, Washington D.C., 1984).

Burton, R. 'The Vlasov Movement of World War II: an Appraisal' (The American University, Washington, D.C. 1963).

Buss, P. H. 'The Non-Germans in the German Armed Forces 1939–1945' (University of Kent, 1974).

Chavchavadse, D. 'The Vlasov Movement. Soviet citizens who served on the German side 1941–45' (Yale University, 1950).

Hayes, N. 'The Intelligentsia in Exile; Sovremennye Zapiski and the History of Émigré thought 1920–40' (University of Chicago, 1976).

Koons, T. 'L'histoire des doctrines politiques de l'émigration russe 1919–30' (Paris, 1951).

Petelchuk, P. 'The National Alliance of Russian Solidarists – A Study of a Russian Freedom Movement Group' (Syracuse University, 1970).

INTERVIEWS

Andreyev, N. E., M.A., Ph.D. Late Emeritus Reader in Russian Studies at the University of Cambridge. In Prague 1928–45. Knew many leading émigrés.

Artemova, A. N. Very active member of the NTS. During the war had a Dutch passport, therefore able to travel easily within the Third Reich.

Bourgina, A. M. Widow and archivist of B. I. Nikolaevsky.

Dudin, L. V., Member of ROA, writer.

Dudin, R. V. Member of KONR youth organisation.

Filippov, B. A. Engineer and literary critic, met Vlasov before the war and also in the occupied territories during the war.

Fröhlich, S. B. Baltic German of Russian culture. Sonderführer, liaison officer with Vlasov.

Galkin, D. D. Worked in press office at Dabendorf, author of *Bloknot Propagandista*.

Grulesky, P. Head of SBONR, post-war Vlasovite organisation.

Kazantseva, M. R. Widow of NTS member (see bibliography) and member of Russian Liberation Movement.

Kiselev, A. Orthodox priest, member of Russian Liberation Movement.

Konstantinov, D. Orthodox priest, member of Russian Liberation Movement.

Kroeger, E. Liaison officer between Vlasov and Himmler.

Kromiadi, K. G. Russian émigré, head of Vlasov's secretariat.

Kruzhin, P. I. Member of KONR youth section.

Krylova, V. N. Widow of instructor at Dabendorf.

Levitsky, D. A. Russian émigré from Riga. Associate member of KONR, head of Malyshkin's secretariat.

Meyer, Y. K. Member of first emigration from Berlin. Worked in KONR civilian department, dealing with aid to *Ostarbeiter*.

Muzychenko, Y. A. Member of KONR, on Ukrainian committee.

Noreikis, N. A. Member of the Dabendorf Press Department, involved in the composition of the Prague Manifesto.

Novosiltsev, I. L. Member of the first emigration, personal friend of Vlasov.

Pryanishnikov, B. V. Member of the first emigration, worked in KONR Civilian Department also on staff of *Volya naroda*.

Rahr, L. A. Member of NTS, worked in Vlasov's secretariat.

Redlich, R. N. Member of NTS, during war known as Captain Vorob'ev, worked in prisoner-of-war camps, visited Kaminsky at Lokot.

Rumyantsev, M. V. Colonel in Red Army, member of the Russian Liberation Movement.

Samarin, V. D. Journalist on staff of *Volya naroda*.

Schatoff, M. V. Head of Vlasov's bodyguard. Founded ROA archive at Columbia University.

Shtifanov, N. G. Lecturer at Dabendorf, involved in composition of Prague Manifesto.

Solzhenitsyn, A. I. Writer.

Steenberg, S. German officer during Second World War, now writer and journalist.

Woyciechowsky, S. Head of Russian émigrés in Warsaw.

Zaitsev, A. N. Lecturer at Dabendorf, member of the NTS, involved in the composition of the Prague Manifesto.

Zherebkov, Y. S. Appointed head of émigrés in Paris by Germans, member of KONR, head of KONR foreign section.

Ten additional people asked not to be named.

PUBLISHED SOURCES

Akten zur Deutschen Auswärtigen Politik 1918–45, Series D, Baden-Baden, 1950. Series E, Göttingen, 1969.

Biblioteka Propagandista, Izdanie kursov propagandistov Russkoy Osvoboditel'noy Armii, 1944.

Bloknot Propagandista Osvoboditel'nogo Dvizheniya Narodov Rossii, no. 5–6, January 1945. Izdatel'stvo glavnogo upravleniya propagandy Komiteta Osvobozhdeniya Narodov Rossii, Galkin, vvedeniye Pershina.

Dvinov, B. L. *Vlasovskoe dvizhenie v svete dokumentov*, New York, 1950.

Evraziistvo, (*Opyt systematicheskogo izlozheniya*), Prague, 1926.

Evraziistvo, (*Formulirovka*), Moscow, 1927.

Fischer, G. 'Besprechung des Führers mit Generalfeldmarschall Keitel und General Zeitzler am 8.6.1943 auf dem Berghof', *Journal of Modern History*, 23, no. 1 (March 1951), 58–71.

Goebbels' Diaries, L. Lochner (ed.), London, 1948.

Goebbels' Diaries, H. Trevor-Roper (ed.), London, 1978.

Heiber, H. *Hitlers Lagebesprechungen: protokollfragmente seiner militärischen Konferenzen 1942–45*, Stuttgart, 1962.

Hitler, A., *Mein Kampf*, translated by R. Manheim, introduced by D. C. Watt, London, 1972.

'Auszug aus der Ansprache des Führers an die Heeresgruppenführer pp.am 1.7.43. abends', *Vierteljahrshefte für Zeitgeschichte*, 2 (1954).

Hitler's Table Talk 1941–44, translated by N. Cameron and R. H. Stevens, introduction by H. Trevor-Roper, 2nd edn, London, 1973.

International Committee of the Red Cross. Report on its activities during the Second World War, Geneva, 1948.

Iskhod k Vostoku. Predchuvstviya i sversheniya. Utverzhdenie Evraziitsev, Sofia, 1921.

Kleist, P. *Zwischen Hitler und Stalin 1939–45*, Bonn, 1950.

Krasnov, P. 'Pis'mo', *Kazach'ya zemlya*, 12 (16 March 1945).

Krest'yanskaya Rossiya, Trudovaya Krest'yanskaya Partiya, Vvedenie. Ideologiya. Programma. Taktika. Ustav, Prague, 1928.

Krest'yanskaya Rossiya. Sbornik statey, New York, 1953.

Kriegstagebuch des Oberkommando der Wehrmacht 1940–45, H. Grenier and P. E. Schramm (eds.), Frankfurt am Main, 1965.

Malyskhin, V. F. 'Doklad na 1-oy antibol'shevitskoy konferentsii voenno-plennykh komandirov i boytsov Krasnoy armii, stavshikh v ryady Russkogo Osvoboditel'nogo Dvizheniya', *Zarya* (18 April 1943).

'Russkiye dni v Parizhe'. Rech' gen. Malyshkina, *Parizhskiy vestnik* (31 July 1943).

'Doklad na konferenzii sozvannoy germanskim institutom mezhdunarod-noy politiki', *Volya naroda* (24 January 1945).

Natsional'no-Trudovoy Soyuz (NTS) Publications:

Natsional'ny Soyuz Novogo Pokoleniya, 1935.

Za chto borot'sya, 1938.

Programmnye polozheniya i Ustav, Belgrade, 1938.

Natsional'no-Trudovoy Soyuz Novogo Pokoleniya. Za Novy Stroy, 1940

Kursy Natsional'no-Politicheskoy Podgotovki. I. 'Osnova natsional'nogo miro-vozzreniya' (1939). III. 'Sotsial'naya, ekonomicheskaya i politicheskaya zhizn',' (1937). IV. 'Istoricheskiy otdel' (1938).

Skhema Natsional'no-Trudovogo Stroya, Slovakia, 1944.

Nazi Conspiracy and Aggression, 8 vols., US Government Printing Office, Washington, D.C., 1946–8.

Petrichenko, S. M. *Pravda o Kronstadtskikh sobytiyakh*, 1921.

'V Kronstadtskie dni', *Revolutsionnaya Rossiya*, no. 16–18, Prague (1922), 6–8.

'O prichinakh Kronstadtskogo Vostaniya', *Znamya bor'by*, Berlin (1926). (All published in abridged form in *Kontinent*, 10 (1976), 206–34.

Pozdnyakov, V. V., *Rozhdenie ROA*, Syracuse, New York, 1972.

A. A. Vlasov, Syracuse, New York, 1973.

Pravda o Kronstadte, Izd. Volya Rossii, Prague, 1921. Appendix: Izvestiya Vremennogo Revolutsionnogo Komiteta Matrosov, Krasnoarmeytsev i Rabochikh Gor. Kronstadta, 1921.

Reichgesetzblatt 1934–35.

Russkoe Osvoboditel'noe Dvizhenie Narodov Rossii. On the back cover: Deutsche Informations Stelle, 7, Chang An Lui, (Gt. Western Road) Shanghai, 1944.

Schatoff, M. *Materialy i dokumenty Osvoboditel'nogo Dvizheniya Narodov Rossii v gody vtoroy mirovoy voiny 1941–45*, New York, 1966.

Spiridonov, A. I. *Formy i metody ustnoy propagandy*, Izd. KONR, 1945.

Trukhin, F. I. 'Vooruzhennye sily Osvoboditel'nogo Dvizheniya', *Volya naroda* (18 November 1944).

Vlasov, A. A. 'Novye metody boevoy ucheby', *Krasnaya zvezda*, Moscow (3 October 1940), reprinted in *Novoye v podgotovke voysk*, Kiev (1940), 95–8.

'Krasnoe znamya', *Krasnaya zvezda* (23 February 1941).

'Pochemu ya stal' na put' bor'by s bolshevizmom', *Zarya* (3 March 1943); *Dobrovolets* (7 March 1943).

'Ob antibolshevistskom povstancheskom dvizhenie', *Volya naroda* (9 December 1944).

'Novy pod'em Osvoboditel'nogo Dvizheniya', *Volya naroda* (17 December 1944).

Wladimirow, W. *Dokumente und Material des Komitees zur Befreiung der Völker Russlands*, Berlin, 1944.

Zhilenkov, G. N. 'My pobedim', *Volya naroda* (15 November 1944).

'Interviyu s inostrannymy korrespondentami', *Volya naroda* (15 November 1944).

'Nasha tsel' svoboda narodov', *Volya naroda* (17 January 1945).

'Das ist die UdSSR', *Völkischer Beobachter*, Berlin (20 January 1945).

BIBLIOGRAPHICAL GUIDES

L'émigration Russe en Europe. Catalogue collectif des périodiques russes. Vol. 1, 1855–1940, ed. T. Ossorguine-Bakounine, Paris, 1976. Vol. 2, 1940–1979, ed. A-M. Volkoff, Paris, 1981.

Foster, L. A. *Bibliography of Russian Émigré Literature 1918–1968*, 2 vols., Boston, 1970.

Lubenksy, S. 'Evraziiskaya bibliografiya 1921–31', *Tridsatye gody*, 7, *Utverzhdenie Evraziitsev*, Prague (1931), 285–317.

Schatoff, M. *Bibliografiya Osvoboditel'nogo Dvizheniya Narodov Rossii v gody vtoroy mirovoy voiny 1941–45*, Trudy Arkhiva ROA, New York, 1961.

Half a Century of Russian Serials 1917–68, parts 1–4, Russian Book Chamber Abroad, New York, 1969–72.

NEWSPAPERS AND PERIODICALS

(It was not possible to find all the Russian language newspapers published by the Germans during the Second World War, nor full runs of either wartime 'Vlasovite' newspapers nor all the publications of the post-war émigré 'ex-Vlasovite' organisations.)

Bloknot instruktora po ideologicheskoy vospitatel'noy rabote, Soyuz Molodezhi Narodov Rossii, Germany, 1947–53.

Bor'ba, organ SBONR, Munich, London (Ontario), 1947– .

Byulleten' antikommunisticheskogo tsentra osvoboditel'nogo dvizheniya narodov Rossii, Munich, 1948–50.

Chasovoy, Paris, Brussels, 1929–45, 1947– .

Dobrovolets, Berlin, 1943– .

Dobrovolets, Organ vnutrennoy svyazi kadrov ROA, Munich, 1953–6.

Evraziiskaya khronika, Berlin, Paris, 1925–7.

Fakel, izdanie SBONR, Canada, 1948.

Golos naroda, SBONR, Munich, 1950–7.

Informatsionny listok SBONR, Munich, 1948–50.

Izvestiya, Petrograd, 1917; Moscow, 1918– .

Kontinent, vol. 1, Berlin; vol. 2, Munich, 1974– .

Krasnaya zvezda, Moscow, 1924– .

Mayak svobody, SBONR, Bradford, 1950–4.

Mladoross, opoveshchanie Parizhskogo ochaga, Paris, 1928–9, continued as:
   Mladoross, ezhemesyachnik, Paris, 1930–2.

Mladorosskaya iskra, Paris 1931–5.

Narodnaya volya, Munich, 1953.

Novoe Russkoe Slovo, New York, 1910– .

Novy grad, 14 vols., Paris, 1931–39.

Novy zhurnal, New York 1942– .

Oboroncheskoe dvizhenie, Paris 1936–7; continued as: *Golos otechestva*, Paris
   1939–9.

Parizhskiy vestnik, Paris, 1942–4.

Possev, Frankfurt am Main, 1945– .

Pravda, Moscow, 1912– .

Rossiya i Slavyanstvo, Paris, 1928–34.

Sbornik Krest'yanskoy Rossii, 9 vols., Prague, 1922–4.

Signal, izdanie SBONR, Belgium, 1952.

S narodom za narod, 5 vols., Munich, 1962–5.

Sniper, byulleten' okruga Schleissheim. Soyuz Andreyevskogo Flaga,
   Munich, 1949.

Sotsialisticheskiy vestnik, Berlin, Paris, 1921–40; New York, 1940–63.

Volya naroda, Berlin, 1944–5.

Vozrozhdenie, Paris, 1949–74.

Za Rossiyu, Sofia, 1932–5; continued as: *Za novuyu Rossiyu*, Sofia, 1935–7;
   continued as: *Za rodinu*, Sofia, Belgrade, 1937–40.

Zarubezh'e, Munich, 1965–79.

Zarya, Berlin, 1943–5.

Znamya Rossii, Vestnik Krest'yanskoy Rossii, Prague, 1933–9.

ARTICLES AND BOOKS

Abdank-Kossovsky, V. 'Russkaya emigratsiya III', *Vozrozhdenie*, 54 (1956),
   128–38.

Abramovich, R. 'O chem my vse sporim', *Sotsialisticheskiy vestnik*, 607/8 (20
   May 1948).

Agursky, M. *Ideologiya natsional-bolshevizma*, Paris, 1980.

Aldan, A. G. *Armiya obrechennykh*, New York, 1969.

Aleksinskaya, T. 'Russkaya emigratsiya 1920–1939 godov', *Vozrozhdenie*, 60
   (December 1956), 33–41.

Alexeev, W. and Stavrou, T. G. *The Great Revival: the Russian Orthodox Church under German Occupation*, Minneapolis, 1976.

Alexeev, W. and Armes, K. 'German Intelligence: Religious Revival in Soviet Territory', *Religion in Communist Lands*, 5/1 (1977), 27–37; 5/2 (1977), 109–16.

Altai, A. 'Ehrenburg o Vlasove v sorok vtorom', *S narodom za narod*, 5 (1965).

Anders, W. *Hitler's Defeat in Russia*, Chicago, 1953.

Andreyev, N. E. 'The reality of national bolshevism. A review of M. Agursky, Ideologiya natsional-bolshevizma', *Soviet-Jewish Affairs*, 12/1 (February 1982).

'O russkoy literaturnoi Prage', *Russkiy Almanakh*, Paris (1981), 332–50.

Anon. 'General Vlasov v Rige. Vospominaniya morskogo ofitsera. Aprel 1943', *Russkoe vozrozhdenie*, 10 , New York (1980).

Na sluzhbe Rossii, Possev-Verlag, Frankfurt am Main, 1978.

'Nesostoyavsheesya vystuplenie generala Vlasova', *Bor'ba*, 13 (September 1948).

'Poslednie dni generala Vlasova (svidetel'stvo ochevidtsa.) 8.7.1945', *Rossiskiy democrat*, 1 (1948), 23–7.

'Tragediya vlasovtsev', *Svobodnoe Slovo*, 1, Paris (1946).

'Yuridicheskiy otdel. Proekt', *Bor'ba*, 13 (September 1948).

'Zagadka maiora Zykova', *Chasovoy*, Brussels (January 1952).

Antonov, R. 'Praga, Pilsen, Schlusselburg', *S narodom za narod*, 5 (1965).

Armstrong, J. A. *Ukrainian Nationalism*, 2nd edn, London, 1963.

Soviet Partisans in World War II, Madison, 1964.

Aronson, G. Ya. 'Beseda s vlasovtsem', *Sotsialisticheskiy vestnik*, 601 (23 October 1947).

'Chto nado znat' of vlasovskom dvizhenii', *Sotsialisticheskiy vestnik*, 606 (23 March 1948).

'Otvet kritikam', *Sotsialisticheskiy vestnik*, 610 (30 July 1948).

'Parizhskiy vestnik. Progitlerovskiy organ na russkom yazyke', *Novy zhurnal*, 18 (1948), 331–41.

'Po povodu statey B. I. Nikolaevskogo o vlasovskom dvizhenii', *Novy zhurnal*, 20 (1949), 272–81.

Pravda o vlasovtsakh, problemy novoy emigratsii, New York, 1950.

Artem'ev, V. P. 'Poslednie dni', *S narodom za narod*, 1 and 2, Munich (1962).

Pervaya Diviziya ROA, London (Ontario), 1974.

Artemov, A. N. '15-letie Prazhskogo Manifesta', *Possev*, 46 (1959).

'Skhema NTS i evreiskiy vopros', *Possev* (June 1975), 40–3.

'Vokrug NTS', *Novoe Russkoe Slovo* (18 November 1979).

Ausky, S. A., *Vojska Generala Vlasova v Cechach 1944–45*, Toronto, 1980; translated into Russian as: *Predatel'stvo i izmena. Voyska generala Vlasova v Chekhii*, San Francisco, 1982.

Avrich, P. *Kronstadt 1921*, Princeton, 1970.

Balashov, A. 'General Vlasov i sovetskaya istoriografiya', *Bor'ba*, 63 (February 1962).

'Kommentarii k "Smolenskomu Manifestu"', *S narodom za narod*, 2 (1963).

'Lubyanskaya operatsiya i general Vlasov', *Bor'ba*, 69 (June 1964).
'General Popel' o Vlasove i vlasovtsakh', *Bor'ba*, 71 (July 1965).
Bartosek, K. *Prazske povstani 1945*, translated by E. Thiemann, *Der Prager Aufstand 1945*, Berlin, 1965.
Berkhin, B. *Voennaya reforma v SSSR. 1924–1925*, Moscow, 1958.
'Beseda za kruglym stolom', *Possev*, (February, March, 1975).
Bethell, N. *The Last Secret*, New York, 1974.
Bitva za Leningrad, S. P. Platonov (ed.), Moscow, 1964.
Bitva za Moskvu, E. Sokolova (ed.), Moscow, 1958.
Blackstock, P. 'German Psychological Warfare against the Soviet Union 1941–1945', in W. E. Daugherty, *A Psychological Warfare Casebook*, Baltimore, 1958.
Bobrov, M. 'Kak eto bylo', *Rossiskiy democrat*, 15, Paris (1948), 15–23.
'Strashnoe bezmolvie Rossii', *Vozrozhdenie*, 5 and 6 (1949).
Bogatyrchuk, F. P. [see also Dr N—] 'O Vlasovskom dvizhenie', *Vozrozhdenie*, 28 (1953).
'Natsional'naya politika KONR', *Novoe Russkoe Slovo* (18 October 1971).
Moy zhiznenny put' k Vlasovu i Prazhskomu Manifestu, San Francisco, 1978.
Böss, O. *Die Lehre der Eurasier. Ein Beitrag zur russischen Ideengeschichte des 20 Jahrhunderts*, Wiesbaden, 1961.
Bräutigam, O. *Überblick über die besetzten Ostgebiete während des 2ten Weltkrieges*, Tübingen, 1954.
Brunst, D. V. *Zapiski byvshego emigranta*, Moscow, 1961.
Buchbender, O. *Das tönende Erz. Deutsche Propaganda gegen die Rote Armee im Zweiten Weltkrieg*, Stuttgart, 1978.
Bullock, A. *Hitler: A Study in Tyranny*, London, 1972.
Butenko, V. 'Partinaya zhizn. (Itogi 1930–1931 goda)', *Vestnik Krest'yanskoy Rossii* (June–July 1931).
Bystryanskiy, V. and Myshin, M. (eds.) *Leninizm, khrestomatiya*, Leningrad, 1933.
Calvocoressi, P. and Wint, G. *Total War*, London, 1972, reprint, 1979.
Carell, P. *Hitler's War in Russia*, London, 1964.
Caroll, W. 'It takes a Russian to beat a Russian', *Life*, New York (19 December 1949).
Chakovsky, A. *Blokada*, 5 vols., Leningrad, 1975–6.
Cherkassov, K. *General Kononov. Otvet pered istoriey za odnu popytku*, 2 vols., Melbourne, 1963.
Chernyak, Y. B. *Zhandarmy istorii*, Moscow, 1969.
Cohen, S. F. *Bukharin and the Bolshevik Revolution. A Political Biography 1888–1938*, New York, 1975.
Conquest, R. *The Great Terror*, revised edn, Pelican Books, Harmondsworth, 1971.
Craig, G. A. and Gilbert, F. (eds.) *The Diplomats 1919–1939*, Princeton, 1953.
Curie, E. *Journey Among Warriors*, London, 1943.
D.B. 'Po arkhivnym sledam (Gitler o vlasovtsakh), *Sotsialisticheskiy vestnik* (30 November 1949, 30 December 1949).
Dallin, A. *The Kaminsky Brigade*, Harvard Russian Research Center, 1952.
German Rule in Russia 1941–1945: A Study in Occupation Policies, London, 1957, 2nd edn, 1981 with additional postscript, 679–89.

Dallin, A. and Mavrogordato, R. S. 'The Soviet Reaction to Vlasov', *World Politics*, 8 (April 1956), 307–22.

'Rodionov, a case study in wartime redefection', *American Slavic and East European Review*, 18 (1959), 25–33.

Dallin, D. J. *Soviet Russia and the Far East*, London, 1949.

Daniels, D. V. *The Conscience of the Revolution*, Cambridge, Mass., 1960.

Davidowicz, L. *The War Against the Jews 1933–1945*, London, 1977.

von Dellinghausen, E. 'Dva goda s Vlasovym', *S narodom za narod*, 3 (1962).

Denike, Yu. 'K istorii vlasovskogo dvizheniya', *Novy zhurnal*, 35 (1953), 263–79.

von Dirksen, H. *Moscow, Tokyo, London: Twenty Years of German Foreign Policy*, London, 1951.

Dmitriyev, I. D. *Zapiski tovarishcha D*, Leningrad, 1969.

Dneprov, R. 'Vlasovskie li?', *Kontinent*, 23 (1980), 287–312.

Dudin, L. 'Velikii mirazh', *Materialy k istorii Osvoboditel'nogo Dvizheniya Narodov Rossii 1941–1945*, 2, London (Ontario) (1970).

Dvinov, B. L. 'Spor o porazhenchestve 1941', *Novoe Russkoe Slovo* (27 April 1951).

'Porazhenchestvo i vlasovtsy', *Novy zhurnal*, 39 (1954), 253–68.

Dwinger, E. E. *General Wlassow, eine Tragödie unserer Zeit*, Frankfurt am Main, 1951.

Ehrenburg, I. 'Pered vesnoy', *Krasnaya zvezda* (11 March 1942).

'Lyudi, gody, zhizn', *Novy mir*, 1, Moscow (1963).

Elliot, M. *Pawns of Yalta*, Urbana, Illinois, 1982.

Epstein, J. *Operation Keelhaul*, Old Greenwich, Connecticut, 1973.

Erickson, J. *The Soviet High Command*, London, 1962.

The Road to Stalingrad, London, 1975.

The Road to Berlin, London, 1983.

Fevr, N. *Solntse voskhodit na Zapade*, Buenos Aires, 1950.

Filippov, B. 'Chuzhye gnezda', *Skvoz' tuchi*, Washington, D.C. (1975).

Fischer, G. 'Der Fall Wlassow', *Der Monat*, Berlin (1951).

Soviet Opposition to Stalin, Cambridge, Mass., 1952.

Fischer, G. (ed.) *Russian Émigré Politics*, New York, 1951.

Fletcher, W. C. *The Russian Orthodox Church Underground. 1917–1970*, London, 1971.

Florovsky, G. V. 'Evraziisky soblazn', *Sovremennye zapiski*, 34, Paris (1925), 312–46.

Fominykh, Ye. 'Kak byl poyman predatel' Vlasov', *Izvestiya* (7 October 1962).

Gaev, A. 'Vlasovtsy v sovetskoy literature', *Materialy i soobshcheniya*, Institut po izucheniyu SSSR, Munich (1960), 38–55.

Galkin, D. 'Predislovie. Ideologicheskaya doktrina osvoboditel'nogo Dvizheniya', *Bor'ba*, 6/7 (June/July 1949).

'Manifest voli narodnoy', *Bor'ba*, 15 (November 1948).

'Voprosy osvoboditel'nogo dvizheniya', *Novoe Russkoe Slovo* (19 October 1952).

Gardner, M. *A History of the Soviet Army*, London, 1972.

Gaucher, R. *L'opposition en URSS 1917–1967*, translated by C. L. Markmann as *Opposition in the USSR 1917–1967*, New York, 1969.

Gehlen, R. *Memoirs*, translated by D. Irving, 1972.

Geller, M. and Nekrich, A. *Utopiya u vlasti*, 2 vols., London, 1982.

Getzler, I. *Kronstadt 1917–1921*, Cambridge, 1983.

Ginzburg, E. *Krutoy marshrut*, Frankfurt am Main, 1967.

Grigorenko, P. G. *V podpol'e mozhno vstretit' tol'ko krys*, New York, 1981.

Haimson, L. H. (ed.) *The Mensheviks*, Chicago, 1974.

Hayes, N. 'Kazem-Bek and the Young Russians' Revolution', *Slavic Review*, 39, no. 2 (1980), 255–68.

Hecht, G. *Ich bin General Wlassow. Millionen Russen vertrauten ihm*, Limburg/Lahn, 1961.

von Herwarth, J. *Against Two Evils*, London, 1981.

Hilger, G. and Meyer, A. G. *The Incompatible Allies*, New York, 1953.

Hoffmann, J. *Deutsche und Kalmyken 1942 bis 1945*, Freiburg, 1974.
Die Ostlegionen 1941–1943, Freiburg, 1976.
Die Geschichte der Wlassow-Armee, Freiburg, 1984.

Hoffmann, P. *The History of the German Resistance 1933–1945*, translated by R. Barry, revised edn, London, 1977.

Hohne, H. *The Order of the Death's Head*, translated by R. Barry, London, 1969.

Holmston-Smyslovsky, General. *Izbrannye stat'i i rechi*, Buenos Aires, 1953.

Huntington, W. C. *The Homesick Millions*, Boston, 1933.

Huxley-Blythe, P. *The East Came West*, Caldwell, Idaho, 1964.

Istoriya Velikoy Otechestvennoy voiny Sovetskogo Soyuza 1941–1945, P. N. Pospelov, V. A. Andreyev, A. I. Antonov (eds.), 6 vols., Moscow, 1961–5.

Istoriya vtoroy mirovoy voiny 1939–1945. A. A. Grechko (ed.), 12 vols., Moscow, 1973.

Johnston, R. H. 'The Great Patriotic War and the Russian Exiles in France', *The Russian Review*, 35 (1976), 303–21.

Junin, A. 'La défaite psychologique allemande sur le Front de l'Est. Vue à travers le Mouvement Vlassov 1942–1945', *Revue d'Histoire de la Deuxième Guerre Mondiale* (1962), 1–12.

Kagan, V. 'Postskriptum k prikazu', *Kontinent*, 14 (1977), 301–5.

Kamyshin, V. 'O pozitsii porazhenchestva', *Bor'ba*, 9 (9 May 1948).

Katkov, G. 'The Kronstadt Rising', *St. Antony's Papers*, 6, Oxford (1959), 11–74.
Russia 1917: The February Revolution, London, 1967.

Kay, H. *Salazar and Modern Portugal*, London, 1970.

Kazantsev, A. S. *Tret'ya sila*, 2nd edn, Frankfurt am Main, 1974.

Kazem-Bek, A. L. 'O porevolutsionnom monarkhisme', *Mladoross*, 1 (February 1930).
Rossiya, Mladorossy i emigratsiya, Paris, 1935.

Kerr, W. *The Russian Army, Its Men, Its Leaders and Its Battles*, New York, 1944.

Khozin, M. S., 'Ob odnoy maloissledovannoy operatsii.' *Voenno-istoricheskiy zhurnal*, 2, Moscow (1966), 35–46.

Kievskiy krasnoznamenny. Istoriya krasnoznamennogo kievskogo okruga 1919–72, Moscow, 1974.

Kiselev, A. *Oblik generala Vlasova*, New York, 1977.

Kitaev, M. *Communist Party Officials*, New York, 1954.

Materialy k istorii Osvoboditel'nogo Dvizheniya Narodov Rossii 1941–1945, SBONR, London (Ontario), 1970.

Kak eto nachalos', New York, 1970.

Kolakowski, L. *Main Currents of Marxism*, 3 vols., Oxford, 1981.

Kolomatskiy, M. 'Portret kapitana Zykova', *Golos naroda*, 118, Munich (1 May 1953).

Konev, I. S. *Sorok pyaty*, Moscow, 1966.

Konstantinov, D. *Zapiski voennogo svyashchennika*, Canada, 1980.

Kopelev, L. *Khranit' vechno*, 2nd edn, Ann Arbor, 1978.

Kornatovskii, N. *Kronshtadskiy myatezh*, Leningrad, 1931.

Korol'kov, Y. *Cherez sorok smertey*, Moscow, 1960.

Kovach, A. *Ukrainskaya vizvol'na borot'ba i vlasovshchina*, Germany, 1948.

Kovalevsky, P. E. *Zarubezhnaya Rossiya*, 2 vols., Paris, 1971.

KPSS i stroitel'stvo sovetskikh vooruzhennykh sil 1917–1964, Moscow, 1965.

KPSS o vooruzhennykh silakh Sovetskogo Soyuza, Moscow, 1969.

Krasnov, N. *Nezabyvaemoe*, San Francisco, 1957.

Krasnov-Levitin, A. E. see A. E. Levitin-Krasnov.

Kromiadi, K. G. 'A. A. Vlasov i tserkov'', *Possev*, 20 (20 August 1950).

'Sovetskie voennoplennye v Germanii v 1941', *Novy Zhurnal*, 32 (1953), 192–202.

'Kak rasskazyval ob etom Vlasov', *S narodom za narod* 2 (1963).

'Vlasovtsy i narod', *S narodom za narod*, 5 (1965).

'Vmesto venka k podnozhiyu pamyatnika generalu A. A. Vlasovu', *Zarubezh'e* (March/June 1976).

Za zemlyu, za volyu …, San Francisco, 1980.

Kruzhin, P. I. 'Dvadtsat' let nazad', *S narodom za narod*, 2 (1963).

'K biografii A. A. Vlasova', *S narodom za narod*, 4 (1964).

'Khronika KONR', *S narodom za narod*, 4 (1964).

'Tragediya 2-oy udarnoy armii', *Radio Liberty Dispatch* (27 February 1974).

Kuskova, E. D. 'Emigratsiya i inostrantsy', *Novoe Russkoe Slovo* (28 October 1949).

'O russkikh pochemu', *Novoe Russkoe Slovo* (28 January 1950; 3 February 1950).

'Boleznennoe yavlenie', *Novoe Russkoe Slovo* (18 November 1950; 22 November 1950).

Kuznetsov, B. M. *V ugodu Stalinu*, SBONR, London (Ontario), 1968.

von Lampe, A. A. *Puti vernykh*, sbornik statey, Paris, 1960.

Laqueur, W. *Russia and Germany*, London, 1965.

Fascism, a Reader's Guide, London, 1976.

Lenin, V. I. *Polnoe sobranie sochineniy*, 5th edn, 55 vols., Moscow, 1958–65.

Lesueur, L. *Twelve Months that Changed the World*, London, 1944.

Letters from Russian Prisons, published by the International Committee for Political Prisoners, London, 1925.

Levitin-Krasnov, A. E. *Likhie gody 1925–1941*, Paris, 1977.

Ruk Tvoikh zhar 1941–1956, Tel Aviv, 1979.

V poiskakh novogo grada, Tel Aviv, 1980.

Levitsky, S. A. 'The ideology of the NTS', *The Russian Review*, 31, no. 4, New York (October 1972), 398–405.

Liddell Hart, B. H. (ed.) *The Soviet Army*, London, 1956.

Littlejohn, D. *The Patriotic Traitors: A History of Collaboration in German Occupied Europe 1940–1945*, London, 1972.

Longworth, P. *The Cossacks*, London, 1969.

Luckett, R. 'A Million Russians Fight for Hitler', *Sunday Times* (14 May 1972).

Lukin, M. F. *Ogonek*, no. 47 (1964), 26–30.

Lyons, E. *Our Secret Allies*, Boston, 1953.

Malet, M. *Nestor Makhno in the Russian Civil War*, London, 1982.

Manuil'sky, D. Z. *Itogi sotsialisticheskogo stroitel'stva v SSSR*, Moscow, 1935.

Melgunov, S. P. *Tragediya admirala Kolchaka*, Belgrade, 1930.

Meretskov, K. A. 'Na Volkhovskikh rubezhakh', *Voenno-istoricheskiy zhurnal*, 1, Moscow (1965), 54–70.

Na sluzhbe narodu, Moscow, 1968.

Meyer, Y. 'Vlasovskoe dvizhenie i ego moral'nye osnovy', *Russkiy zhurnal*, no. 1, New York (1956), 19–27.

Milyukov, P. N. *Emigratsiya na pereput'e*, Paris, 1926.

Rossiya na perelome, 2, Paris, 1927.

N—, Dr [pseudonym of F. P. Bogatyrchuk]. 'Po povodu tak nazyvaemogo vlasovskogo dvizheniya', *Vozrozhdenie*, 7 (January–February 1950), 105–13.

N.N. 'Istoki vlasovskikh nastroenniy', *Sotsialisticheskiy vestnik*, 613 (30 October 1948).

Nadezhdin, N. 'Politicheskoe mirovozzrenie Vlasovtsev', *Bor'ba* (11 December 1948).

'Put' k svobode', *Novoe Russkoe Slovo* (9–19 January 1961).

Naumenko, V. *Velikoe predatel'stvo. Vydacha kazakov v Lienze i drugikh mestakh 1945–1947*, New York, vol. 1, 1962; vol. 2, 1970.

Na Volkhovskom fronte 1941–1944g., A. I. Babin (ed.), Moscow, 1982.

Nielsen, J. P. 'Miliukov and Stalin. P. N. Miliukov's political evolution in emigration 1918–1943', *Meddelelser*, no. 32, Slavisk-Baltisk Institutt, Universitet i Oslo (1983).

Nikolaev, A. *Tak eto bylo*, Germany, 1982.

Nikolaevsky, B. I. 'O novoy i staroy emigratsii', *Sotsialisticheskiy vestnik* (26 January 1948; 28 February 1948).

'Porazhenchestvo 1941–1945 godov i Gen A. A. Vlasov', *Novy zhurnal*, 18 (1948), 209–34 and 19 (1948), 211–47.

'Otvet G. Ya. Aronsonu', *Novy zhurnal*, 20 (1949), 281–92.

Istoriya odnogo predatelya, reprint, New York, 1980.

North, R. C., *Moscow and the Chinese Communists*, Stanford, 1953.

Notes of a Political Prisoner, East European Fund Inc. Research Program on the USSR, New York, 1952.

Novosiltsev, I. L. 'A. A. Vlasov', *Novy zhurnal*, 129 (1977), 183–90.

Ogin, P. and Korol', B. 'Komandir peredovoy divisii', *Krasnaya zvezda* (9 October 1940) and in *Novoe v podgotovke voisk*, Kiev, 1940.

Okuntsev, I. K. *Russkaya emigratsiya v Severnoy i Yuzhnoy Amerike*, Buenos Aires, 1967.

Orlov, S. 'Na ch'i den'gi sozdavalos' Russkoe Osvoboditel'noe Dvizhenie?', *Zarubezh'e*, 53–4 (February–April 1977).

Osipov, N. 'Litso dvizheniya', *S narodom za narod*, 5 (1965).

'O sud'bakh Rossii', *Mosty*, 12, Munich (1956), 323–5.

Osokin, V. *Andrey Andreyevich Vlasov.* (*Kratkaya Biografiya*), izdatel'stvo shkoly propagandistov Russkoy Osvoboditel'noy Armii, August 1944, republished New York, 1966.

Paly, P. N. 'Neispol'zovannoe i gibnushchee nasledstvo', *Novy zhurnal*, (146 1982), 194–207.

'Voennoplenniy No 7172', *Novy zhurnal*, 133 (1978), 48–77.

'Olovyannye soldatiki', *Novy zhurnal*, 152 (1983), 68–107.

'Razmery zla', *Novy zhurnal*, 153 (1983), 213–30.

Pern, L. *V vikhre voennykh let*, vospominaniya, Tallin, 1969.

Petrov, V. *My Retreat from Russia*, New Haven, 1950.

Petrovich, P. *Mladorossy*, London (Ontario), 1973.

Pipes, R. *Struve, Liberal on the Right, 1905–1944*, Cambridge, Mass., 1980.

Pismenny, Y. 'Ob odnom voprose svyazannom s Manifestom', *Vlasovets*, no. 3, Munich (1950), 7–8.

'Dvadtsat' let spustya', *S narodom za narod*, 4 (1964).

Plyushchov, B. *General Maltsev*, San Francisco, 1982.

Poltoratzky, N. P. (ed.) *Russkaya literatura v emigratsii*, Pittsburg, 1972.

Polyakov, I. A. *Krasnov-Vlasov, vospominaniya*, New York, 1959.

Pozdnyakov, V. V. [see also Volgin and Volzhanin]. 'Po povodu odnoy teorii', *Vozrozhdenie*, 28 (July/August 1953), 166–70.

'A. Vlasov o natsional'nom voprose', *Novoe Russkoe Slovo* (26 December 1971).

'Generaly ROA v amerikanskom plenu', *Novy zhurnal*, 108 (1972), 218–36.

'Meletii Aleksandrovich Zykov', *Novy zhurnal*, 103 (1971), 153–68.

Prychodko, N. 'Germany's disastrous Eastern policy and the role of General Vlasov', *The Ukrainian Quarterly*, 6, New York (1950), 49–56.

R.N. 'Kak sozdavalsya NTS', *Possev* (July 1983).

Radkey, O. *The Unknown Civil War in South Russia*, Stanford, 1976.

Redlich, R. N. [see R. Vorob'ev].

Reitlinger, G. *A House Built on Sand: Conflicts of German Policy in Russia 1939–1945*, London, 1960.

Rekunov, A. M. (ed.) *Sovetskaya prokuratura*, Moscow, 1982.

Riasanovsky, N. V. 'The Emergence of Eurasianism', *California Slavic Studies*, 4 (1967), 39–72.

von Rimscha, H. *Russland jenseits der Grenzen 1921–1926*, Jena, 1927.

'Die Entwicklung der russländischen Emigranten nach dem Zweiten Weltkrieg', *Europa Archiv*, 7 (August/November/December 1952).

Rosenberg, W. G. *Liberals in the Russian Revolution*, Princeton, 1974.

Rudnev, V. V. 'Novy grad', *Sovremennye zapiski*, 50 (1932), 432–55.

S.B. 'O chem zabyl gospodin Aronson', *Bor'ba*, 9 (May 1948).

Saburova, I. 'Drug generala Vlasova', *Novoe Russkoe Slovo* (13 November 1974).

Salisbury, H. *The 900 Days: The Siege of Leningrad*, London, 1969.

Samarin, V. D. *Civilian Life under German Occupation 1942–1944*, Research Program on the USSR, New York, 1954.

'Antibol'shevitskie vosstaniya', *Russkoe vozrozhdenie*, 15, New York (1981), 125–215.

Samoylov, E. M. 'Sud nad predatelyami', in L. N. Smirnov, V. V. Kulikov and B. S. Nikiforov (eds.), *Verkhovny Sud SSSR*, Moscow, 1974, 371–80.

Samsonov, A. *Velikaya bitva pod Moskvoy*, Moscow, 1958.

Schapiro, L. *The Origin of the Communist Autocracy*, London, 1955.

The Communist Party of the Soviet Union, 2nd revised edn, London, 1970.

Schultz, E. K. 'Vlasov v nemetskom osveshchenie', *Vozrozhdenie*, 28 (July/August 1953), 170–5.

Schwartz, S. 'Tragediya vlasovskogo dvizheniya', *Sotsialisticheskiy vestnik*, 658 (January 1953); 659 (February/March 1953).

Seaton, A. *The Russo-German War 1941–1945*, London, 1971.

Sergeev, A. 'O porazhenchestve', *Novoe Russkoe Slovo* (15 May 1951).

Shandruk, A. *Arms of Valor*, New York, 1959.

Shkarenkov, L. K. *Agoniya beloy emigratsii*, Moscow, 1981.

Shtifanov, N. 'Dabendorf', *Novoe Russkoe Slovo* (18 February 1974).

Shub, B. *The Choice*, New York, 1950.

Simpson, Sir John Hope. *The Refugee Problem*, London, 1939.

Smena vekh. Sbornik statey, Y. B. Klyuchnikova, N. V. Ustryalova, S. S. Lukianova, A. V. Bobrishcheva-Pushkina, S. S. Chakhotina and Y. N. Potukhina (eds.), Prague, July 1921.

Solzhenitsyn, A. I. *Arkhipelag GULag 1918–1956*, vols. 1–2, Paris, 1973.

Stalin, I. V. *Sochineniya*, vols 1–13, Moscow, 1946–55; vols. 14–16, R. H. McNeal (ed.), Palo Alto, 1967.

Steenberg, S. *Wlassow. Verräter oder Patriot?*, Cologne, 1968, translated by A. Farbstein as *Vlasov*, New York, 1970.

Stephan, J. J. *The Russian Fascists*, London, 1978.

Streit, C. *Keine Kamaraden. Die Wehrmacht und die sowjetischen Kriegsgefangenen 1941–1945*, Studien zur Zeitgeschichte, 13, Stuttgart, 1978.

Strik-Strikfeldt, W. *Gegen Stalin und Hitler. General Wlassow und die russische Freiheitsbewegung*, Mainz, 1970, translated by D. Footman as *Against Stalin and Hitler*, London, 1970.

Struve, G. P. *Russkaya literatura v izgnanii*, New York, 1956, 2nd revised edn. Paris, 1984.

Sukhanov, N. *Zapiski o revolutsii*, Moscow, 1922.

Svetlanin, A. *Dal'nevostochny zagovor*, Frankfurt am Main, 1953.

Tel'nov, Y. 'A. A. Vlasov na severo-zapade okkupirovannoy Rossii', *Novy zhurnal*, 157 (1984), 268–71.

Thorwald, J. *Wen sie verderben wollen …*, Stuttgart, 1952.

The Illusion: Soviet Soldiers in Hitler's Armies, translated from the German by R. and C. Winston, London, 1975.

Tishkov, A. V. ''Predatel'' pered sovetskim sudom', *Sovetskoe gosudarstvo i pravo*, Moscow (February 1973), 89–98.

Titov, F. 'Delo Vlasova i drugikh', *Na strazhe sotsialisticheskoy zakonnosti*, N. F. Chistyakov (ed.), Moscow (1968).

'Klyatvoprestupniki', *Neotvratimoe vozmezdie*, N. F. Chistyakov and M. E. Karyshev (eds.), Moscow (1973), 214–34.

Tolstoy, N. *Victims of Yalta*, revised edn, London, 1979.

Trepper, L. *The Great Game*, London, 1977.

Tys-Krokhmaliuk, Y. *U.P.A. Warfare in the Ukraine*, New York, 1972.

Ulam, A. *Russia's Failed Revolutions*, London, 1981.

V., Podpolkovnik. 'Poslednie dni generala Vlasova', *Sniper*, Munich (22 May 1949).

Varshavsky, V. S. *Nezamechennoe pokolenie*, New York, 1956.

Vasilakiy, V. 'Put k pravde', *Izvestiya* (2 September 1962).

Vasilevsky, A. *Delo vsey zhizni*, Moscow, 1976.

Vasiliev, A. *V chas dnya, Vashe Prevoskhoditel'stvo*, Moscow, 1973.

Verbin, V. 'Zakaz na fal'sifikatsiyu', *Bor'ba*, 60 (February 1961).

Vertepov, D. P. (ed.), *Russkiy korpus na Balkanakh vo vremya II velikoy voiny 1941–1945g.*, New York, 1963.

Vishnyak, M. V. *Sovremennye zapiski*, New York, 1957.

V kruge poslednem, Novosti Press, Moscow, 1974.

Vladimir. 'Na chto rasschityvali vlasovtsy', *Sotsialisticheskiy vestnik*, 611–12 (27 September 1948).

Vlassov, A. A. *Les confidences du Général Vlassov, 'J'ai choisi la potence'*, Paris, 1947.

Vlassov, Frau H. 'Die Tragödie eines Generals', *Schweitzer Illustrierte Zeitung*, Zurich (10 January 1951).

'Mein Mann wurde gehenkt', *Die 7 Tage*, Konstanz, Germany (2 November 1951; 9 November 1951; 10 November 1951).

von Vogelsang, H. *Kriegesende in Lichtenstein*. Freiburg, 1985.

Volgin, V. [pseudonym of V. V. Pozdnyakov]. 'Russkomu chuzhoy kaftan ne po plechu', *Bor'ba*, 27/28 (November/December 1949).

Volkmann, H-E. 'Das Vlasov-Unternehmen zwischen Ideologie und Pragmatismus', *Militärgeschichtliche Mitteilungen*, 2, Freiburg (February 1972), 117–55.

Volzhanin [pseudonym of V. V. Pozdnyakov]. 'Kto Zykov', *Bor'ba* (November/December 1950).

Vorob'ev, R. [pseudonym of R. N. Redlich]. *Filosofskie osnovy natsional'no-trudovogo solidarisma*, Menhenhof, Kassel, 1946.

Voskresenskiy, D. 'Vlasovskoe dvizhenie i rossiskiy solidarism', *Ekho*, Regensburg (29 July 1948).

Werth, A. *Russia at War 1941–1945*, London, 1964.

West, R. *The Meaning of Treason*, revised edn, London, 1982.

Wheeler-Bennet, J. *The Nemesis of Power: The German Army in Politics 1918–1945*, London, 1953.

Williams, R. C. *Culture in Exile*, Ithaca, 1972.

Wrangel, P. N. *Vospominaniya*, 2nd edn, Frankfurt, 1969.

Young, G. *The House of Secrets*, New York, 1959.

Zherebkov, Y. S. 'Popytki KONRa ustanovit' kontakt s zapadnymy soyuzni-kami', *Zarubezh'e* (February/April/June 1979), 16–22.

'Russkie dni v Parizhe', *S narodom za narod*, 2 (1963).

'Finansoviy dogovor', *S narodom za narod*, 4 (1964).

Zhilin, P. 'Kak Solzhenitsyn vospel predatel'stvo vlasovtsev', *V kruge poslednem*, Moscow (1974), 101–11.

Index